Praise for *Love, Africa*
A *Vogue* Best Summer Beach Read

"A passionate debut memoir bears witness to political turmoil. . . . A stark, eye-opening, and sometimes horrifying portrait by a reporter enthralled by the 'power and magic' of Africa."

—*Kirkus Reviews*

"[An] exciting, harrowing memoir that aptly displays why [Gettleman's] a Pulitzer Prize winner and a *New York Times* bureau chief. . . . There's a thrilling immediacy and attention to detail in Gettleman's writing that puts the reader right beside him. . . . Gettleman's memoir is an absolute must-read."

—*Booklist* (starred review)

"Colorful, evocative, and immediate."

—*Publisher's Weekly*

"Africa—that vast swell of nations, languages, landscapes, and histories—has always had a peculiar impact on foreigners, but Gettleman seems to have been hit harder than most."

—*New York Times*

"A romantic, globe-spanning tale, a sort of *Indiana Jones* meets *Casablanca*, coupled with the newsroom drama of *Spotlight*."

—*Dallas Morning News*

"*Love, Africa*, wraps two love stories inside a swashbuckling, some-times hair-rising, account of the author's life."

—*Tampa Bay Times*

"A powerful and revealing memoir."

—*Forbes*

"Jeffrey Gettleman's beautifully written memoir is about many kinds of love: for a continent, for a family, for the truth. The path to love is not always straight, but when Gettleman discovers his true passions, he grabs hold and doesn't let go. *Love, Africa* offers a key to understanding humankind's past and future and a key to understanding our hearts."

—Sheryl Sandberg

"Rarely do you read such beautifully rendered honesty: witness the eyes and heart of Jeffrey transform into a remarkable person and writer for our time."

—Ishmael Beah

"Gettleman's memoir of his life, his love, and the excitement and perils of journalism is a page-turner. The portrait of Africa that emerges is disturbing, tender, and harsh. It's an insight you can't come to without having spent much of your professional life living and covering that continent. A tremendous read. I couldn't put it down."

—Abraham Verghese

"Jeffrey Gettleman's memoir is truly, in all its complicated tragic beauty, a love story made up itself of inextricably intertwined love stories. I was mesmerized."

—Alexandra Fuller

"To feel the fear, sinfulness, and rapture of being a foreign correspondent, read this book! Using self-lacerating truth and high velocity prose, Jeffrey Gettleman has written a compulsively readable new story about what it means to be 'our man in Africa.'"

—Blaine Harden

"Jeffrey Gettleman has true grit. That's why he was in my book, and why you have to read his."

—Angela Duckworth

LOVE,
AFRICA

LOVE, AFRICA

A MEMOIR OF ROMANCE, WAR, AND SURVIVAL

JEFFREY GETTLEMAN

HARPER

NEW YORK · LONDON · TORONTO · SYDNEY

HARPER

A hardcover edition of this book was published in 2017 by HarperCollins Publishers.

P.S.™ is a trademark of HarperCollins Publishers.

This is a work of nonfiction. All the events in this book happened. Some names and identifying details have been changed in order to protect the privacy of the various individuals involved. The author has attempted to render the experiences detailed herein as faithfully as possible. The depiction of personal interactions is from the author's perspective.

HarperCollins books may be purchased for educational, business, or sales promotional use. For information, please e-mail the Special Markets Department at SPsales@harpercollins.com.

FIRST HARPER PAPERBACKS EDITION PUBLISHED IN 2018.

Designed by William Ruoto

Africa map illustration by Malchev/Shutterstock

Library of Congress Cataloging-in-Publication Data has been applied for.

ISBN 978-0-06-228410-5 (pbk.)

19 20 21 22 LSC 10 9 8 7 6 5 4 3 2

TO MY CAMERADO

⋅

◇◇◇◇◇◇◇◇

PREFACE

⬦⬦⬦⬦⬦⬦

One day my sons will ask why they were born in Africa; and now that we've moved on, I see more clearly all the reasons why.

In a big way, their early years in such a warm and beautiful place were inevitable, the accumulation of adventures and misadventures between their mother and their father, in Africa and beyond, together and alone.

I wish we were all back there now. I miss everything about that life. I miss the scruffy airports and the stubby bananas. I miss opening my curtains in the morning and looking out at our garden and seeing the flame tree blossoms lying lightly on the rich green grass. I miss feeling deeply connected to a part of the world where I wasn't from but took me in as if I belonged.

We've gone back several times as a family to visit, and it's always a mix of wonderfulness and frustration. I've never felt as alive as I did living in Africa. I've never felt as at home. But now that we're looking out at the world from another continent, recapturing that feeling is like trying to re-enter a dream.

New Delhi, India
2018

PROLOGUE

◇◇◇◇◇◇

The biggest stories often start with a scrap of paper, a phone number and an obviously fake name. The first hint of this story came from my friend Louis, a French diplomat. Louis was a good source. He had wavy hair, a big, intelligent face, and a weakness for cinnamon liqueur, tall African women, and conspiracy theories. We were sitting on the balcony at Trattoria, an Italian restaurant on a bustling street in downtown Nairobi, having lunch. Most diplomats stayed away from bustling streets—and downtown Nairobi—so Trattoria afforded us a reliable degree of anonymity. We might have stuck out, two *mzungu*s in the heart of the city, looking at each other across a table set with oil and vinegar and a red carnation peeking out of a chipped vase, but no one knew who we were. From where we sat, we could see the taxis and 4x4s edging past curbs painted in black and white. Crowds of people moved through the streets— university students chatting, holding armfuls of books, butchers in white coats, newspaper vendors balancing stacks of papers on their heads, lawyers from the nearby courthouse exchanging greetings in the distinctive Kenyan fashion, arms relatively straight as they shook hands, still clasping each other for a few moments as they chatted. In the doorways of the banks and forex bureaus leaned watchmen with wooden clubs tucked under their arms. They eyed the street cautiously. It was the daily Nairobi churn, lit up by clear sunshine beaming off the storefronts and windshields.

Louis picked up his linen napkin, folded it into quadrants in a practiced European way, and blotted his lips, red from *arrabbiata* sauce. He gazed off.

"Who knows what's going on in the Ogaden," he said, which meant, coming from Louis, *something* was going on in the Ogaden.

When I got back to the office, I called around to aid workers and human rights people who might know something about the Ogaden Desert, the poorest, most remote part of Ethiopia. That led to a meeting with a friend of a friend of a friend of a friend in a flyblown café in Nairobi's Eastlands where I could have easily disappeared. A wispy Somali man named Abdi Farah sat across from me, close enough for me to smell the frankincense smoke he used to perfume his clothes. It was a light but unmistakable scent that cut through the café's other smells of sweat, French fries, and roasting goat meat. He had bright, playful eyes and scars on his cheeks. We were mutually suspicious; we also needed something from each other. Abdi Farah leaned toward me and scribbled out a name and number on the back of a faded café receipt. "When you get to Addis," he said, "call this guy. Tell him Bob sent you."

Before I allowed myself to get too excited, I did a little more research. From a human rights contact of mine, I learned the Ogaden rebels were extremely well armed. Just the week before, I had banged out a quick story about how this same outfit had attacked a government oil field and killed seventy-five, but by the standards of this region, that hadn't immediately registered as major news. Now I knew, from a military source, that the Ethiopian government was receiving covert help from the Americans. The Ethiopian army had sealed off the entire Ogaden Desert and was burning down villages and massacring civilians. It wouldn't be easy getting in, the source said; there were checkpoints everywhere. That made up my mind.

As I heaped my gear into a pile in the middle of the office

floor—my satellite phone, my Internet transmitter, my bug sprays and mosquito nets and notebooks and cords—my hands were shaking from a combination of excitement and dread, though at times like these I honestly couldn't distinguish between the two. I could see the story: secret atrocities; clandestine American involvement; an underdog war, with a religious edge (the Ethiopians were predominantly Christian, the rebels Somali and Muslim).

Several days later, my wife, Courtenay, and I checked over our shoulders before ducking into a taxi in Addis Ababa, Ethiopia's capital. She perched the small bag with video equipment on her knees. We were headed off on a long drive east, toward the Ogaden. The road threaded through the cool misty highlands and flattened out into dry, fruitless plains. For two days we drove, until the lights of Jijiga, the last big town before you hit the desert, disappeared behind us.

Then we started walking.

We had a guide, Musa, a college student working undercover for the rebels. My first words to him were: "Bob says hello." We followed Musa up sandy hills, down sandy hills, through swirling rivers the color of chocolate, the water warm and rich with sediment, strangely soft against our skin. The sky was coated with stars as we moved stealthily through profusions of bushes that bloomed in the dark and yielded a smell like lemongrass and basil that clung to our nostrils and our wet, sticky clothes.

When we finally reached the rebel outpost, located on a small hilltop, Musa took us back to the radio "room." It was a single wire twisted around a thorn tree connected to a crackly CB. There we met the rebel leader in this part of the desert, who also used a nom de guerre: Commander Peacock. He was squatting on the ground, holding the transmitter in his left hand, shouting in guttural Somali, clad in cracked old boots and disintegrating camouflage. When he saw us, he slowly stood.

"Welcome to the war," he said.

Now, at this point, if you're wondering if we were absolutely insane to march out into the middle of the desert and place our lives in the hands of a band of freshly bloodstained outlaws led by a man named Commander Peacock, I can offer an explanation: the transitive property of trust. Reporters deposit their lives in it all the time. People I'd trusted had hooked me up with people they'd trusted who hooked me up with people they'd trusted. Peacock and I were simply two terminal points on a long line drawn by trust.

This is one of the things I've experienced most deeply in Africa, and I've felt it from Khartoum to Kinshasa, from the Indian Ocean to the Atlantic: that chain of connections, the surprising openness, the ease of movement—and I'm not talking about going from A to B, because it's still hard as hell getting most anywhere in sub-Saharan Africa. I'm talking about movement *across worlds*. There's this notion, lived just about every day out here, that nothing's easy but anything's possible. I had been dazzled by my first hit when I was eighteen, captivated by the spirit, the energy, the differences, the feel. I realize now that those words conjure up nothing specific in anyone else's head, but behind them are some of the brightest memories of my life: walking along Lake Malawi holding a stranger's calloused hand, moving through villages with packs of people, the sandy paths littered with mango peels, feeling so connected to strangers it was like there was a set of jumper cables running between us.

It was this feeling that made me hop around from newspaper to newspaper for more than ten years until I got the one job I had always wanted, East Africa bureau chief for the *New York Times* (it's a lofty title; there were no other correspondents for thousands of miles). I was put in charge of news from a dozen countries, a huge chunk of territory lying across Africa's waist. And I had a camerado to help me decipher it, process it, survive it. To my surprise and joy, Courtenay had retooled from public defender to video journalist, which meant the two of us could go anywhere a scrap of paper or a fake name could take us. Whatever I had in my heart, I was now doing it.

We followed Commander Peacock to the edge of the camp. He pointed his rifle out at the desert and said, with the slightest flicker of amusement in his eyes: "If they put ambush, never run." He patted his hand down, to mean "lie flat." Courtenay and I exchanged a quick glance. We'd covered a lot of rebels—rebels terrorizing the hills of eastern Congo, fighting for autonomy in Darfur, shelling the towns of Burundi. This region, overly militarized during the Cold War and then basically dumped by the West when it ended, has more than its fair share of antigovernment feeling. But Commander Peacock seemed different. He had a gravelly voice aged far beyond his twenty-seven years and dusty dreads growing out of a receding hairline. He was tall and slightly bent, with questions coming out of questions.

"Mista Jifri, how is your condition?" he'd ask me over the next several days, and when I'd say I was fine, even if my feet throbbed from all the walking, he'd let loose:

"Mista Jifri, are you creationist or evolutionist?"

"Mista Jifri, why Mexico too poor. It next to the US, no?"

"Mista Jifri, how does car insurance work?"

I was really only able to answer the first one.

We covered at least a hundred miles, looking for the Ethiopians looking for us. Peacock appeared to know where he was going. He sometimes flashed me a goofy sideways grin that seemed to acknowledge that being a rebel fighter loping through the desert was a quixotic way to spend one's life, but fuck it, it was interesting. He spoke passionately and repeatedly about creating an independent homeland for his people where the oil and gas resources went to build schools and the children's bellies weren't swollen with worms—standard rebel fantasies. The rebels were eager for ink, which is why they had invited us out here, but I knew what they were up against. The Ethiopians were one of Africa's most ruthless regimes. They had MiGs, helicopter gunships, tens of thousands of infantrymen, and now the CIA helping them too. As I trudged behind Peacock, trying to keep up with him and scribble in my notebook and not trip on a rock, I dashed out, "Heavily armed dreamers."

Courtenay was impressed. "Look at these guys," she said. "They're carrying all of our shit, they're happy we're here, they're blowing up people, but at the same time, they're so nice."

I'm sure she did like them, but in that comment there was a subtle condemnation of me. We had been dealing with some painful fragments of our past, and even though we still shared moments of tenderness, that faith that two people draw from, and share from, was nearly gone. It had seemed as if going on this trip would recement our bonds, or maybe tear us apart. Some couples have a baby to save a marriage. We went into the Ogaden. It was a gamble, not made any easier by the hunger, the heat, the danger, and most especially the thirst, a very greedy thirst that stalked our every step. We walked for hours most days through thick thorn trees whose bone-white needles constantly cut us, the sun burning down, searing every inch of our exposed skin. The only water was the rare stream or mud puddle, and there was only so much we could carry. At each day's end we were left with empty bottles and splitting headaches, our pants streaked with white salt stains, our urine like syrup.

"You need to do something about this," Courtenay said to me one blazing afternoon.

"What do you want me to do?" I croaked back. "I'm thirsty too."

"Don't be a pussy," she hissed. "Do something."

"Like what?"

"I don't know. But get me some *fucking* water!"

The soldiers around us kept their eyes riveted to the horizon. They pretended they hadn't heard her. It grew so quiet, all I could hear was everyone's boots digging into the sand and the clinking of bullets in bandoliers bouncing on backs. This was a nomadic culture where women were dutifully wrapped in cloth all day like marble statues, never to be unveiled; they spoke when spoken to, if they were spoken to. Every once in a while, they were beaten like dusty rugs.

I walked to the back of the line and sheepishly asked Peacock if he had any extra water. It was a serious taboo out here to ask for another man's water. Peacock smiled knowingly and poured me most of his bottle. I jogged obediently back up to Courtenay, who took it from me, closed her eyes, and tipped it back like a can of beer. She handed me back the empty bottle and walked off. I wondered if that counted for anything in her mind.

This wasn't the only reason we decided to leave three days later, but I knew I shouldn't push it. We had spoken to dozens of rebels and villagers, collecting accounts of every abuse imaginable, and we'd probably get only more of the same. Soon enough the rebels might actually run into the Ethiopians, and who knew how that would go. It was time. Courtenay had gotten her video; me, my notes. My dirty-paged notebook detailed everything that I'd heard and overheard. It contained maps, organizational charts, code names and numbers. It was like a guidebook to the insurgency.

As we said good-bye, everyone was quiet. Peacock assembled the rebels into two straight lines. We exchanged a few final words.

"Peacock, man, if you ever come to Nairobi, I'll take care of you."

We both laughed. It was an absurd thing to say; Peacock said he wanted to die out here, and there was more than a good chance he would. But it was all I could think of. And I did mean it.

We hugged, my cheek against his tattered uniform. And Peacock being Peacock, he somehow arranged a dump truck that was working in the area to give us a lift to the nearest town.

We hopped out at Degehabur, a smudge of a settlement on the desert's edge, about an hour away. The main road was dirt, lined with slanted shacks. Courtenay was wearing her yellow linen shirt and a pair of shapeless flesh-colored nylon camping pants that we called the "sexy pants." We walked up to the gate of a guesthouse, one story, about twenty lonely rooms.

The proprietor took my wad of moist bills and handed me a tiny key that looked like it fit a suitcase lock. He barely said a word, faintly smiling. I was so pleased we had made it this far, I wasn't thinking straight. And I was still new—I hadn't been in this job even a year, I didn't know the contours of this region or the brutality and trickery pooled in forgotten places like Degehabur.

I would've never guessed that as Courtenay and I crossed the courtyard, the comforting sound of her nylon pants swishing behind me, our new proprietor friend was slipping out the back door. And as we plopped down the bags in our room and I began to rummage through my backpack, I hadn't the faintest intuition that a platoon of Ethiopian soldiers from a nearby army base was storming out of their barracks.

"Hey," Courtenay said. "Where'd you put the shampoo?"

"I'll find it," I said back. "Let me just take a quick leak."

"And please get something to wash some socks in. Mine are disgusting."

I stepped into the courtyard, searching for a plastic bucket. Right as I spotted one in the corner, a green pickup packed with soldiers zoomed through the gate.

Three men jumped out, their tightly laced boots hitting the pavement hard.

"You!" one of them shouted in clear English. "Get in."

He shouldered his assault rifle and shook it wildly in my face. My mouth went dry.

"Get in truck!"

More soldiers clattered into the courtyard. They carried assault rifles, belt-fed machine guns, rocket-propelled grenades. They were probably no older than Peacock's troops, young twenties, but they looked like grown men, well-fed, crisp camouflage, none of that childlike smileyness in their eyes. They formed a tight ring around me, weapons drawn, and closed in. I didn't know what was happening, but I knew one thing: they were in that bulging-eyed, unreachable state human beings morph into right before they kill.

If I opened my mouth, they'd shoot me. If I didn't move quickly enough, they'd shoot me. If I moved too quickly, they'd shoot me.

I climbed into their truck.

Good things take time, growing, maturing; they need tending. Think of a garden of orchids, or for that matter, a marriage. Bad things happen fast, like a bone snapping. Courtenay stepped out of the room seven seconds after I had left it to find me encircled by a platoon of Ethiopian soldiers, the same ones the rebels were fighting, rifles raised at my chest.

"What the hell is going—"

They grabbed her by the arm and yanked her toward the pickup.

The soldiers jumped in, guns banging against the sides. They ordered us to sit on the floor, in the back half of the truck. I kept trying to tell myself that maybe they'd just drive us to a police station, lock us up for a few hours, shake us down for a bribe, then let us go. Just as long as they leave our—but no, that happened too. Before the driver gunned the engine and the guesthouse disappeared in a swirl of dust, the soldiers ransacked our room, ripping our bags out. We weren't headed to a police station. I started to feel faint. And I still had to pee.

I glanced over at Courtenay. She was wearing a red bandanna around her neck, like a scout. The Ethiopians stood above her, rifles angled at her skull.

The truck idled for another moment and then jerked forward with a roar. These men could kill us, they could do whatever they wanted to us; any illusion of control over our own lives, our own bodies, had been wiped out in an instant. We were hurtling down a bumpy road to an unknown destination, the gray, gravelly desert slipping past us, and I started to hemorrhage energy simply trying not to freak out. And still I was freaking out. I had gotten Courtenay into this, and now I couldn't get her out of it. If we survived, would she lose even more faith in us? Was this where my love of Africa had taken me? I know that a privileged white man falling suddenly—and inexplicably—in love with Africa is a cliché. So much so the French have a term for it, *le mal d'Afrique*, the Africa disease. It puts you under a spell and/or kills you. Maybe so. But I had worked hard to get here, and it took half my life.

As I felt the heat from the soldiers' eyes on us—it didn't seem like they were just doing a job, they seemed enraged at us, as if this were personal, as if we all don't just have roles to play—the words that kept echoing in my mind were from Courtenay's dad, from the evening we had left for Africa. It's a clear memory but it seems to belong to someone else now. We were standing on the curb at JFK, her dad's voice husky with sorrow. He too had been searching for the right last words, until he finally said: "Take care of my girl."

I was doing a bang-up job.

"Excuse me," I asked the Ethiopian soldiers. I swallowed hard. The truck's floor was hot. "Where are you taking us?"

Nobody said anything.

"I want to call the US embassy."

One of the soldiers whipped around, clenching his weapon.

"Shut up."

Courtenay seemed far less scared than I felt. Her wide-set eyes were focused; her forehead was unfurrowed. I felt deeply torn that she was even here. I knew the government soldiers would stop at nothing, that they didn't flinch parting flesh. At the same time, I'd be a liar to say I wanted to be alone. Courtenay was the one with good ideas, the one I had always clung to, the one who could figure a way out of this. Even though we were at a very fragile point, even though for years I had pitted my two loves, Courtenay and Africa, against each other for reasons I struggled to understand, I had finally accepted a truth that now guided me: If you're with the one you love, the rest should be logistics.

I took one more look at her. She quickly looked back. I saw a dart of fear in her eyes. The doors were locked, the rifles hadn't moved an inch, blinding light poured down from the sky. We both sensed it would be easier if we didn't look at each other anymore. Or say anything.

Afoot and light-hearted I take to the open road,
Healthy, free, the world before me,
The long brown path before me leading wherever I choose.

Camerado, I give you my hand!
I give you my love more precious than money,
I give you myself before preaching or law;
Will you give me yourself? will you come travel with me?
Shall we stick by each other as long as we live?

—Walt Whitman, the beginning and end of *Song of the Open Road*

ONE

⬦⬦⬦⬦⬦⬦

ITHACA, 1990

Every day, after my 3:35 class ended, I hurried back to the frat
house to check my mailbox. Many of the letters started the same:
"My beloved friend . . ."

Some asked for a camera, others for clothes. Most asked for
nothing, just sharing the news from rural Tanzania or backroads
Malawi, the two agrarian countries where I had been five months
earlier. One boy, Macfereson Banda, from Karonga, Malawi,
wrote to see how our soccer ball was doing. "When I played with
it," he said, "I was really feeling as if I am on top of the mountain."
I won't lie. We had met thousands of kids driving from Nairobi to
southern Malawi on a homemade mission to bring aid to refugees.
I didn't remember who Macfereson Banda was. But I remembered
that spirit, that drive to get close and stay close.

The letters from East Africa came in slender, tissue-thin envelopes trimmed in red and blue. The envelope was the letter, so I
was careful slipping the blade of a knife under the seam. As I sat
at a long wooden table in our dining room, happily rereading the
week's Africa mail, Michael Laudermilk sauntered in, wearing a
Lakers tank top and thumping a basketball.

"Gettlemern"—*mern* was our word for nerd—"what you doing?"

Laudermilk—Milk—was my same year. He stooped above me. The ball stopped bouncing.

"Those airmail?"

"Yup."

He bent closer, glancing at the stamps.

"Africa, huh? You were there over the summer, right? What's Africa fucking like?"

I looked up at him. His handsome face was framed by glossy black hair. Milk was a star safety on the varsity football team, built like a gladiator, unjustly athletic. We weren't close, and for the first time he seemed genuinely interested in something I had to say.

"It's like . . ." My mind started to race. "Like . . ." I looked out the window, off into the naked Ithaca trees. I hated that question.

How much did Milk really want to know? What was I supposed to say? That question still trips me up, and back then I definitely didn't have the poise to hop over it. My first Africa trip had been like a lucid dream—and I was possessive of this dream, because dreams lose their power if you start sharing them around. It began the moment I'd landed and stood eagerly in the aisle, peering out the windows, waiting for the stewardess to wrench open the door. When that dry canned airplane air rushed out and Nairobi's fresh cool night air rushed in, rich and loamy, like a million wet leaves, it was an immediate intoxication. That's how that whole summer went, our truck chugging down the road, one thing morphing into the next, things just seeming to *happen*, leaving behind this sweet, heavy, mysterious emotional aftertaste.

It felt like every day we discovered something; of course that was an illusion, but the illusion was rarely broken. Our summer was a road trip, we covered a thousand miles over four weeks across eastern and southern Africa, we did see a lot. The afternoon we rolled into Salima Bay, on Lake Malawi, was no more or less eventful than dozens of other long sunny lazy days we shared, but it remains deeply etched. Lake Malawi was an inland sea; you couldn't see across it. The water was coppery, the sand by the shore burning.

We stripped off our shirts and ran in, pushing the water away with our thighs. It seemed to get thicker each step. Immediately we were surrounded by dozens of kids thrashing toward us, belting out "Mzungu! Mzungu! Mzungu!"—the equivalent of gringo. We couldn't communicate, but that didn't stop us from playing with the slippery little kids and throwing them into the water and wrestling on the beach with the bigger ones. They cheered at just about everything we did, and after I toweled off and dressed—in front of a crowd of about ninety-five—scraps of paper were thrust into my hands. Where from! What district! What village! The children wanted to be pen pals, and I scribbled out my address as fast as I could. They tugged us toward their huts, and I peered into one, a little round house, roof black from smoke. There was nothing inside, no toys, no balls, no books, no mattresses even, just blankets bunched up on a clean dirt floor. Malawi was one of the poorest countries on earth; I had never seen anything like this. I felt something on my leg. I looked down. A little boy, about four, was rubbing my shin. People here don't have hairy legs. His warm little fingers tickled like a spider. As I was standing in the doorway of his house, checking things out, he continued to move his fingers up and down the ridge of my shin extremely lightly, feeling my hairs. It was one of the most intense moments of mutual curiosity I've ever experienced.

This was a different world. Personal space didn't exist. Grown men walked down the beach holding hands, and once when I was standing in the middle of a pack of fishermen, I felt a set of rough calloused fingers interlace in mine. I liked that. I squeezed back. Wherever I went, so much warmth enveloped me; I could feel it opening me up. It made me think that maybe out here, you didn't have to move through life hopelessly alone.

Our guide to this new world was just a year older. His name was Dan Eldon and I'd never met anyone like Dan Eldon. He'd blaze into a restaurant, snap a stiff salute to the waiters, flick them a cassette, and the next thing I'd know, there would be one white face in the middle of a circle of waiters, everyone grooving together and singing out loud in one voice with several different accents: "Fight the power! We got to fight the powers that be!"

The first time I saw Dan was in Mombasa, swimming in an ocean that was a shade of bright blue that didn't look like any water I'd ever seen before; it was the color of Windex. Dan was paddling just beyond the waves. When someone pointed him out, I was surprised by how young and delicate he looked, after all I had heard. He was clean-cut, with a long face, dark eyebrows, and a square jaw, but still, there was something fragile about him. We had met through a fluke. I have a childhood friend named Roko, who was friends with this guy Chris, who came on the trip to film it and knew a guy named Lengai, who had grown up in Nairobi with Dan. Dan had organized a mission to help Mozambican refugees, and he invited a dozen students to drive from Nairobi to the border of Malawi and Mozambique, where he planned to donate a car and several thousand dollars to the refugee camps.

Before we left for Africa, I held that same vague patchwork of images in my head that many people hold, of suffering, disease, deprivation, and poverty. That part of Africa is real—but it's only that, part of the picture. Even though we were constantly aware that we had so much more than the people around us—our Nikes, our flashlights, our Walkmans, money—even though we were surrounded by people who were clearly struggling, I rarely sensed any resentment, any bitterness. Curiosity, yes; we were oddities. When we walked through the towns, things would suddenly stop; people around us would turn and stare, shoe-shiners would be suspended in mid-stroke, and I'd hear them whisper to each other, "Something-something-*mzungu.*" It felt like we were being worshiped, which felt wonderful—and disconcerting. It didn't seem right to be regarded as representatives of some alien civilization that had just descended for a quick visit.

I soon learned that the playing, the wrestling, the endless grip-shifting handshaking, helped lower those barriers. My guard began to drop, inch by inch. I realized there was so much less to fear than

I had originally thought. When we camped in the middle of the savanna in Mikumi National Park, animals all around us, big ones, so close we could smell their pungent musk, somehow it didn't feel reckless. It felt as if they had their space, we had ours.

"You guys ever wonder what to do with a landscape like this?" Dan asked after we all sat down by a campfire. "It's, like, beautiful food you can eat; a beautiful woman you can kiss; but what are you going to do with a landscape this beautiful?" Eager for Dan's approval, we gazed out at the acacia trees silhouetted by the moon and the chest-high elephant grass rolling away for miles, wondering if there was any possible way to answer a question so profound.

◇◇◇◇◇◇◇

I heard a thumping on the wooden floor, jarring me back to my senses. Milk. Bouncing his ball again. I had nearly forgotten he was still standing there.

"Interesting, Gettlemern, very fucking interesting."

I don't even know what cow-eyed sentences I'd uttered.

"I'll see you tonight. And don't forget the garbage bags."

That night we called a meeting.

"Get in close, fucking weenies!"—that's what we called the eager young men who wanted to join our house, *fucking weenies.* "You know the rule of this house! We always stay close!"

We shoved the weenies into a corner of the living room and began ripping apart Hefty bags and taping them to the windows so nobody could see in. Sam, another one of my brothers, struggled to crawl up on a table, slow as a grizzly, and then he reared up like one. Sam gazed down at the weenies and then opened his mouth and vomited on them. I was at a safe distance, but one weenie—Derek, from Baltimore—reached up, face distraught, and slowly felt the gooey chunks in his hair. We all pointed at him and howled. That's how it went in our house. True humiliation was how we expressed our false love.

Maybe, looking back, I'm giving myself too much credit. But I think it was around this time that I began to suspect that I was on a collision course with myself. I knew I couldn't keep this up. My fraternity was such a radical reduction of what there was on campus, let alone what I had tasted on that summer trip, let alone what I suspected lay out there in the even wider world. I was nineteen, a sophomore at Cornell University, and like any other teenager, desperate to fit in—and desperate to stand out. I'd allowed myself to be puked on and worse to get into that frat, and for no good reason; frats were simply what I thought you did at Cornell.

So I created my own alternate world: *Africa*. It was perfect. No one knew much about it, especially me. Of its fifty-some nations, I had briefly visited four: Kenya, Tanzania, Malawi, and South Africa. But I kept staring at the pictures in my scrapbook, rereading the Africa mail, writing to my buddy Dan, stoking my appetite.

It was a cold morning when I walked purposefully up our driveway, my worn-out Nike trainers, the same ones that had been such a fascination in Malawi's sun-blasted villages, squeaking in the snow. I climbed the hill to Uris Hall, past icicles hanging in the gorge, a dark trickle running between the banks of ice. Up ahead loomed a nineteenth-century clock tower wearing a toupee of fresh snowflakes. Its hands showed ten o'clock, which felt like the crack of dawn to me. I was headed to the study abroad office. If I had one mission at this point, it was to break free of the confines I had so ardently put around myself.

"There are some excellent programs at Oxford and Cambridge," a counselor suggested when I told her I didn't speak any foreign language but wanted to go to Africa.

When I stared back, she asked: "What about an archaeology program in Crete?"

I trudged home in disbelief that there wasn't a single program south of the Sahara. I was beginning to see that this wouldn't be easy, that I was nurturing an inconvenient passion. So I hatched my own plan. It turned on four classes a week in a room that smelled of chalk dust and mold, located in a small building at the farthest end of campus: the Africana Study Center. The instant I walked into that little classroom, where I had signed up for Swahili, I was back in a world of light, soapy cumulus clouds somewhere on the horizon.

Mwalimu Nanji, our teacher from Tanzania, was short and quiet, with tired eyes and a gray Afro that he combed into a rectangular shape. He never volunteered how he had come from sunny Dar Es Salaam to snowbound Ithaca. I never pried. I desperately wanted him to like me. He was my only link.

"Bwana Jeff, habari yako?" *How are you?*

"Mzuri," I'd eagerly answer—*Good*—forming my whole mouth around the word, like he had taught us: "Mooo-zur-ree."

Swahili is a visceral language. You don't say "I am hungry," you say "I *hear* hunger." You don't smoke a cigarette, you *pull* it. There's no fancy or plain way to say "you," no masculine or feminine words; it's communication stripped down to its essence, just how it felt out there.

I finally learned the origin of *mzungu*, that word a hundred little children had shouted at me on city streets and country roadsides. It comes from the verb *kuzunguka*, to go around and around, and is probably derived from observations of the first honkies in the region, the explorers. Roughly translated, it means "the dude who walks in circles."

Swahili started long before any white men came to walk in circles. About a thousand years ago, when the first Arabs landed on the East African coast in crescent-sailed dhows, hungry for ivory, spices, fragrant woods, and slaves, they needed a way to communicate with the African merchants. A language evolved, part Arab, mostly African, with bits of Hindi, Portuguese, Persian, English, and German eventually sprinkled in. It was an Esperanto that people actually spoke—today, more than a hundred million speak it.

As the months passed, my interest in Swahili provided endless amusement for the guys in the frat. One night the following October, we were all gussied up for a sorority formal at the Waterfront, a club in downtown Ithaca. I was wearing a tie, a wide floral one that I had bought on the streets of Manhattan from a homeless man for a dollar. I had even spritzed some Calvin Klein Obsession on my neck. I looked—and smelled—the part.

There were a bunch of us sticking to the bar as usual, drinking the usual. Colored lights flashed across the wood-paneled room, which had big windows looking out on a smooth, black Lake Cayuga. The windows were partly fogged up, and the techno music was blasting so loud that if you held your cup real gently, you could feel the plastic sides vibrating to the bass. *Boosh, boosh, boosh, boosh.*

"Gettlemern," O'Hare shouted. "Tell me again why you're taking Swa freaking Hili?"

Our backs were to the bar, elbows on it. O'Hare was a redheaded kid from a town on Long Island that everyone seemed to have heard of but me, Port Something or Other. He was a bit of a ringleader. We didn't like each other.

"I don't know," I said. "The teacher's pretty cool. It's an easy A."

"Gentlemen." Milk leaned in—and people tended to listen to Milk. "He likes it, he's been to Africa. What's the b.f.d.?"

"Seems weird to me," O'Hare went on. "Why don't you say something? Say something in Swahili."

"Just shut 'em up," Milk said. "Say something. It doesn't have to be long."

Everybody looked at me. The last thing I wanted was to perform like a circus bear. College was constantly creating these predicaments: in the morning, you're an interested, earnest student trying to understand John Rawls's veil of ignorance, in the evening you're a dumb-ass five beers deep and peeing on the hood of Carl Sagan's Volkswagen Rabbit. Youth knows no contradictions. I took a swig of my Sex on the Beach, a sweet pink drink with the viscosity and charm of cough syrup.

"I don't know, man," I said. "What do you want me to say? *Jambo* means 'hello.'"

For some reason, that set off a burst of wild cackles, and I seized the opportunity to get the hell out of there. I walked across the club to near the dance floor. I felt much better standing by myself, sipping my drink, watching the swirl of colored lights and people moving back and forth.

As my eye traveled across the faces, I kept coming back to the same one. It belonged to a girl with high cheekbones, wide-set eyes, heavy eyelids and dark hair; her features looked Eurasian, maybe even Eskimo. She was wearing a red dress that showed off her back; she was lithe and freckly. As she danced, the blacks of her eyes shone. There was something in them that I had seen before. She seemed deeply, freely happy, like those kids on Lake Malawi. I could tell she really dug dancing. I was terrified to approach her directly, so I chose a moment when a girl I knew was talking to her, went up to them both, and lamely shook her hand.

A few days later, standing with a pack of guys in front of Rockefeller Hall, I saw the same girl. She caught me looking, and as she walked by, she lifted her eyes and dropped a casual "Hi."

"You know her?" my buddy Ethan said, punching me hard in the arm. "She's kinda fly."

The next afternoon, I returned to my room to find a note tucked in the door. I took one look at it but instantly folded it up and wheeled around.

"Who wrote this?" I said, stomping down the hallway, brandishing the note. "Who *really* wrote this?"

No girl would venture into our den, alone, in the harsh light of day, braving the one enormous groin-scratching meathead who always lounged on our front stoop with his lacrosse stick like the Cyclops guarding his cave.

But the brothers swore that they hadn't written that letter.

I went back to my room and shut the door. It was an unusually bright autumn day, light flooding through the windows. I opened the note again and studied the handwriting, strong and clear, perfectly straight on lineless paper.

"Hi, Jeff, how are you? We met the other night. Maybe we can have dinner sometime? Here's my number. Courtenay." Her telephone number was scribbled under her name, neatly as the rest.

Was I hallucinating? I stepped back into the hallway to ask again if this was a prank. Part of me still hoped it was. It would be so much easier that way. It was like those colliding feelings of thrill and terror I'd always get sprinting down the side of the lacrosse field as fast as I could, wide open, in perfect shooting range, dying to crank the ball through the back of the net but hesitating to call out for it because I dreaded choking. If the letter was a fake, well, that meant I could just slip back to the safe routine of waiting for the *meep . . . meep . . . meep* of the beer truck backing up to the front of the house on Friday night with two thousand cans of Coors or Beast or whatever it was before a party. But if it were real, I actually had to do something.

The brothers huddled in the hallway, eager to share their hard-earned wisdom.

"Call her, you dumbshit," one said.

"This is your lucky day, asshole," said another.

A few nights later, I picked Courtenay up. We drove to a Vietnamese restaurant at the bottom of the hill, near the Ithaca Commons. I was wearing my typical outfit—ripped jeans, yellow-rimmed Ohio State baseball cap on backward, slightly funky sweatshirt—I prided myself on going three or four days without a shower. Of course I was eager to make an impression, but even more I was fearful of seeming anything less than nonchalant. The last thing I wanted was to come across like I was trying too hard. Evidently she was less hung up on things like that, radiant in a snug-fitting Arctic-blue Nordic sweater with big brass buttons on her chest, borrowed from her roommate, the prettiest thing either of them had in their shared closet. In the car, I smelled her still-wet hair.

She sat down and smoothed out her napkin in her lap. She was beautiful to listen to and beautiful to look at. She didn't wear a drop of makeup—she didn't need to, with her dramatic coloring—

pale skin, full red lips, and that very dark hair, starting from a sexy widow's peak. Her eyes were light brown, flecked with dark spots, like tiger lilies. With those wooden chopsticks, she lifted glass noodles to her lips. She handled them like she had been born in Hanoi. I ate with my hands.

I can't tell you what I learned about her over those spring rolls and little bowls of noodle soup, perhaps because I was too nervous or too busy looking at her. But I don't think it mattered. We were at an age when all key decisions are made in small parts of seconds, and we had already decided, in one of those small parts, that we wanted something from each other.

As we drove back, I started getting nervous. What should I do when we got to her house? I pulled up along the curb, and she was just sitting there, gazing up the road. I put the car in park, eyeing those swollen lips. I leaned over, moved toward her, shut my eyes. She did the same.

We bumped teeth.

TWO

⬦⬦⬦⬦⬦⬦

THE WORLD, 1992

I set off for the airport with $5,000 wadded up in my right front pocket; an around-the-world ticket in my hands; a new backpack; a new pair of great big Italian mountain boots; several pairs of allegedly sweatproof polyester socks; thirty-eight rolls of film; and my dad's Olympus OM-1 camera, which he had kept in immaculate condition for the past fifteen years, not a scratch or ding on it. My parents had spooled out the leash farther, much farther, God bless them, even though I wasn't getting any college credit, and what I was about to embark on ran the risk of making me never want to come back. "What were we going to do?" my mom later told me. "After that first summer, you had gone to another world we knew nothing about."

This time I was going for a whole glorious year. I had been working the previous summers to make this happen. It felt very bold at the time, but once I made my decision, I never second-guessed it: I was dropping out. Dan approved. He had done the same thing, right after high school. His guidance counselor at the International School of Kenya, a beautiful school on a hillside outside Nairobi, had responded to his decision dismissively. "Oh, I see," she had said. "You're taking a year off."

"No, no," Dan corrected her. "I'm taking a year on."

Nineteen ninety-two was the perfect year for a Year On. It was a new dawn, one of those hopelessly optimistic periods where past mistakes are eclipsed by a future not yet here. The Soviet Union had just said *dasvidaniya* to itself, the Cold War had suddenly ended, the United States was embarking on the longest-running economic expansion in its history, and al-Qaeda was barely a twinkle in Osama's eye. People liked us, at least that's how it felt. In Egypt, all I had to do was walk down the sidewalk, hold out my right hand, and bark "Eedack!" and I'd get the loudest, friendliest smack (*eedack* means "your hand" in Arabic). The ease of a high five says a lot, and in 1992, for the most part, it was a world of easy high fives. For one, none of us had a cell phone in our hands. This was right before the communication revolution—about sixteen civilians knew what e-mail was. The result was an immersion that was about to be rendered impossible for forever onward. I felt so free that year, so blissfully severed from my world back home. From England to New Guinea, I hit four continents and seventeen countries, spending more time in Kenya than anywhere else. I arrived in Nairobi in the spring.

"Amazing, man, just amazing," Dan said from his porch, where he was waiting for me. "I just heard you talking to the *askari*."

It was only the Swahili basics that I had inflicted on Dan's guard, my accent plywood, none of that music native Swahili speakers make the instant they open their mouths. But Swahili was like a little key, unlocking that other world.

"You learned all that, *in a classroom*?"

I beamed.

"Come on, man," Dan said, clapping an arm around my shoulder. He was a little thicker now, some stubble on his chin. His hair was combed straight back, and he wore a white T-shirt, black jeans, and a black leather vest. He looked like a handsome greaser. "Let's bring your shit inside, and then let's go. Deziree has got a little problem . . ."

Deziree—or Dez, Dan's 1977 Land Rover jalopy—always had a little problem. It was like the safari had never ended.

"Got my rear viz?" Dan asked.

"Yes sir!" I answered, turning around to make sure he wouldn't whack anything as he threw it in reverse. We backed out Deziree and roared off. I asked Dan where exactly we were going and all he said was "To see the *jua kalis*."

That confused me. From Swahili class I knew that *jua kali* meant "fierce sun," but I didn't know what it would mean plural, or in this context. We cut through downtown, past an ochre-colored skyscraper—much of Africa had the architectural misfortune to win its independence in the mid-1960s, which meant many big buildings went up with heavy cement facades and in some interesting hues—and Dan hung a hard left on River Road. The streets were teeming with people and smelled of garbage and sweetly rotting fruit. Dan stopped in front of a crowd of men in ripped jumpsuits, unbuttoned to the navel, no undershirt. We were immediately swarmed.

Jua kali, I soon found out, refers to the artisans and craftsmen who perform their trades out on the street under the fierce sun, thus the name. The *jua kalis* included auto mechanics, carpenters, welders, shoemakers, sign painters, upholstery specialists, and experts in plastics and resins. They were a huge part of Kenya's informal economy (probably bigger than the formal economy); many were highly skilled, illiterate engineers. The crumbling curbs of River Road were like their office park.

Within seconds, twenty broad-handed men were sticking to Dez's fenders, yelling "Unataka nini? Nini? Nini?" *What do you want? What? What?* My eyes jumped from man to man. What was stopping them from ripping us out of the truck, turning us upside down, and shaking all the money out of our pockets? They weren't necessarily hostile, but they were determined. In a place like this, if you didn't work, you didn't eat. Dez had a slight problem with her accelerator cable, and I started to wonder why Dan hadn't taken her to a real garage.

Dan calmly explained the issue, and from that unruly crowd stepped one man who looked right at us. "I can do it," he said.

He was wearing the same set of grubby, torn rags stained with engine grease, and his face radiated a certain fundamental pride. The other men dropped back respectfully.

All eyes were on us, sitting stiffly in the front seat. Decision time.

Dan stepped out of the truck, climbed up on the hood, and looked down at the crowd. He pointed to the man with the firm gaze and said in a loud stage voice: "Can anyone here vouch for this man's character?"

The men stared up at Dan. They didn't say a word.

"No bother," Dan said, laughing. "You got the job."

Typical Dan. He loved this part of the world and slightly mocked it at the same time. He was making fun of the fact that *jua kali* work was a leap of faith—that anyone could say he was a mechanic and then disconnect every single engine hose and still demand payment. That tension is what made Dan particularly alive in these moments. He interacted with people, especially in crowds, in a way that I probably never would. He was able to take all their curiosity and play with it, like a toy. It was the same whenever he whipped his latex monster mask out of his backpack and pulled it over his head and sent the kids scattering like a burst of starlings, chirping with laughter. He took for granted that if he raised his hand to the sky, so too would every single African. Somehow, he did this without making a fool of himself. Or them.

"Dude, you got to realize something," he said as we stepped out of his truck—he could tell I'd been nervous. "With crowds, it can always go either way. You have to be respectful. But the energy of a crowd, man, the way it moves as one, there's nothing like it."

He walked me around the various *jua kali* zones, and standing in the middle of all those handsaws munching through wood and metal tinging out against metal made me suddenly want to pound nails and saw wood. The economy here wasn't hidden, like it was back home. When was the last time you saw someone on the street making a door? Or a coffin? "This is real life," Dan pronounced. The men in front of us were making or fixing things, eager for work, living one day at a time, hand to mouth, without any real ability to control what happened to them or their families tomorrow but they did it with a certain moxie. That was real life, and Dan didn't have to proselytize. I could see how growing up in this place had made Dan different from the other guys I knew. My eyes narrowed with a new envy. Lucky bastard, I thought. I would give my left nut to have grown up in Kenya like you.

◇◇◇◇◇◇◇

Dan was a peer but he naturally wore the mantle of an elder. He taught me how every evening there's a changing of the guard in the insect world: flies out, mosquitoes in. He introduced me to *matatu* minibuses, chicken tikka, and reggae rap. He helped me appreciate Nairobi's dreamy climate, which made every day like a perfect September day back home, mid-seventies, low humidity, sunny with a few clouds. And he took me to White Night, apparently the thing for *mzungus* to do in Nairobi, which was quite segregated.

The Carnivore disco played different music on the big nights of the week, catering to Nairobi's segmented party scene. Saturday was disco, popular with Indians; Friday was Lingala, the sweet and smooth music from Zaire, popular with Africans; and Wednesday was Rock Night, more commonly known as White Night. From the howls of recognition I heard in the parking lot and the long hugs out on the dance floor, I deduced that White Night was something of a weekly reunion. The few blacks that attended were on the clock, in one way or another. While I was sitting at the bar and Dan was dancing, a young Somali woman came up to me and took my hand. She put it in her lap and grabbed me with two liquid-caramel eyes that said, *What are you going to do now, Mzungu Boy?*

Mzungu Boy was rock-hard and terrified. This woman oozed a practiced ease. Mzungu Boy was a virgin. Mzungu Boy guarded that secret as closely as his virginity itself.

Courtenay had been the closest, but we hadn't even been that close. We had survived the teeth-bumping episode to go on several dates; we'd even slept in the same bunk bed a couple times, in the frat house, in what she and I called the Alcove. Once I rolled over and found her looking at me. I smiled, kissed her cheek, closed my eyes, and turned my head away, pretending I was going back to sleep. But I couldn't. There was something growing in the Alcove, pressing against my closed eyelids, gently trying to lift them. Courtenay wasn't scared of intimacy; I could see that staring right at me. But as much as I was intrigued by her, I wasn't ready to open up. I rushed our good-bye in her sorority's driveway as we sat in my car, heater blasting, windshield wet with feathery Ithaca snow. We had barely exchanged addresses before she got out and walked away.

"Dan!" Mzungu Boy eventually blurted out. "Get your ass over here!"

I finally extracted myself from the young woman and Dan from the dance floor, and soon enough we were back at his house, up on the second-floor veranda off his bedroom, lying out on foam mattresses in the open air.

The air smelled like perfume.

"What's that?" I asked.

"Night jasmine," Dan said.

I took a big draft, trying to commit the smell to memory.

◇◇◇◇◇◇◇◇

The three months I spent with Dan flew by. What we did in all those days, I couldn't tell you; they were as jumbled as the journals he loved to make. He sat at his desk for hours, listening to the low, sultry tones of Edith Piaf trickling out of a boom box, turning things over in his hands that he had found, sticking things to paper, copying down phrases that meant something to him. His journals were bound collages, series of photos stuck to paper, smears of different colors and different materials, different ideas—letters, postage stamps, airline tickets, newspaper clippings, receipts, paint, feathers, blood, high-quality black-and-white images, all glued together. There was one picture I couldn't stop staring at: Dan, in a gorge, shirt off, carrying a pretty girl in his arms. He was wading waist-high through opaque water and his eyes were fixed and dark. A single shaft of sunlight speared down behind him. The girl was clutching Dan's neck, her head tilted back, eyes rapturously closed. It was as if she were giving her body over to him.

I think Dan got interested in journals when he was around fourteen. At the time, his parents were getting divorced. Retreating to his room and closing the door and sitting at that desk, alone, for hours, must have been his way of finding a safe place in the world. He did his best thinking with a pair of scissors in his hands, and those three-dimensional heaps he was constantly building could have told me more about Africa and the world than the stack of Lonely Planet books and Michelin maps I lugged around with me—provided I knew how to read and interpret them, which at that point I didn't. Dan may not have known either. Maps carefully divided things up, plotted things out, measured things. Maps were what the colonizers used; they made the conquest of Africa possible. Dan didn't live by maps. Dan just went.

It amuses me to remember how stubbornly intent I was to not appear as if I worshiped Dan. You never get what you want from those you admire, so I affected a pose of nonchalance. I still eschewed daily bathing and pretended not to notice the slight flare of Dan's nostrils when he opened the door to the downstairs guestroom where I had decamped and took in a noseful of my cheese-smelling socks. I enjoyed testing things, especially in his world. Dan didn't seem especially interested in the fact that several people, trusted family employees at that, lived in utter poverty on the Eldon property, and he discouraged us from asking too many questions. The cook, the gardener, and the guard stayed behind the main house in a cold-water shack with a rusted roof, like a piece of a slum that had somehow gotten lost and stopped behind the mansion to ask for directions. Shreds of laundry flapped on a line. It was Yoknapatawpha County back there. Dan called it the SQ, the servants' quarters. I called it the slave quarters. I guess if you grew up with an SQ, you didn't question it.

One day Benjamin, the gardener, took me back there. Benjamin was my all-weather friend on the compound, always game to play soccer or teach me more Swahili. I stood in his doorway.

"Nice room," I said.

I was shocked. Benjamin's room was a dingy cell with a torn foam mattress. His few possessions stuffed in the corner—two gunnysacks, some ripped shirts, and some old newspapers—could have easily passed for garbage. There wasn't a picture on the wall; it was a home without pride. I wasn't supposed to be back there. Everybody here, on both sides, had his role and his techniques for overlooking the obvious. But I enjoyed poking a membrane I knew I shouldn't touch.

My time with Dan ended with the clicking of a slide projector. Chez Eldon was often a free hotel for talented drifters. One day it was a tall, pale Englishman who called himself an explorer and whose back was covered in scars that looked like the nuggets on a crocodile's back—he had been initiated into a tribe in the Indonesian jungle that revered crocodiles, and part of the initiation involved being pinned down on a canoe and cut several hundred times with extremely sharp blades of bamboo. The Englishman let me run my hands over his shoulders; it felt like braille.

The next day, one of the most beautiful women I'd ever seen walked through the door. Her name was Penelope Roy; she was a former Miss India. Dan whispered to me that if I carried in her bags I might be able to score, so I dashed outside and lugged in a couple of heavy suitcases. But after she asked me to make her a cup of tea, and I put milk *and* lemon in it, she laughed at me. Penelope had reformed herself from high-paid call girl to photojournalist. She was elegant, well dressed, well traveled, and expressed an affection for danger that made me nervous. One night we gathered in Dan's living room, and Penelope showed us some slides.

"Those are all bodies?" Dan whispered.

"Those are all bodies," Penelope said.

Penelope Roy was in the first wave of photojournalists to get into Mogadishu after Somalia's government imploded. Many of her pictures were pictures of the dead. As she clicked through her carousel of slides, she told us about how "warlords"—I had never heard that term before—were blocking food supplies, massacring civilians, and creating mass starvation. She had many images of rolled-up gray blankets, cinched with string at both ends. After she paused on one picture of a half-lit warehouse stacked with corpses, Dan asked her what f-stop she had been using. Frankly, I found it a little strange to turn the conversation to the fine points of composition. But I kept my mouth shut.

The end of the Cold War wasn't such a cause for celebration in Africa. While people were still partying in Berlin, they were being shot to death in Somalia, disemboweled in Liberia, hacked up in Rwanda. Africa had the rotten luck to gain its freedom at the height of the Cold War, which meant dozens of young nations had been instantly reeled into the maelstrom, on one side or the other, and instead of building courthouses, highways, or universities—exactly what these fragile, artificially created countries needed—the United States and USSR built arsenals.

The superpowers took some of the least developed areas on earth, like the Somali desert or the Congo River basin, and pumped in first-world killing equipment. They installed leaders of these tinderboxes on the basis not of genuine popularity but merely of who would do their bidding. In Zaire (now Congo), America should have bent over backward to help Patrice Lumumba, the charismatic and democratically elected prime minister who had fought so hard for independence. Instead, it helped kill him. JFK then cozied up to a cunning army man, Joseph Mobutu, who promptly changed his name to Mobutu Sese Seko Kuku Ngbendu Wa Za Banga, "the All-Powerful Warrior, Who, Because of His Endurance and Inflexible Will to Win, Will Go from Conquest to Conquest, Leaving Fire in His Wake." Courtesy of our millions, Mobutu became one of Africa's worst disasters, ruling for decades like a late-stage Roman emperor.

But as soon as the Berlin Wall came crumbling down, the Mobutus became an embarrassment. There was suddenly no reason to prop them up. The West abruptly disengaged from Africa, and the Mobutus toppled over, one after the other, like evil little dolls. Upheaval and war erupted everywhere, marking the most seismic moment in Africa since the continent tore itself off from Gondwanaland 150 million years ago. Sierra Leone became so Hobbesian, with its drugged-up rebels running around terrorizing people and drugged-up government soldiers running around terrorizing people, that the Sierra Leoneans invented a new, quite clever term: the sobel. Soldier? Rebel? To a brutalized civilian, it was all the same. And it had never been easier for a sobel to get an automatic weapon.

In the early 1990s the former Soviet Republics were on their knees, and the arms business had been one of their biggest industries. Nearly overnight, from warehouses on both sides of the Urals, crates of AK-47s, RPG-7s, Katyusha rocket launchers, F-1 grenades, and Dragunov sniper rifles began to vanish. They were stuffed into rickety, rear-loading Antonovs piloted by vodka-stinking Moldovans who chugged in low across those stunning, wide-open African skies. Add to this the forces churning inside people's hearts, the hope and gutsiness that the spread of democracy in Eastern Europe had invigorated in Zambia, Kenya, Sudan, Rwanda. I can't think of another part of the world as primed, by outsiders, to explode.

But while all of this was happening, my appreciation of these events was peripheral, at best. As I squeezed out push-ups in Dan's living room, my ripe feet up on the couch, blasting whatever music Dan was listening to that day—music was like salt to him, he added it to everything—I was only vaguely aware that several civil wars were raging a few hundred miles from where I was grunting on the floor.

But for Dan it was different. He had tried three colleges by this point—none fit, none would ever fit. Dan now knew it, and he had no problem saying it. His pictures were getting better, cleaner, he was learning to play with light. He would get much closer to his subjects than other photographers; he was really good at portraits. When he told me of his plans to tag along with Penelope and pick up freelance work in Somalia, I took it as a subtle hint to hit the road.

◇◇◇◇◇◇

In 1992 a Lost Battalion composed of several thousand twenty-somethings wandered the surface of the earth with a single mission: to see the world. Typically broke, usually carrying a Lonely Planet guidebook, and always smelly, the battalion's members slowly made their way east to west or west to east, eternally searching for the cheapest way to keep going. The great dream was to land a "courier" ticket—deeply discounted passage for carrying documents for this or that stupid company. Everyone on the circuit spoke about it like the Holy Grail.

Tom and Dom were sergeants in the Lost Battalion, travelers par excellence. They were searching for what Kerouac and his gang called the It. I met hundreds of fellow travelers that year, but no one quite like them.

My Tom and Dom days began one rainy afternoon in Jerusalem. I was checking into a drafty hostel in the Old City, given a bed in a dorm. As I plopped down my backpack, I heard a loud sigh from the bunks above.

"Welcome to the dog's bollocks," said a guy with a proper British accent.

"Shut yer gob," another said. "You picked it."

They introduced themselves as Thomas and Dominick, from London.

"But you can just call us Tom and Dom," they both said, at the same time.

For the next half week, whenever I saw one, I saw the other. As two friends often do, Tom and Dom genuinely resembled each other—tall, scruffy, and lean, mid-twenties, ponytails to the middle of their backs, immutably clad in jeans and jean jackets. I half expected to see them carrying a guitar case with stickers on it: that's what they looked like, not backpackers but members of a band.

A few weeks later I bumped into Tom and Dom again, several hundred miles away in Dahab, Egypt. We stood on the beach, our ankles getting washed by the warm Red Sea, laughing at the randomness of it.

Two months after that I saw Tom and Dom several *thousands* of miles away, this time in Nairobi's industrial area, walking as one, a gangly, eight-limbed denim-clad creature loping its way across the sidewalk.

"We just bought the world's greatest Land Rover!" Dom yelled out.

"We're going to Cape Town, the bottom of Africa!" Tom yelled out.

"Wanna come?" they both yelled out.

They were as hopelessly smitten by the idea of Africa as I was. Before committing, though, I had to consult my travel buddy. Roko, whom I have known since sixth grade, had come with me on the first Dan trip in 1990. He was one of my best friends growing up, and when I told him I was thinking of dropping out of college to travel the world, we immediately began scheming.

Roko had long, greasy hair, heavy eyelids, sharply pointed incisors, and a large head. He got a charge out of helping people and used to get excited when we passed a broken-down car on the road because he loved to jump out and help push. He was a Balkan mutt, half Czechoslovakian, half Yugoslavian. His mother escaped shortly before Russian tanks rolled into Wenceslas Square and his father was a distinguished cardiologist from the Dalmatian Coast, determined to row across the Atlantic. We used to see the good doctor at his house in Winnetka, training on his patio, mustache, headband, face a grimace of sweat, yanking on that erg as if his life depended on it.

Roko had arrived in Nairobi after me, also shacking up at Chez Eldon. He listened closely to my proposal to go with Tom and Dom to Cape Town.

"I like those fucking guys," Roko said. "I say we do it."

Dan stood on his porch and watched with a knowing smile as we chugged out of his driveway in the Tom-and-Dom-mobile, an aged Land Rover of Deziree's vintage. The asphalt soon thinned to dust. We cut through the mixed light, waving to Maasai herders adhering to a way of life that seemed hundreds, maybe even thousands, of years old, pulling into thatch-roofed villages devoid of any sign of the contemporary era except dozens of bright red Coca-Cola signs, every storefront red, leaving the distinct impression that Coke was the emissary of progress, the icebreaker of change. First comes Coke, then asphalt, then power lines, then maybe education, justice, and human rights. It was mostly true, though I later learned that Coke gave out free red paint. In the bigger towns, when we entered a restaurant, flocks of kids swarmed the windows to watch us eat. Eventually they grew bored, and by the time we were finished, all that remained of the crowd outside were prints of forehead grease smudged on the glass.

We modeled our road trip on the safari Dan had led. We gave ourselves plenty of time to meander aimlessly through villages, wrestle with strangers, take bad pictures, and get drunk on warm flat beer poured out of old bottles whose lips were as smooth and soft as sea glass. A key difference of this safari, though, was that Tom and Dom were the pilots, and they didn't know anything about East Africa.

"Jeff, go speak some Swangeelee to those fine fellows and sort this out," they'd say whenever we got lost, which was daily.

Cresting one hill, we stopped to figure out where we were. There was no one around to ask. A great plain stretched below, a great green ocean of grass. We could see flat-topped acacia trees sticking up like thumbtacks and zebras sprinkled around. We were perched on the lip of Kenya's Great Rift Valley, the cradle of mankind, though at the time we had no idea.

Dom cut the ignition, stepped out. He peered over the edge of the escarpment.

"I've never seen so much of the world in one gulp," he whispered.

We stood behind him, shirtless, barefoot, in patched, vagabond shorts, nodding solemnly.

◇◇◇◇◇◇

As my Lonely Planet guidebook said, few travelers to East Africa don't dream of climbing Mount Kilimanjaro, summiting at dawn, and looking down at the miles and miles of bushland lighting up with the glory of a new day. Nearly two thousand years ago, Ptolemy wrote about "mountains of the moon" in Africa, and in the 1840s, when Johannes Rebmann, a German missionary, sent back reports of seeing a glacier on the sweltering equator, learned geographers in Europe ridiculed him.

When I got my first unobstructed look at Kili, from a campsite in northern Tanzania where we were staying with Tom and Dom, I couldn't believe it either. Kili is the tallest mountain in the world that's not part of a mountain range. It was huge, lonesome, and startling. The snowcap, which has since significantly melted, shone a brighter white than the clouds. It was higher than the clouds. I knew then I'd never get tired of looking at it.

"I don't think we have the right shit to make it to the top," I told Dom.

"No," he said, looking at me in my ripped shorts and the faded dress shirt that I had bought at a Nairobi flea market for 20 shilingi—Kenyan shillings—the equivalent of less than a dollar. "You don't."

"But Roko and I thought it would be fun to get a little closer—"

"Cool, well, I think Thomas and I will skip it. While you boys are up there sweating your bollocks off, we'll spend some quality time with our"—Dom reached into his jean jacket—"our new little friend." He produced a joint as fat as a cigar. "Have fun."

As Roko and I tromped off toward a roadhouse at the foot of the mountain, I turned around to wave good-bye. Tom and Dom's arms moved slowly back and forth, their faint blue jackets fading away into the rich green hills.

White smoke puffed from the roadhouse's chimney. The windows were clouded with steam. As we walked in, the smells of wet wool, beer, popcorn, and wood smoke sprang at us.

Roko and I didn't have enough money to pay for the official Kili dream—$500 apiece, including permits, guides, and park fees. But we figured that mountain's pretty damn big, there's got to be a way to sneak on. We grabbed two stools at the bar, trying to glance around for someone who could give us a little intel without looking like two young men about to break the law. The roadhouse, with its sawdust on the floor and happy growl of sounds, was where all the climbers hung out. We started talking to a tall white guy named John, mid-thirties, a sportswriter from Denver. He had just summited and was in high spirits. He bought us each a drink.

"Man, you guys are traveling for a year? That's spectacular! You getting sick all the time or what?"

"Yeah," I said.

"Man, when I was in Sumatra in 'eighty-two, I got typhoid."

"How bad was it?"

John paused.

"I lived."

John the Sportswriter didn't know a thing about sneaking up

Kilimanjaro. He had a decent job and had done the whole thing legit—proper guide, proper papers, even some porters. But he seemed on our side.

"The last thing I want to tell you guys, and it might sound weird, but just hear me out," he said, avoiding our eyes. "When I was your age, I did the same thing. I traveled around the world. It was the best two years of my life. I think about that trip every day, even now. You will too."

It was the first time any adult had said that what we were doing had some value. Life would go on, we'd get locked into a job, maybe even end up in some strange place like Denver. But we would always have this trip to call on, no matter what we went on to do.

Fortified, we loaded up on peanuts, Cadbury Fruit and Nut bars, and a reckless amount of cream wafers. We were about to undertake the most physical challenge of our lives on a diet the equivalent of s'mores.

The first morning we tromped through Himo, a little town nestled in the lush green foothills at Kili's feet. It couldn't have been much past eight, but a parade was about to begin, and a fat man with a shiny face plodded woefully down the main road, swinging a perforated can of incense that smelled woody and wonderful. Another man wearing a shiny black tux with dagger lapels, like an announcer at a prize fight, banged a goatskin drum so slowly, *thump-thump*, so softly, *thump-thump*, that my arms were mapped in chills. Behind them, hundreds of villagers lined up, about to march down the road.

All the people were decked out in their best duds. Many looked like they had been pulled straight out of a Middle America shipping container, circa 1978. One guy was wearing five-inch platform disco shoes. There was a certain vulnerability on display that I had never noticed before: all dressed up, the poor looked poorer. The collars on their shirts were rubbed bare; the kids were wearing cracked plastic shoes; every woman in a pretty dress had gaping holes under her arms. At first I was delighted to stand there, watching the parade go by, but then I started to feel like I was peeking behind a curtain. People walked sheepishly past us, as if they were trying to see if we bought it, if we were judging them, if we could tell that their Sunday best was actually somebody else's rags. It was as if they were saying with their downcast eyes, We must look poor, *to you*. The poverty had always been there. But for some reason that day, and thereafter, I couldn't overlook it as easily.

When we arrived at the first checkpoint, we found the path blocked by a big hunk of wood. I stepped inside the warden's hut, which had sheets of old newspaper glued to the walls as wallpaper. Easing down onto a busted couch, I opened with "Habari gani?" *What's up?*

When the warden asked to see our permits and I shook my head, he leaned back on the busted couch.

"Kuna taabu kidogo," he said. *There's a little problem.*

"Might twenty dollars be enough to fix it?" I said, in gravelly Swahili.

He just looked at me.

"Thirty?"

My last sight of the warden, as he lifted the gate and we tromped through, was the flash of a roguish grin.

We opened our map on a mossy rock. Several trails ran up Kili's stomach, and the Marangu route was the gentlest and most popular. We didn't even have to discuss it.

"Fuck the Marangu route," Roko said.

Instead, we marched off on the Umbwe route, the steepest, slickest, rockiest way up, one of the mountain's most neglected trails. We were scaling this thing without permits, so we didn't want to bump into anyone. As we ascended, the trees grew taller, the mists thicker. Soon we heard little else than creeks of melting ice rushing through the woods. The trail was so poorly marked that sometimes all we were working off was a gash in two trees a half mile apart.

We didn't see the mountaintop for several days, but we could always feel it looming above us, that giant, lonely block of ice.

The wonder of climbing a glacier on the equator is that in the span of a few days you slip through several entirely different worlds, one after the other—scratchy savannah, lush jungle, cool misty cloud forest, high-altitude desert, rocky plateau, and finally arctic snowfields. Roko and I fell into a rhythm. We didn't talk much while climbing: the physical exhaustion was total and pure, no annoying joint pain, no fear, no sense of time, nothing but the good clean burn of muscle tissue being pushed as far as it could go.

"Man, to travel with a purpose, that's what we need," Roko said as we lay on a tarp in the woods one night.

"Yeah," I said. "I guess we're just fucking around."

"Now, don't get me wrong," Roko was quick to say. "There's nothing wrong with fucking around, nothing wrong at all. But I'm talking about somebody *paying* us to fuck around."

Lying out there next to my best friend, looking up at the stars, seeing the Southern Cross bolted into the sky, the proportions perfect—it made me sad to think this had to end.

But that night I started to wonder: Was there a way to keep going? Could I figure out a way to construct a life where I was traveling with purpose?

Roko stood up in the darkness, and I heard him reach into his backpack. He pulled out one of our last Cadburys and cracked it in half—dinnertime. In many ways, he was like the brother I never had. I felt very close to him, as close as I had to anyone.

"I don't want anyone saying this shit is easy," Roko said, handing me my half of the choc, which we pronounced "chalk." He eased back down. I bit off a corner and sucked it under my tongue, letting it slowly melt.

"But we can make it," Roko said. "We can make it."

The air thinned out. We were closing in on 15,000 feet. By day four, we were looking down at the tops of the marbled clouds.

But I was struggling to breathe. We were actually ascending too quickly. Any expert would have told us to stop for a day or two and "acclimate," though of course we hadn't consulted any experts—John the Sportswriter didn't count. My chest and throat felt tight; I had a ringing in my ears and experienced strange blackouts where suddenly I couldn't see anything, even though my eyes were wide open, like when you've been sitting for too long and stand up too fast. I later found out that I had AMS, acute mountain sickness, and people die from it on Kilimanjaro. I was also carrying far too much weight, all the crap for my Year On: a three-pound zoom lens, spare shoes, a bottle of Listerine, candles and vitamins, even a large Swahili Bible a Tanzanian priest had given me.

"You okay?" Roko asked when he saw me bent over on a rocky path, the sun blazing all around. I was about to puke, though I had eaten nothing for hours. "Let me take some stuff from you." I unbuckled my pack, and it dropped to the ground with a thud. Roko picked it up, inspected the straps for a minute, then figured out a way to clip my whole pack to the top of his. "You can handle that?" I wheezed. "No sweat," he said. He took one step forward, and his knees nearly buckled. I'm sure the Bible didn't help. "No problem." He grimaced. "Now let's do this thing."

For ice axes, we used triangular rocks we had dug up from the ground. To keep away the frostbite, we wore white athletic socks on our hands. To stay hydrated, we drank snowballs. We could no more see the end of the path, which was buried somewhere in the lofty mountain's head, than we could see the end of our own lives. Sneaking onto Kili was among the stupidest, most reckless things I've ever done, and that's saying something.

At 19,000 feet, at the top of the glacier, we ran into a fence of frozen waterfalls. We were very close now, the summit only a few hundred feet above, if that.

"Dude!" Roko yelled. "Don't go that way. It's dangerous."

"Which way?" I groaned back, spread-eagled over a chute of loose rocks about as easy to scale as a wall of golf balls. The angle of the slope couldn't have been less than 60 or 70 degrees. Each time I moved, up or down, the scree kicked loose. With a shudder, I watched the rocks tumble down, gathering velocity, and as they crashed into boulders a thousand feet below, they made a terrible conking sound.

There's exactly one difference between an adventure and a tragedy: death. I started thinking about the phone call, the news being broken across a muffled line, my parents slowly sitting down at the kitchen table, the quiet engulfing the room. What would everyone think? How embarrassing. But there wasn't much I could do about it now. It was just as terrifying moving down as up. And Roko's chronic chipperness was beginning to annoy me. He was about twenty yards away, slowly but surely making his way across a set of rocks, grinning back at me. It didn't help that I was cold, wet, sweaty, and starving, nearly vertical now, clinging like a shivering rat to a sheet of ice.

Then the sun went down.

"Maybe we should take a break," Roko yelled over.

"Fine," I groaned back. "Khalas"—the Arabic and Swahili word for "That's it."

We crawled toward each other, found a tiny, icy ledge to erect our tent on, and to keep warm, we huddled together on one side of the tent; the other was dangling off the ledge. We were on the roof of Africa. The tip of Mount Kenya poked through a mattress of clouds 200 miles to the north—between those two mountaintops is supposedly the longest span between any two points on earth that a person can see. But this earthling barely had the strength to lift his woozy head. It grew cold, I don't know exactly how cold, but I remember waiting for the school bus when I was a kid and it was 10 degrees outside, and it was colder than that. The air bit through the socks on my hands and the seven layers of clothing I was wearing—I had put on every article in my backpack, down to three pairs of underwear. The sweaty socks I took off to dry quickly froze. So did my leather Italian boots. I puked all night.

"You hear that, man?" I moaned when the sun finally rose—there was light, blinding white snow light, hours before any heat.

"What?"

"Voices."

When I unzipped the tent, a frozen crust of ice and snow slid off. We descended by skidding down on our butts so fast we almost took out the other climbers at the foot of the glacier. We got to our feet and sauntered up to them with pride—even though the skin on our noses was peeling, we were still wearing socks on our hands, and I had dried vomit on my face. They were four middle-aged American climbers, well equipped and accompanied by a team of twenty-five Tanzanian guides, cooks, and porters—the porters had even hauled a toilet on their backs so the *mzungus* could shit up there in true mountain peace. It's as apt today as it was back then—there are essentially two ways to travel Africa: one for the dirt cheap, the other for the filthy rich. We chatted about the mountain and where we were from and the climbers offered us some hot tomato-and-cheese sandwiches, which we wolfed down, two bites each.

What dorks, I thought, looking over at them in their puffy jackets. At least *we* shat in the woods.

Their chief guide, a man with a rough beard, yellowish, malarial eyes, and expensive boots—Remy was his name—looked us over.

"You really American?" Remy said. "Can I see your passports?"

Like the twenty-year-old morons we were, we handed them to him. Remy deposited them in his pocket.

"Kuna taabu kidogo," he said.

"What kind of problem?" I asked.

◇◇◇◇◇◇◇

Two days later, Roko and I were ushered into park headquarters. For breaking several Tanzanian laws and being caught on Mount Kilimanjaro without permits, we were fined $1,200, which we didn't have. "You'll go to jail if you don't pay it," the head of the park told us before locking our passports in a drawer.

Roko and I glanced at each other. *Jail?* There were still a lot of adventures on our joint to-do list, but doing time in a Tanzanian prison was not among them. My mind started to race. If I had to call my parents and they had to get the embassy involved and the embassy had to call the Tanzanians and they found out about the bribe, then that would be the end of the dream. I'd be on the next plane out—if I was lucky.

I apologized profusely, both in English and Swahili, and begged the boss for leniency. He shook his head. Fine, I said. We'll pay the money. But we need to go to the next town to get it from a bank. He reluctantly agreed. As soon as we walked out of his office, I suddenly realized: We're free. Instead of going to the next town, we snuck off on the next bus to Dar Es Salaam, hundreds of miles away. We still had no passports, so we marched into the American embassy to present our version of events.

"That's the problem with this place," the counselor woman grumbled. "It's so damn corrupt. Everybody wants bribes. I can't believe Kilimanjaro National Park, of all places, was trying to shake you two down for twelve hundred dollars."

I nodded, struggling to keep a straight face. At this stage of my evolution, I didn't see the conflict in ripping off and lying about a place I purported to love.

"I'll get you new passports," the counselor said. "Just give me a few minutes."

Roko and I turned into the waiting room and flopped down in two chairs, flicking through a stack of three-year-old *Reader's Digest*s.

"Yeah," I whispered to Roko. "We got the US of fucking A on it."

We slipped each other a quiet, celebratory low five.

Twenty minutes later the counselor woman came back and rapped on the window.

"Come here, boys."

We put down the *Reader's Digest*s.

"I just talked to park headquarters. And I don't know what the hell happened up there. But here's what I'm going to do. I'm going to give you new passports, and I'd advise you get out of Tanzania. Now."

Now seemed harsh. I grabbed my stiff new passport, flexed its cover a couple times, making it my own, jabbed it into my back pocket, and breezed out. There are moments when you're on the fulcrum, when any number of factors can tip the scales, and in Africa being a *mzungu* usually helps.

Roko and I agreed to split up for a couple weeks. I guess we felt it necessary to show we were still tough. We spent one last night in Dar, at the Holiday Hotel—never, ever to be confused with the American chain of a similar name—a guesthouse in the Indian quarter with big, old rooms and high-gloss paint on the inside walls. "Kwa heri," we said to each other the next morning, good-bye, and hugged before walking off in opposite directions.

There comes a moment in the lives of most young men when, for the first time, they move away from the comfort and fellowship of good friends for something those friends can no longer provide. I wasn't aware of it at the time, but as I walked slowly south toward the harbor, the Holiday Hotel shrinking behind me, I was taking the first steps to discovering what that was.

I hopped on a ferry to Zanzibar. I don't think there's a more spellbinding island, or maybe it was simply the fact it was the first place in East Africa where I ventured alone. Even the name—Zan-Zi-Bar—conjures up all the good stuff: the daggers, the spices, the sense of a far-off place that one has heard of, over the years, but has no idea what it is. Or what it was.

A century and a half ago, Zanzibar Island was one of Africa's most prosperous centers of commerce, the capital of a bustling worldwide empire in cloves, nutmeg, elephant tusks, and human beings. Its largest town, Stone Town, was a wealthy, whitewashed city on the Indian Ocean, a maze of narrow, snaking streets linking the port, workshops, apartment buildings, mosques, and the sultan's palace. Its people were Africans, Arabs, Indians, and Persians, and the Swahili-speaking offspring of all those groups combined. Now it was a bit down-at-the-heels, more congruent with the rest of Tanzania, which has always struggled economically, but it still delivered a distinctive sense of place. Its streets were tiny and enigmatic, sometimes no wider than a couple pairs of shoulders, smelling of pungent jackfruit and frankincense smoke that curled out from under the huge, obsessively carved, half-open doors.

You could see the sea, or at least feel it, from almost anywhere on the island. A fringe of fine white sand ran all the way around, forming Zanzibar's legendary beaches. I found a small hotel perched on a coral bluff near a fishing village, but when the manager told me the price, I was torn. I really wanted to stay there, but it was several times more than I had paid anywhere else. It's easy to lose perspective when you're traveling in the developing world. But then I thought, screw it, life is short. I handed over the eight bucks.

At night, bats cruised the moonlit sky, printing their shadows on the sand. A little rectangular carpet of warm yellow light stretched out from the door of each hut, and when I walked past, I could hear people eating their dinner, by gas lantern. I looked out at the ocean, across the sand, out at the boys slipping quietly through the low tide, clutching spears, hunting flounder in the shallows, moving silently as smoke, and my thoughts turned inward.

I saw myself out on that beach, with a girl, all that powdery white sand sticking to her sweaty body. And while I was watching those boys slip through the moonlit water, stabbing the fish with their dull spears, the iron point pushing through the flesh, I was overcome by the idea of how we're all bound together—the boys, the waves, the moon in space pulling those waves around the boys, the mysterious woman pulling me deeper in. I stood on the coral bluff for several minutes, staring out at the dark water. When I got back to my room, I lit a candle, tore a few blank pages out of my journal, and scribbled down as much of this as I could. Later

I popped it into one of those thin-as-tissue airmail envelopes and sent it off to the one person in the entire world who might appreciate what I was feeling.

It was around this time that I had an unusually vivid dream. One night I swear Courtenay crept into my room. As I slept, I willed it to happen, her hair on my cheek, her flickering tiger-lily eyes watching over me.

◇◇◇◇◇◇◇

Roko had left me a note at the American Express office in Dar about where to meet him next—that's how we communicated, wrinkled notes scribbled out for each other at American Express travel offices and at the free poste restante of various post offices around the world. It usually worked. Our plan was to meet up on the shores of Lake Tanganyika, near the same spot where Henry Morton Stanley found a shaggy *mzungu* standing with some Arabs and supposedly said "Dr. Livingstone, I presume?" As I emerged from a colonial-era train carriage that had been packed with dozens of travelers, children, and squawking chickens, my face dirty, my hair floppy and dusty, I saw a shaggy *mzungu* standing along the tracks with a huge smile. Roko didn't bother with "Mr. Gettleman, I presume?" He yelled out "Waz upppp!" We walked off together, arms around each other's shoulders, the crowd thinning out. We spent a couple days with some fishermen we met on the lake, then picked the smallest, dingiest border post to cross back into Kenya. I slunk up to the immigration desk.

"Habari, bwana," the officer said.

"Habari," I returned cautiously.

I produced my passport with a shaky hand. Was he about to type my name into a computer and realize I owed the United Republic of Tanzania $1,200?

There was no computer. Or even a phone.

We proceeded to a noisy, litter-strewn bus station with dozens of battered vehicles lined up, engines revving, clouds of diesel smoke wafting into the sky. Touts for the various operators waylaid travelers, pulling and pushing them toward the open doors. It looked only partly like a game. Roko and I jostled our way past the touts, hands thrust deep in our pockets so no one could pickpocket us. We shouldered our way deep into a jacked-up bus back to Nairobi that was nearly full. Buses here don't have precise schedules; they depart only when full. When we arrived in Nairobi, we jumped out, feeling good: we had just stiffed an impoverished African nation a thousand dollars. We began walking to Dan's house.

As we strutted through Uhuru Park, one of the biggest parks in the city, I heard loud footsteps behind me.

"Bwan," I said to Roko, grinning—that's what we called each other, bwan, short for bwana, or sir in Swahili—"we about to get jumped."

"Yeah, bwan," Bwan said. The idea that someone would contemplate jumping *us* was laughable.

I didn't hear my camera strap snap in two, my dad's lovingly cared-for Olympus tumbling away into the abyss of Nairobi's underworld. I didn't feel the fabric of my pants splitting as the muggers slammed me to the ground and tore out my wallet and money belt and passport and around-the-world ticket. People were all around, but no one came rushing in for the rescue. I kicked screamed yelped wiggled, but it didn't matter. Adrenaline is just like anything else: it has its limits. I had four grown men on top of me, grinding me into the sidewalk, their hands racing all over me like they were trying to defuse a hidden bomb. Everything's fine, until it's not—I would learn this again and again.

Anger came. But my initial reaction was the opposite. I was overcome with joy that we hadn't been beaten up. *Getting mugged ain't so bad* was really my first thought. Later I realized that the amount of cash we lost was the exact same amount we owed. The Motherland was simply claiming its debt with what Mafia loan sharks and Yiddish grandmas call "vigorish."

Dan was amused.

"Uhuru Park, huh? What'd I tell you boys 'bout walkin' around dis town at dusk?" he said in his mock southern drawl.

Roko went on to Bombay. I had to wait several days in Nairobi for a new passport; if you lose two passports in a short time, a bored counselor at the embassy has something to investigate. I spent my final night in Africa at Dan's, up on the veranda again. A lot had happened since our last midnight meeting. I had bribed my way up the continent's greatest mountain. Dan had talked his way into Somalia. I had seen the anarchy of an African bus station. Dan had seen anarchy in the streets.

There was so much I wanted to share with him. I had an irrational certainty that this part of Africa would become part of my life, had to be, would never not be. Getting mugged or nearly falling off Kilimanjaro didn't decrease it. Those episodes, if anything, made me feel like I could hack it here. But I didn't dare voice this to Dan; my adventures seemed microscopic compared to his. So I just lay quietly on my back on the foam mattress, breathing in the night jasmine. Dan was right next to me, but I had the sense he had quietly slipped across the border to adulthood. His eyes were firmer, that glimmer of mischief dimmer. I thought it was simply the maturation process, how at some point you have to simmer down the kid and rev up the man and step into the adult world with a new voice and a new way of being. Childhood ends. The rest of life begins. But at the time, it hadn't happened to me, so what the hell did I know.

Dan looked off into the darkness.

"Well, Jeff," he said. "I guess this is it."

And it was.

THREE

◇◇◇◇◇◇◇

EVANSTON, 1993

Coming in from Chicago on Sheridan Road, the first thing you hit is Calvary Cemetery, established before the Civil War and a beautiful sight at night, with the mist rolling over the graves, the oak trees shivering in the wind, and the granite angels gazing out at Lake Michigan.

Keep snaking up Sheridan Road into the heart of Evanston, and the apartment buildings give way to lakeside mansions with carports and enormous imposing doors. Five minutes farther north, you come to the corner of Ridge and Colfax. There's a relatively modest brick house with a ginkgo tree out front. That's where I grew up with my sister Lynn, two years older, who alternately beat me over the back with a LeSportsac bag and tried to make sure no one else ever messed with me. The window on the top left, facing out toward Ridge Avenue, was my room.

A mix of maples and oaks arched over the street, and at 2:00 a.m. in the summer the window-unit air conditioners churned, the cicadas buzzed high in the trees, and a few insomniacs watched *Letterman* reruns—the sounds of a suburb putting itself to sleep.

The trailer was parked not far from there, on Lincoln Street.

Kevin and I exited his Volvo. His hands were empty. Mine held a foot-long wrench.

"Time to liberate," I whispered.

We had been eyeing the equipment trailer that belonged to Campus Painters, one of our rivals, for nearly a week. We were just at that stage of life where it was beginning to dawn on us that the world wasn't nearly as complicated as we had been led to believe. You didn't need any specialized felonious know-how to break into a locked trailer. All you needed was a big wrench.

I handed it to Kevin. He slipped the mouth over the padlock at the trailer's rear end, tightened, and began twisting. We weren't picking the lock; we were simply going to rip it off. I glanced up and down the street. "Come on, man!" I whispered. "Do it!" Finally I heard the lock clank to the asphalt, and we giggled so hard diving into that treasure of drop cloths, brushes, 5-in-1s, and ladder jacks that we nearly pissed our shorts. There was no house painters' honor code, not for us. We cleaned out other crews with an unrepentant giddiness.

All that I had said before about feeling more connected to my fellow man, being more in touch with what mattered, the wisdom of East Africa, well, I wasn't quite ready to actually live like that. I tried not to think about what I was doing, stealing when I hardly needed to, stealing for kicks. I know from the experiences of most guys I grew up with that I wasn't alone; mischief was our muse. Scanning the leafy streets, plucking things from the aisles of 7-Eleven, crank calling, hurling roll after roll of toilet paper into the trees outside some girl's house, illegally climbing mountains in Africa were all part of our quest to feel a little risk. Fear, trepidation, nervousness, dread—at some level we knew these were portals to something greater, and we craved them. The fact someone else was on the receiving end of our self-development was rarely a factor.

Da Vinci Brothers was the key to my overseas operations. Hanging off the back of a Land Rover yelling "Habari!" on the dusty roads of Kenya was possible only because I slathered Benjamin Moore paint—black, brown, hunter green—on Tudor houses every summer in Evanston. Our band of Da Vinci Brothers consisted of me, Roko, Kevin, Benny, and another childhood friend named Beef. We were usually joined by a few other college students; we lost numbers whenever someone landed a real job. None of us were brothers, none of us was remotely Italian, and none of us could execute a clean, dripless brushstroke, though our motto was "If your house isn't a masterpiece, we didn't paint it." Believe it or not, we got a few jobs.

In the mornings we hit the paint stores—we didn't steal paint—and we often crossed paths with the professional painters, the ones with the tool belts, chirping pagers, and bristle-brush mustaches. "Check those dudes out," Benny whispered to me one day as we waited in line for a gallon of custom-colored high gloss to be mixed in a machine that straps the cans into a metal vise and shakes the shit out of them. Three adult painters stood in spotless overalls. "The real fucking thing," Benny said. "The real fucking thing."

Not one of the original Da Vinci four, but a close friend who needed a job, Benny came on at thirteen bucks an hour and rose up to crew chief. He was a bit loose with the brush, but was a gifted entertainer. As we worked, he read aloud swatches of the dirty plays he was writing or led us in another round of a game of his, "Would You Rather . . ."

Of all of us, Benny probably had the most Kerouac in him. He dropped out of college, moved to the Left Bank for a year, lived on a barge on the Seine, and then came home and announced he was going to be an actor. He was full of joy and a very good listener. He talked of coming to Africa one day. "I think I'd dig that place."

Benny was my second friend to die. He was diagnosed with ALS at thirty. The disease started messing with his wrists at first, then his fingers, then his tongue, then the nerves in his legs. It strapped him into a wheelchair, thinned his hair, and turned his once-beautiful face into a liver-spotted skull. None of us could believe how fast that disease cut through him.

When I saw Benny for the last time, years later, he was parked in a wheelchair in a nearly empty apartment on the north side, the fall afternoon sinking into twilight, a Jamaican nurse softly drying dishes in the kitchen. Benny was down to skin and bone, his vanishing body a host to his never-ending will. All that was left was a thin, creaky voice, more like the vapor of a voice.

"Scoop," he whispered. That was his name for me. "This shit is worse than AIDS."

But in the Da Vinci Brothers' heyday, the summer of 1993, Benny was still very much with us, broad-shouldered, trim-waisted, topped with dark, curly hair. It was his idea, as crew chief, to change the radio station we had always listened to, B96, the Killer B, sure to be playing classics on the order of "Dreamlover" and "Whoomp! (There It Is)" to National Public Radio. "Good for client relations," Benny explained, and he was right. Listening to NPR bestowed upon us smelly mini-men an erudite air that we otherwise lacked.

One morning we were "throwing paint," as we used to say, on a large house in South Evanston. Benny was on the ground, digging out old glaze from a windowpane and laying in new sludge, and I stood on a ladder, sloshing a shutter with rust-colored oil paint that all of us Da Vincis agreed was an ugly-ass color, but the owners had rejected our learned advice. It was mid-July, the searing season. We all had our shirts off. Our backs were beginning to turn a stupid shade of brown.

"Hey, Jeff!" Benny hollered up.

"Yeah!"

"Something about Somalia."

"Sweet, man. Turn it up!"

All the Da Vincis knew I had a friend in Somalia. I had told each of them, about fifty times. My buddy Dan this, my buddy Dan that, it was the most lopsided buddyship in the history of buddies. I am fairly certain that Dan never told a soul in Mogadishu that he had a friend named Jeff slapping paint on houses in Chicago.

But that didn't stop me from eagerly scanning the papers, looking for Dan's name in tiny lettering beneath the black-and-white photos, checking the mailbox for one of his letters. In the relatively short span since I had been to East Africa, Somalia had gone from an African country that nobody gave two shits about to the biggest story in the world, as act 1 of the New World Order went up. Banking on the notion that a little food and a couple of Black Hawks could fix any overseas problem, George H. W. Bush sent 25,000 American soldiers to help pass out supplies to starving Somalis and restore some order to a land cast into chaos by the warlords. It was a humane act, one of his last as president.

Dan had finagled his way into Somalia before the Black Hawks, before the marines staged their melodramatic storming of the (unoccupied) beach. He cruised the pockmarked alleyways of what the marines called Skinnyland, photographing a country on the verge—jeeps whizzing around with heavily armed ten-year-olds, tanks on fire, a cathedral in ruins, women with AKs under their tea tables and luscious sneers across their faces that said in every language known to man, "Just try me, motherfucker."

One of the youngest foreign journalists in Skinnyland, Dan loved it. From the few photographs he had sent, I saw him in cutoff shirts, arms marbled with veins, strutting around Mog with a Stetson, Nikons dangling from his neck, and a 9mm pistol—something journalists would never do today. He couldn't have looked much cooler. He landed spreads in the world's biggest magazines while at the same time hustling postcards and T-shirts he had printed that said "Doing the Mog." At age twenty-two, Dan had cracked a key segment of life's code: how to get paid for being yourself.

"UN forces attacked from the air . . . entire operation took less than twenty minutes . . . press photographers went to the scene. . . ."

"Benny, turn it up, I can't hear it at all!"

" . . . a mob attacked them and killed two. Two others are missing and presumed dead."

Those last words—*missing and presumed dead*—sent a jolt up the ladder. Dread, fear, revulsion, shot through me, along with something cheaper and less savory, an electric feeling that I hate to admit was a variety of excitement, like the kind we were constantly trying to make. Wait, Dan was just killed? *In Somalia?* But the instant I thought that, I knew it wasn't true. Dan would be here for a long time. He'd tell me about what happened to those four journalists when I talked to him next. I finished the day, painting several window frames, sealing up the paint, folding up the stolen drop cloths.

When I returned home that night, I found a note on the dining-room table.

"Hayden called," my mom had scribbled.

Innocuous words, but I hadn't heard from Hayden in a year. She had been on that first Dan safari, traveling across Kenya with a Maasai boyfriend. As I squinted at my mom's scrawl, I felt something I hadn't before: I was deeply afraid for another person.

Hayden's phone rang and rang. So I raced into my room, somehow found my old Africa journal, punched into the phone, 011, 254 . . . Nairobi.

"Yes," a man answered, not Dan's dad.

"Hi, um, I'm a friend of Dan's and I'm calling from Chicago . . ." Silence.

"I wanted to know if anything happened to Dan today. Is he okay?"

The only sounds I could hear were cars softly whooshing down Ridge Avenue.

"No," the voice finally said. "Things are not okay. Dan is dead."

I stood in that room by myself for some time. *Dan? Gone?* I closed my journal and drifted downstairs and into the garage. It was around midnight. I fumbled with the keys to a U-shaped Kryptonite bike lock and wheeled the bike out. About a half mile away was the lake, and when I rode down there, it was deserted and muggy, a haze gathered around the streetlights. I sat on a big rock at the edge of Northwestern's campus, staring across the water, waiting for dawn.

I had closer friends, but Dan had been better at life than anyone else I'd ever known: he was himself, he explored, he had fun doing good things. I don't see how anyone could have spent time with him and not been significantly altered. Until I went on that first safari, I had simply assumed that I was going to be a lawyer in Chicago when I grew up, just like my dad. But Dan was like an abrupt left turn. He made that all-important introduction: Jeff, World. World, Jeff.

I heard a voice whispering out to me over a dying fire, smelled those *jua kalis* in oily rags from River Road, saw him standing on that beach, the Windex sea rising gently behind him. And then I saw Dan sprinting frantically down a shot-up alley with the strangest of looks on his face. No one had given him his rear viz. I later learned that an American military helicopter had hovered overhead as the mob closed in. A warning shot, even a measly smoke grenade, would have made the difference. The pilot flew away.

What happened next has never been made clear, and I obsessed about it for years, asking many people, in many different places, for anything they could tell me. Did Dan drop to his knees and beg for his life as the mob closed in? Or die on his feet? Was he smashed in the back of the head with a rock? Or a rifle butt? Was he stabbed? I'm not sure any of it matters. What does is that Dan died in a moment of chaos and anger. His last feeling, so antithetical to his life, was fear.

I now see that Dan took too big of risks for his age. But at the time, while Dan was burning up in front of us, none of us did anything. We all just stood back, admiring the pretty flame.

When the night finally ended, I looked for meaning in the sunrise, but the sun didn't rise. The cloudy sky gradually turned a mild pink. I looked south, toward Chicago's skyscrapers emerging from the mist. Never again would I think that it was into one of those buildings that I would eventually disappear. I pedaled home slowly.

Dan's sudden exit had upended everything I thought I knew about luck and life. He had done so much for others—the refugees, the people he photographed, all those lives he changed. Dan loved Africa. How could Africa not love him back? As I arrived back in the garage and locked up my bike, I settled on the one thought that remains the only thing that makes any sense about his death, because it doesn't: the mob made a mistake that day. They got the wrong guy.

I didn't go to his funeral—I'm sure I could have, but it wasn't as if anyone invited me. I was told it was like the passing of a beautiful king. People flew in from all over the world and stood together in the Ngong Hills, where Karen Blixen had had her farm, under one of those life-changing skies. Dan had been a sensation in Somalia, this talented, charming, witty kid, and correspondents from the biggest media houses in the world came to say good-bye. I could see them all standing there, shoulder to shoulder, hands clasped in front of them, though their faces were fuzzy. I didn't know what such people looked like.

Months later, the Eldon family sent me an envelope, a little heavier than normal. I opened it carefully, sliding a knife beneath the fold, as I always did with every letter that came from East Africa. Inside was a single postcard, a picture of an old Moroccan steamer that Dan had madly decorated with squiggles of ink. It was with him when he died, found with his cameras, some old receipts, and a folded-up Emerson poem.

It was addressed to me, but blank.

⬦⬦⬦⬦⬦⬦

It just so happened that the same week Dan was murdered, Courtenay flew back to the United States from her Year On in London. We hadn't seen each other for eighteen months—an epoch when you're in college.

Our writing had picked up as the day of our reunion drew

near, an intense flurry of longer and more provocative letters. "All I could dream about was me, on that dark beach, lying beneath you," she had written about the Zanzibari dream I had shared. "You were kissing my neck and they were my hands in your hair." It was an incredibly sexy thing to write, and we hadn't even had sex. But if Dan's life—and death—had taught me anything, it was to eliminate the what-ifs, to jump into the car when it was time to jump into the car and drive when it was time to drive, even if the object of that drive was eight hundred miles away. We usually regret inaction, not action. I credit Dan with planting that seed in me, the notion that when presented with a choice, there's really only one way to decide: take the path of least regret.

After one night in Manhattan, I drove across the Tappan Zee on a perfectly clear Saturday morning, the sun turning the rusty girders into a delicious gold. I turned off the bridge at Grandview, curled beneath it, popped out onto a narrow curvy road. River Road. Another River Road. I was excited but nervous about what was going to happen, unsure of where we were going with all this epistolary buildup, but somehow certain that this was going to be different—how, or from what, I didn't know.

When Courtenay stepped out of the back door, in khaki shorts and a sleeveless denim shirt, her eyes shining like polished obsidian, her arms splattered with freckles, I got a hitch in my throat. Someone was smiling at us from the kitchen window—Courtenay's five-foot-two grandma, in her floral muumuu. Grandma knew.

I was walking from my car, Courtenay from the side of her house, and under a great big pine on her front yard we reached for each other. Courtenay hugged me like no one had ever hugged me—long, hard, eager. She was it. I knew it that instant. I squeezed the hell out of her. That certainty, my face in her hair, the breeze— there would never be a better moment in my life.

The rest just flowed—sitting with her parents, joking with Grandma, strolling out by the Hudson, so majestic up there, nearly at its widest point, peeling off each other's clothes. I had saved two condoms from my first safari, one red, one blue, given out free at a border post in Malawi. I'm sure they were expired—they had been waiting in my wallet for three years. When I tore open the foil of the first one, Courtenay and I just looked at each other steadily, for a second. Those two days of that weekend, I felt there was every reason in the world why we were together.

"You get laid?" Benny asked as we were up on two new ladders, side by side—we now had more "liberated" equipment than we knew what to do with. I kept dabbing the eave. I may have been back in Evanston two days later, throwing paint, but I didn't go ten minutes without returning to Grandview. I read her letters at night.

How close the sensation was of my nightgown slipping off, of my body pressing against yours. I cannot wait for August to press on until I am able to be with you again.

When school started, we reunited for good. It hadn't been easy reentering college after my Year On; I had felt adrift, disinterested. Everything seemed of lower voltage compared to what I had felt traveling around the world. But now I was in love, and that changed the very geography of campus. Courtenay led me on walks along the gorge, the two of us quietly following leaf-scattered paths that I hadn't even known existed. She took me into cozy restaurants that smelled of warm food that I had walked by a hundred times but never bothered to look into. Fall passes through Ithaca quickly, and soon the nights were so cold and crisp that when we kissed standing on her porch, our bodies shivering, the inside of her mouth felt supremely warm.

I was fascinated by every inch of her—her long, curly hair, the India-shaped birthmark on her right knee, her flat stomach, the dark stubble of her armpits.

One morning, after she had left for class, I climbed out of her bed and started to snoop around. There was a black book on the floor of her closet. I opened it. It was filled with drawings—women in long dresses, ballet dancers, couples intertwined. I was stunned by how well she could draw—she was a Russian lit. major, not an artist—at least, I hadn't thought of her that way. I sat on her bed, slowly turning the pages, and for some reason I felt this surge of happiness so intense that it triggered a kind of sadness at the same time. Here was proof, page after page, of a pure and searching heart that seemed to belong to a different, less cynical era when love didn't spring from drunken hookups or stupid parties. And this heart was drawing, day by day, closer to mine. There was even a black-and-white picture she had made of a guy with big eyes, a biggish nose, and a goatee. The resemblance was unmistakable.

Over the next few months, Courtenay taught me so many things I didn't know I didn't know—how to eat Chinese food with chopsticks, how to make dinner with spaghetti and a can of olives, how with salads, it was all about the dressing, and how to move in sync with her in such a way that she saw colors.

"What was that one?" I asked, after an especially intense moment.

"Purple."

She was the president of the Cornell Democrats, and one night a famous journalist came to town—of course I had no idea who he was.

"Hello, everyone." Courtenay smiled, in front of a packed auditorium. In such circumstances, I always got egg voice. Courtenay didn't quiver. She was so clear, so alert, her eyes confidently sweeping the room, drawing everything in. People were nodding as she spoke. When she finished her introduction and handed over the mic, heads turned and trailed her back to her seat. It was hard to believe she was my girlfriend.

I still toggled between the frat house and the classroom, though Courtenay gently pulled me more toward the latter, or at least made me feel good in the middle. We went to a few more dances, and sometimes Courtenay would suddenly shout, "Ooh, I love this song. Come on!" and tug me onto the dance floor.

"Courtenay!" I yelled over the music as we danced. "Did you want to dance with me? Or did you just want me out here so *you* could dance?"

She'd laugh, her eyes bright, as if I'd caught her out, and then she'd drape her slender arms around my neck, giving me a squeeze.

We usually avoided the scene at the library and did our homework up in her room. She was an astute reader and proofread all my papers.

"You have to be clearer," she was always telling me. She'd be lying in bed, knees up, circling things on my dot-matrix printouts with a felt-tip pen. "The world does not have enough topic sentences."

Her intellect was part of the attraction, as was the fact that she was as opinionated as me. She took her Cornell Democrats seriously, trudging through the New Hampshire snow and knocking on doors for Tom Harkin, the most liberal candidate in 1992. Bill Clinton, she said, was "a big fat sellout."

She was quick-witted, hot-blooded, highly expressive, and slightly unpredictable. Once when I was lying on her bed, arguing with her about something, she suddenly stopped talking. An odd expression crossed her face, almost like a faint, unwanted smile. She took one large step toward me and socked me in the stomach. I milked her guilt for two and a half days. When you learn to love, you learn to fight.

◇◇◇◇◇◇◇

The morning of my big interview, we stopped underneath the clock tower, where our paths diverged.

"You all set?"

"I think so."

"Got your résumé?"

(It was a joke that I even had a résumé. Da Vinci Brothers was part of it—I even had the gall to mention something about how I was a "project manager" in charge of "equipment acquisition.")

"Yep."

"You know what to say, right? Tell him about Dan, tell him about your Swahili, and tell him why you want to be over there. Don't be nervous."

"I'll try not to be."

"Don't worry, you'll do great." She hugged me tight.

The Peace Corps recruiter was sitting in an empty classroom, reading a book. The Peace Corps was the easiest route back to Africa, and I wasn't opposed to taking it—there were hundreds of jobs all across the continent in countries such as Tanzania, where JFK had sent some of the first volunteers. The recruiter asked me to tell him about myself, and I started with my summer in Malawi and how I was now in my fifth semester of Swahili and nearly fluent—or at least I could fool you that I was fluent—and I followed Courtenay's advice and dropped Dan's name. "I love Africa," I said. I didn't know what else to say—the guy was annoyingly quiet.

He nodded and said I sounded like a "neat kid"—both words highly offensive.

Then he looked away.

"I'm sorry, but we need soil scientists, not philosophy majors."

The guy was clean-cut, he worked for the Peace Corps, and he didn't even have a beard. Now where was I supposed to turn? The Peace Corps was like my safety school.

I stepped outside, feeling suddenly weary. I looked around the Arts Quad at the students walking under the leafless trees with their Birkenstocks and wool socks. The limestone buildings seemed so classy and permanent, like they would never change. I have three months left, I thought, and my college transcript—American Indian literature, Indonesian, Swahili, Kant, ethics and public life, black-and-white photography, modern Japanese history, capped with Nautilus weight training—is a map to nowhere, drawn by a blind cartographer.

I had the Where, but no idea about the What.

"You ever think of working for a newspaper?" a creative writing teacher suggested.

"Newspaper?" I blanched. And I actually said the following: "Who wants to write for a boring newspaper?"

Photographs for newspapers, however, had some potential. At least you were out of the office, capturing action. I shot some pictures for the *Cornell Daily Sun*, sports mostly, and after every shift, late at night, after I had developed my film and blow-dried my negs, I sat down at the AP LaserPhoto machine and printed out wire photos from Africa. It was one of my ways of staying in touch.

One evening in the spring of senior year—this was April 1994—I dropped by the office to grab a couple rolls of T-Max to cover a lacrosse game. The AP machine began spitting out images, on its own, somehow, of churches full of bodies, schools full of bodies, rivers thick with twirling bodies. The post–Cold War mayhem was convulsing across the continent, from the Horn of Africa, where it started, to Africa's lush green heart. More people were slaughtered, hour by hour, in Rwanda than during the height of the Holocaust, and the Hutus didn't have cattle cars or gas chambers. They used machetes and nail-studded clubs.

The photo editor walked by the AP machine and glanced at the photos.

"Shit, man, that's nasty," he said. Then he lifted his eyes to the schedule on the wall. "Princeton on Saturday. You got it?"

"Yeah," I said. "I got it."

◇◇◇◇◇◇◇

I made a lot of calls those next few weeks, searching for a way back. Finally one person answered. When the time came to break the news to Courtenay, I found her reading in bed in her room on the top floor of an old house, branches with tight little buds gently scratching the glass of her window. I got in next to her and began stroking the smooth underside of her arm.

"The whole summer?" she said.

"Yeah, the whole summer."

She turned away to gaze out the window.

"Why didn't you tell me about this? I thought we were going to spend the summer in New York together."

"I don't know. I didn't think it was really going to happen."

"Ethiopia? *Really?*"

"Yeah, Ethiopia's really cool. It's the only country in Africa with its own alphabet, it's got all these old churches . . ."

I didn't understand that her objections weren't about Ethiopia the place. I didn't realize the full extent of how betrayed she felt. She had spent the past year formulating a life together, thinking we were going to move in with each other that summer and get married, and here I was ambushing her with the news that I had just accepted an internship for Save the Children across the world. I say I didn't understand, but I had kept my plan under wraps because at some level I knew how hurtful it would be. This was the beginning of my spiraling off, of my throwing away years of us being together. Often it's not the bad things that split people apart but the opportunities. I guess this is what happens when you fall in love, for the first time, with two things at once.

On my last day in Ithaca, we walked down to the park with a Frisbee—Courtenay loved Frisbee. We stood as far apart as we could, the disc spinning smoothly from her hands to mine, an immensely comforting rhythm. I waited with my head tilted back as it floated down from the mostly clear skies—that was one of Courtenay's favorite expressions, mostly clear skies. All our months together were now collapsing into a few hours left, then just a few minutes. That's when it hit me with tremendous force: What the hell am I doing?

I cried the whole way to the Syracuse airport. She remained sweet and dry-eyed, following the curves of Route 13, the farmland sliding away from the sides of the highway. Her face was riveted to the road, our windows down, the air cool and fresh.

Right before I took off for Ethiopia, I reread her last letter.

I can't believe I won't see you for dinner. My life is going to be very different now but I know we will be together again. Do you know how much you mean to me? Do you know? I am in that car with you, Jeffrey.

FOUR

◇◇◇◇◇◇◇

ADDIS ABABA, 1994

The light came in thin and gray. I could see it at the top of the windows, where the curtains didn't quite fit. Traffic began to move outside. I was awake, but the gauze of my dream still clung to me.

If I moved a finger or even a toe, it would send electric impulses through my body and awaken all my senses and she would disappear. But if I was really careful, and lay perfectly still, it was like Courtenay remained with me. This happened many times that summer, never to happen again.

One morning I was so sure that I had just felt her cool leg against mine, smelled her hair, that I was confused for several seconds before I realized that I was lying on my back alone in a bare room with a naked lightbulb dangling from the socket above me. This was strange new territory for me: I was here, thinking of there. Jesus, I said to myself, rolling over on my stomach. Time to go to work—in Ethiopia.

Electricity was an infrequent visitor, water a total stranger. My "shower" was one sharp icy bead that I had to carefully position myself under to get clean. Outside, it was mid-fifties, wet, misty, an algae-like chill dripping over everything. As soon as I walked out the door, I was sighted.

"Ferengi! Ferengi!" the beggars yelled, using a term that means just what it sounds like, "foreigner," and lacks the merry mystique of *mzungu*, the man who walks in circles, though that was exactly what I did all summer. Addis was like an unfinished thought. Many of the streets didn't have names. "Take the one that goes to the airport" or "Follow the one that runs by Meskel Square." Everywhere I looked, something was broken: a window, a railing, a car cruising around with no hood, a woman trudging along with no eyes. A putrefying menagerie of dead rats, dead cats, dead dogs, even dead donkeys, lay strewn about the streets. Oh, I missed Nairobi. Where was that tidy grid? Where was that night jasmine? Addis's Candyland maze stank of death and diesel.

The country had just emerged from thirty years of civil war, and disbanded soldiers saluted me from the curb, half of them with legs sawed off. Begging was Ethiopia's leading economic activity. From that sea of penniless wanderers one man emerged whom I'll never forget: Naked Man. I'd see Naked Man striding through traffic with a staff of bleached wood, looking like a prophet, his massively swollen balls hanging low. He'd present himself to an unwitting minibus, and the passengers would recoil in horror, frantically pushing coins out the window. I could hear them clinking on the pavement. I rooted for Naked Man because he was on to something. He knew what the entire giving business turned on: shame.

My shoulders were tight by the time I arrived at work at the rehab center in the Kirkos slum, where Save the Children provided several hundred street children goopy *injera* meals, Ping-Pong, and an allegedly safe place to play. The whole compound smelled like fresh, wet mud. I lied to myself every day of that summer, calling this a job—it was an unpaid internship, and nobody cared whether I showed up or not. Sometimes it wouldn't be until lunch that the head of the rehab center, a portly Ethiopian man, bothered to say *tadias*, hello. I dreaded lunch. It would be me, the social workers, our guard with the heavily scarred knuckles, and eighty-five street kids taking our seats on hard wooden benches. The grub was traditional Ethiopian food served by a homeless priest with black fingernails who insisted on tearing off a swab of *injera* bread and dragging it through a plate of *mesir wat*, a molten, spicy red lentil stew, and then stuffing the food directly into our mouths. I didn't appreciate that this was a standard Ethiopian gesture of hospitality. I just thought it was gross.

An hour later I would stand up from my desk, mumble to the guard that I had to go to the bathroom, and dash to the latrines, ripping off my pants as fast as I could, trying my best to not sound as though I were exploding like a grenade. Once on the way home, during rush hour, I was so sick I couldn't make it back to my apartment and threw up on the sidewalk, hunched over, my legs shaking, a crowd of people parting around me, frowning at the spreading puddle at my feet. "Don't worry, Jeffrey," the head of the office said when I called to tell him I was deathly ill. "It's just a twenty-four-hour bug. By tomorrow night, you will be fix-ed." Ethiopians pronounced the "ed" like that, as a separate word. I felt like I had cholera, though of course I didn't.

Time moved through my apartment like sludge. Most evenings passed with me sitting in my living room as the light slowly died, mindlessly chewing discs of semi-stale bread and mushy wedges of Laughing Cow cheese, the only food that didn't give me the shits. I ate and missed Courtenay. I spent two thousand dollars that summer, the last vapors of my Da Vinci fortune, calling her in New York, and when the time came to hang up, neither of us could ever bring ourselves to do it.

"You go first."

"No, you."

I begged her to take a couple weeks off so we could meet in Zanzibar.

"I have visions of white beaches and blue water, little houses and mosquito nets," she wrote in one of her faxes—this was when faxes were still big, and every afternoon when I stopped by headquarters, I went right to the accountant's desk where the new fax machine sat, covered in ancient Ethiopian dust. "Our fascination endured

18 months, it can endure more. Know that I love you, my sweet baby, and I will count the days until I see you again."

It ended up being a lot of days. Courtenay had landed a job on a political campaign in New York, the candidate she worked for was headed into a tough primary—Eliot Spitzer was an opponent—and she couldn't get any time off. I was sick with longing for everything we did—Frisbee, the sushi dinners, lying in bed at night and sharing our days, the kissing (one of the few things no one can do alone). It was in this apartment that I discovered something I would inflict on myself several more times: the primacy of loneliness. If you're working hard and lonely, or traveling a lot and lonely, or even chasing down a dream and lonely, you're still, at the heart of it, just lonely.

On the rare night, if I was lucky, Jose Lorenzo called me up to watch the World Cup (Brazil beat Italy that summer, again). Jose Lorenzo was a cheery Filipino in his mid-thirties with black plastic-rimmed glasses and a Frito Bandito mustache, running one of the world's biggest condom distribution programs—the AIDS pandemic was just about to hit Ethiopia. He used to be an executive at a razor company, and it was all the same to him: he was a salesman, a damn good one. He taught me more about aid work than anyone else. He knew that it took strategy, not heart.

"Just look at Coke," he said as we settled down in front of his TV, a cooler at our feet holding a six-pack of Bud that he had somehow scored from the American embassy.

"Back in the seventies, or maybe it was even earlier, some chumps in Atlanta figured out how to convince poor people in Africa that they needed Coke."

It was true. How could I forget all those little towns, one after another, with the red Coke signs everywhere, like shrines?

"Just think about it." Jose Lorenzo paused for emphasis—and a swig. "For eons Africa had been absolutely fine drinking tea and brown water, but all of a sudden they just had to have a Coke. A little sugar, a little caffeine, a few bubbles. It was magic. Remember that seventies slogan? 'Coke adds life'? That'd be fucking nice."

I nodded, happy I wasn't chewing those discs of semi-stale bread by myself again.

"It's all about marketing, man. If you're trying to get people to *use* condoms, you have to make them *want* condoms. You got to package it right, come up with a story, make people think that if they use your products, they're the coolest amigo around. Coke nailed it. So did Anheuser-Busch."

Jose Lorenzo grinned at the tin can in his hand.

"You actually think this shit is drinkable?"

◇◇◇◇◇◇◇◇

Jose Lorenzo wasn't the only expat I glommed onto. There were others, though I can barely see their faces: the strung-out Canadian ecologist whose fingers twitched as he gobbled fries at Burger *Queen*; the fifty-year-old Kenyan cowboy who danced with teenage hookers at the discos, his liver-spotted hands around their fluted necks; and one doughy American embassy employee who never told me what he did or where he came from or what his real name was, who unfortunately I remember quite vividly. "Just call me Captain Jack," he insisted. We converged at muddy bars and mediocre restaurants, equally lost, equally unhappy, tenuously connected by two things: a profound loneliness and a lack of melanin. Captain Jack got his kicks by humiliating Ethiopian waiters, and I have always felt that you know everything you need to know about a guy by seeing how he treats waiters.

"You know Africans," Captain Jack snickered one night after sending the waiter back to fetch something he didn't actually need or want. "They can't learn. It's not their fault. Their IQs are just lower. Shit, they can't even swim."

Looking at his puffy face, it occurred to me: Why exactly am I hanging out with Captain Jack? Courtenay would have stood up and walked out.

I was thinking of her, as I often did, as I stared out the mud-streaked windows of an old bus groaning up a hill, past peasants on their knees in barren fields. I needed to get out of Addis. Someone had told me about a religious festival in a place called Kulubi, and when I climbed off the bus ten hours later, it was like I'd stepped into the pages of a storybook. The hillsides teemed with white tents, thin blue smoke rising into the sky. As I walked into the crowd, I started to feel better. People lifted their chins and nodded to me, the only foreigner around. I could smell fresh eucalyptus and roasting coffee. Soon I befriended a guy named Gebre who slapped into my hand two pieces of *tere siga*, chunks of raw beef, a delicacy served on special occasions. Heavy as D-cell batteries, they took five minutes to chew. But they were salty, bloody, juicy, and good. And in that extended movement of mastication, I finally felt like I was back on the road.

Gebre insisted we fight our way through the moist throngs to the center of Kulubi's action, a small and blocky church that didn't even look that old. It was ringed by a moat of beggars—the blind, the crippled, the half-dead, the almost dead, the mad, the beautiful, all doing spectacularly, their bowls heaping with silver. All cultures have their own internal aid system, and many Ethiopians, both Christians and Muslims, believe it's good luck to give to beggars during the Kulubi festival. For one day each year, beggars became kings. One legless guy asked me if I wanted to *fly* home with him.

Gebre soon disappeared, leaving me for hours drifting through the crowds, looking for his face before it dawned on me that he probably had better things to do than serve as guide to a clueless *mzungu*. That's how the whole summer went, brief intermissions of camaraderie separated by vast stretches of solitude. It was so different from my first summer in Africa. There was a misery here that wasn't leavened by thumping reggae rap or close physical contact. I didn't walk hand in interlaced hand once. I'm fully aware that my impressions of Ethiopia were tinted by the most bottomless loneliness I've ever felt. I found it cold and suspicious, anathema to the Africa I had constructed in my mind.

As night fell, a cool wind swept down from the hills, and I trudged toward a two-story shack. I needed a place to sleep, and there weren't many options. The wise beggars had booked up all the proper guesthouses, paying their bills in waterfalls of change.

"Room?" asked a pretty young woman standing in the doorway. There were actually a few pretty young women standing by the doorway.

"Yes, a room," I said.

"Come with me, ferengi."

We plodded up a narrow flight of stairs, like in a Wild West saloon. She wore a loose-fitting Ethiopian robe, like a toga, and she moved well and knew it. She opened a door into a dark room and leaned over to light a stub of wax. She wore no bra. I saw all the way down her shirt.

She lifted her face to mine but remained bent over.

"You like?"

I couldn't think for a second.

"Yass, sister," I mumbled. "I like, I like."

Gently, she lifted back the bedcovers and looked at me. Two wrapped condoms had been thoughtfully placed on the bedside table, probably passed out by the likes of us.

"So?" she said.

My girlfriend was ten thousand miles away. What were the odds Courtenay would ever find out? What were the chances this would lead to anything?

But I didn't even need to ask those questions.

"I'm sorry." I looked away.

I had no urge to be with this woman. I just wanted to get into bed—by myself. She sneered at me, twisting her face into an ugly expression I wouldn't have thought possible—her features actually transformed, sharper nose, beadier eyes, crooked teeth—and then she yanked the sheets all the way back. She grabbed a large aerosol can from the floor and fumigated the bed, sending up a cloud of toxic particulates between us.

"Night," she said, swishing away.

◇◇◇◇◇◇◇

Ethiopia used to be an empire. It was one of the few places where the Africans had repulsed the *mzungus*—Adwa, northern Ethiopia, 1896—and it had never been colonized, save a couple years of military occupation under Mussolini. Many of its kings claimed to have descended from an affair between the Queen of Sheba and King Solomon; this storied history, going back hundreds of years, fed into the fierce national pride. But the whole Horn of Africa—Ethiopia, Eritrea, Sudan, Somalia—has a pox on all its houses. The Horn sits at a strategic intersection, where Africa and Arabia, the Red Sea and the Indian Ocean, Christianity and Islam, white and black, all meet. Superpowers fight for this space.

In the 1960s and 1970s, the United States propped up Haile Selassie, Ethiopia's last emperor, an elegant little misanthrope who traveled around with an enormous retinue of sycophants, modernizing parts of his country while starving others, until a cabal of army officers strangled him and buried him under a toilet. Upset about losing its guy in the region, the States halted a multimillion-dollar arms shipment to Ethiopia, and the Russians stepped in. They started supplying arms and sending in Cubans. In response, the United States soon began backing Somalia, Ethiopia's archenemy, which had been a stalwart Soviet client state. It made absolutely no sense—or perfect sense. The two superpowers simply switched sides. So it goes in Africa.

Ethiopia and Somalia went to war over the Ogaden Desert in 1977, and ever since, the border area has been hot. Toward the end of my time with Save the Children, I pleaded with the bosses to send me down there. The Ogaden rebel movement was just beginning to hatch, but I didn't know that. I just wanted something to do.

"I'm glad you asked," one of Save's administrators said. "Because it's actually a cool project, with these nomads becoming farmers. This way, when there's another famine, or if there's another war, they'll have more resources at their disposal. They're terracing the hills, and you can grow a ton of crops that way. Maybe get some pictures of that?"

I nodded enthusiastically. From what little I knew of the aid world, this was an essential duty: to document. If there isn't a picture, there isn't a project. Donors need to see proof that their krona, yen, pounds, or dollars have been transformed into a new feeding center or a series of neatly terraced hills if they're going to keep writing checks.

I was matched up with a field officer named Solomon; he had no interest in going, but the whims of the *mzungu* had to be indulged. For the two-day drive to the Ogaden, Solomon and I didn't talk much. The silence was broken when we pulled into Dolo Odo, a small town encircled by Somali refugee camps, and we saw a little boy dash out of his tent with a splatter of green diarrhea dripping down the back of his leg, his mother running after him. "These people," Solomon grumbled. Like most of our staff, Solomon was Amhara and despised the Somali nomads. He likely feared them too.

The project site was still hours away, and we made what now seems an odd choice: we left our truck in a crowded refugee camp and drove off with a local aid worker, in his car. When we arrived at what we thought were "our" hills, we found nothing—no terraces, no crops, no nomad-farmers.

We drove around some more. The landscape was mostly flat, though there were a couple of crumbly little hills here and there.

"Maybe this one," Solomon said, looking up at another hill. "Maybe that one."

He had been casual at first, but I soon noticed that he was clenching the strap dangling from the window tighter than he needed to.

Then we ran out of hills.

We motored back to the initial spot and cranked open the doors.
I cupped my hand over my eyebrows and could now see, barely, a
few faint steps crudely hacked into the hillside and some tendrils
of red, white, and blue plastic sheeting flapping in the wind, the
torn-up terrace material, donated by American taxpayers.

"Those bastards." Solomon glared at me. "I was just here a few
months ago. I saw them. And now they've taken them down."

If that summer had worked out, everything afterward might
have been different. When you're young, each summer is a bridge,
and that summer I was crossing that great middle-class *mzungu*
bridge from college to life. What Save the Children was trying to
do out in that desert wasn't easy, offering alternatives to a deeply
rooted, wandering way of life that had its own real adventures and
freedoms. And I would never say *all* the projects were a bust; back
in Addis, I'd taken pictures of vaccination and feeding programs
that were running just fine. But at that moment, I wasn't thinking about those other projects. I was standing at the base of a hill,
staring up at a heap of sand where, I had been led to believe, there
would be signs of progress, but instead saw only flapping pieces of
plastic. I realized then that I had been aiming all summer toward a
place I didn't even want to go to. I scratched aid worker off the list.

I later learned that the nomads had played us for fools. They had
zero interest in becoming farmers but went through the motions of
terracing the hillsides every so often to get the sacks of grain that
came as part of the deal. They probably didn't even eat that grain,
but sold it on the open market to buy guns—you need guns to
rustle camels. Then they'd tear down the terraces and do it again.
The intentions of the project were not so dissimilar from what Jose
Lorenzo had been saying about Coke. We were trying to rebuild
people in our image, convincing them that *our* way of doing things
was superior to *their* way, that they should put down *their* tea and

pick up *our* Coke. The Somalis were proud people too, and they'd essentially said, *Screw that*. Or maybe it was simply that we had done a poor job at marketing.

⬦⬦⬦⬦⬦⬦

I knew something was wrong even before I smelled smoke. As we motored back into the refugee camp where we had left the Save the Children truck, we were surrounded by shouting children. They jabbed their fingers at us, laughing, "Dab! Dab! Ferengi dab!"

When we cut through the crowds, we found our truck a blackened husk, not a fleck of paint on it—a stunning work of postmodern art: tires melted into shiny black puddles, seats burned into cages, side windows reduced to icicles dripping from the tops of the window frames.

"That's glass." I didn't know what else to say to the gleeful crowd pressing around me. "Glass."

There had been an accidental cooking fire, someone said. The fire (*dab* in Somali) spread, another said. Our car had been trapped, the first guy said.

I scanned the compound. Several extremely flammable thatched huts were positioned around a square of hard-packed dirt. None of the huts had been burned. Actually, nothing else was burned, not a straw.

More people started gathering around, yelling at each other in throaty Somali, shooting me hard looks.

"Stop staring!" I hissed. "I'm just the fucking intern!"

We were two days' drive from safety, on the edge of the Ogaden Desert, in a small town without a phone, no other foreigners around—and now we had no way out.

A few times in life you want to click your heels and go home. This was my first. I still loved East Africa, I was even thinking of climbing Kili again, but I hated this place. I had let it come between Courtenay and me. I had indulged myself in silly dreams of solving my confusion about life by committing myself to solving others' confusion. But what if they weren't confused? What if they didn't even want my help? From pit latrines to condoms, we were trying to assist countless people in every aspect of their lives, from how they shit to how they fuck. And many didn't even like us. And now they were torching our cars.

◇◇◇◇◇◇◇◇

Night rose around us. Dolo Odo's darkening flats lit up with the small red pinpricks of cooking fires. I looked for what Dan had taught me, the sudden absence of flies, which meant the mosquitoes were coming. Soon I was swarmed by malarial mosquitoes feasting on my bare arms. I swatted as many as I could, furious at myself for forgetting to pack bug spray.

I was so exhausted by the time we found a truck that minutes after we started to rumble down the road, I passed out in the backseat. It must have been around midnight when I was jolted awake by a loud metallic *thwack*. The wheels of the left side jumped up, and the driver gunned it. Solomon and the driver kept looking back nervously.

"What's going on? What happened?"

"We hit a soldier!" Solomon shouted back to me.

"What? Is he dead?"

"I don't know! And we're not stopping!"

The next morning the three of us—me, Solomon, and the driver—stood wordlessly in the sunlight, in a grassy courtyard of a guesthouse somewhere near Awasa. A long, green, greasy smudge stretched from the truck's front fender to the gas tank—probably from the painted clip of the soldier's gun. The evidence was right in front of us. We had killed a man. But I brushed that away. What was this going to mean *for me*? I could feel my stomach bubble, the pressure and panic building.

We found out later that the man, or boy, had bled to death. The prevailing wisdom in rural Africa is that it's dangerous to stop if you hit someone because a mob could adjudicate the case on the spot.

Anyway, that's what we told ourselves.

◇◇◇◇◇◇◇

My final assignment for Save the Children was to compile a newsletter. No one was going to read this thing. It would be stuffed into an envelope and tossed in the trash. Or maybe I should have spared the recipient the paper cuts and sent it prefolded, as a paper airplane.

I resumed my solo voyages around Addis, but this time I was supposed to be interviewing people who lived on the street. I had an excuse now to talk to any stranger and go beyond the standard traveler's curiosity, so I tried it. I spent more than an hour with one family who lived in a cardboard hovel that looked like a fort American kids would make for fun, and I hung out with a pair of former child soldiers looking for honest work. Midway between the wet feeding site near Mercato and the street children center in Kirkos, I realized the day was half over and my notebook nearly full.

So I went out the next day, and the day after that, visiting more cardboard colonies, then a leather workshop set up specifically for ex-combatants, raising my head to make some notes of my own about the belts dangling on the wall, how the whole workshop smelled of rawhide and something akin to nail polish. It was nice, for once, just to watch those boys hang their heads over their workbenches and do their thing without me trying to counsel them. The aid industry has saved millions of lives, but it is complicated (and maybe this is a necessary evil) by a set of feelings that often leave the getters feeling patronized and the givers feeling a little cynical.

But the simple and oddly satisfying task of collecting information felt different. To some degree, it leveled out the *mzungu* factor.

Granted, on this continent, I would always be a soft, privileged outsider. But at least now I was dependent on the cooperation and openness of others, and my notebook wasn't full of prescriptions. It had been blank. They were filling it.

After the child soldiers, I found myself sitting across a desk from a man named Tewodros who ran a small street children project, asking him the name of his center, where the kids were from, who funded it, future plans.

"You see . . . Jeff, you said, right?"

"Yes, thanks, that's right."

"Well, Jeff, what we're hoping to do is build a fifteen-by-twenty annex for the boys to . . ."

The older I get, the more I believe that the only thing we have to offer is what we've been through. People listening can take it or leave it. That day I listened.

I sat in a chair with no back, scribbling notes, thinking of the next question. There's always that thrill of learning something new, feeling your brain grow inside your head, no matter what that something is. But this was far more powerful. It came on quick, and inexplicably, like anything remotely profound. I suddenly cared about what Tewodros was saying, and he cared that I cared, and the way his eyes lit up when he told me about that annex lit up something in me. A current shot up between us. That's exactly the sensation a good interview delivers: it gives you a surge, it makes you feel connected, it adds some purpose to life.

Tewodros saw from how hard I was pressing my pen into my notebook that I was with him all the way.

As I flipped to a clean page, one of my last, because Tewodros was really streaming now, a smile crossed my lips. I thought: Wait a second, wait a second, wait a second here. Maybe this is it.

FIVE

◇◇◇◇◇◇◇

CENTRAL FLORIDA, 1998

Amanda Brown, seven years old, went missing on Friday, September 11, 1998, from her trailer home in Seffner. The night before, her mother, Kathy, a part-time junkie, had gone to a bar, met a crabber named Willie, invited him home, and the three of them hunkered down in front of the TV to watch *Titanic.* Kathy told Willie that her back hurt; Willie prescribed her five Valiums. When she came to the next morning, Willie—and Amanda—had disappeared.

Kathy panicked, called 911. When the deputies ran his name, she learned she had brought home a child molester. Willie Crain, who looked like Ichabod Crane, gaunt and hunched, with wild black hair, had gone to prison for raping several little girls. He warned one that if she ever said a word, he'd slice her into crab bait. He should have been in prison for fifty years. He did about six.

The police began looking for Amanda in Willie's crab traps. They slogged through the mangroves, dragged rakes along Tampa Bay's mushy bottom, brought out the bloodhounds to stand on the decks of airboats, the K-9s sniffing for all those oils and juices that rise to the surface when a body begins to soften up and rot.

They found nothing. They searched Willie's skiff, his crab shack, and his double-wide mobile home. Nothing. They cut off the covers of his mattresses, they swabbed and dusted. Nothing. I'd covered a few homicides by this point, and I'd never seen the deputies so helpless. They couldn't even make Willie give a blood sample, because although he was the prime suspect, there wasn't any real evidence against him. Willie denied knowing anything about Amanda's disappearance, saying the last time he saw her she was sleeping in her mama's bed, and maybe she just done up and run away, though that seemed odd—what seven-year-old runs away in the middle of the night? Then he retreated from the fray. No one knew where he was hiding.

I drove out to the Crain family business, the Crab Hut, a slapboard shack hanging over the bay. I found his adult daughter standing behind the register, boxing up some blue crabs.

"Sorry you got to deal with this," I said. "It must suck. But my boss sent me out here to see if there was any chance I could talk to Willie."

Those first few words are all that really matter—and often it helps to hang it on the boss. It's also the tone you strike, the eye contact.

The daughter looked at me hard, and I stared earnestly back. I swear we connected for a second. She was still watching me closely as she picked up the phone and dialed.

"Dad, got some kid here from the *St. Pete Times.* Talk to him, will ya? I got customers."

It was a Thursday afternoon, nearly a week after Amanda's vanishing, when I pulled up to Willie's double-wide. Sheets of aluminum foil were spread over the windows to reflect the sun. Redneck AC, it's called.

I stood on his rotting porch, stomach muscles tight, my knuckles raised to rap on the screen. I caught a whiff of something. Overpowering, industrial, toxic. I was racking my brain, trying to place the smell, when the screen door flung open.

"Howdy, Gee-off!" Willie said. "Come on in!"

The screen banged behind me. Willie turned the lock in the door, sealing the two of us in, together.

"Come on back," Willie said.

He was about five ten, wiry, sharp-shouldered, wearing Levi's and a purple T-shirt. I followed him back to the dining room, walking the length of the trailer. It wasn't all that long, but I certainly wouldn't have wanted it one foot longer. The linoleum sank a little beneath each step, but the place was spotless—the VHS tapes on the bookshelves were perfectly straight, the counters on the kitchen looked like they had been freshly wiped, the rugs were sparkling white. Bleach. That's what I'd smelled on the porch. It was even stronger inside, that nose-tingling, hyper-clean swimming-pool smell nearly obliterating all the other swampy smells of dense humidity, stagnant water, and endless foliage.

He sat down at a table, in front of a plate of pork chops. I eased myself into a chair. My back was to the door, which I didn't like.

"Woo," Willie said. "Woo-wee. Steamy one out there, huh?"

"Yeah," I said. "It's hot. Bet it's gonna rain."

"Don't mind if I keep eatin', do ya, sir?"

"No, no. Please."

The sauce got all over his fingers and his face as he cut the meat into chunks.

"Hey, Willie, what's going on with those?" I said, pointing to two black stripes running up the sides of his wrinkled neck.

"Yas sir, them my jugulars." He was oddly formal, a lot of *Yas sirs*, *No sirs*. His eyes were flat. "If the po-lice want my blood, yas sir ree, the po-lice can come and fuckin' git it—all of it."

He had traced his jugular veins with a marker pen, so it would be easier to slit his own throat. An open Buck knife sat on the table, next to a freshly oiled whetting stone and a pack of Juicy Fruit. I was twenty-seven years old, and now on a suicide watch. I had no idea what to ask next. Part of me wanted to ask him: Wouldn't it be easier to slit your wrists or drink some of that bleach than to cut your own throat?

Instead I said, "Willie, you seem real hungry."

He put his fork down, looking up at me.

"Damn skippy, I'm hungry. I'm starving. This is the second meal I've had since the kid died."

He resumed shoveling the pork chops into his mouth.

I might have missed it. I was so nervous, and this had all been the small talk, the warm-up for the interview, words exchanged that you don't always remember because you're just getting settled. But he'd just said "since the kid died." Up until then Willie had stuck to his story—that Amanda must have run away.

He knew I had heard him correctly, that I knew what this implied. His right eye started twitching.

My toes curled in my shoes. A shiver, like the kind you get when you see someone bleeding real bad, ran up the back of my leg. The Buck knife still sat six inches from his hand. I thought of the locked door, the bleach, the crab traps. How many crab traps would my body fill?

Both of us tried not to seem aware of what we were both aware the other person was aware of. I wanted to bolt, but I knew he could grab me and that the door was locked. So as dry as my throat grew, I rasped out more bullshit questions. I focused on the lines in my notebook, how straight they were, how imperative it was to follow them, how if I wrote perfectly on them, I might make it out.

Not once did I lift my eyes to meet his. I was afraid of what I might see. And terrified of what he would know.

◇◇◇◇◇◇◇

Journalism was the What. Some type of writing life had always been in the suburbs of my consciousness, but without that jolt in the Addis slum, I don't think I would have ever seized it. Journalism was traveling, journalism was adventure, journalism was having an excuse to talk to whomever you wanted, journalism was sticking up for the little man and making powerful people scared of you, and journalism was, most of all, my ticket back.

From the mists of the future, a path was emerging, backward toward me: if I wanted to be a foreign correspondent based in Africa—make that East Africa—I'd have to get to a big paper, and to do that, I'd have to work at a medium paper, and to do that, I'd have to start at a small paper. It would probably take three to five years, but I could do this, I was thinking, I could do this. I should have listened to that creative writing teacher at Cornell, but back then I was too cocky to listen to anybody.

I wasn't instantly transported from the Addis slum to Willie's trailer. There were a few steps between, which time has since compressed into slim volumes on my mental shelf. After that lonesome summer in Ethiopia, I did a master's degree in anthropology at Oxford, where the dons assigned me stacks of books on linguistics, kinship, structural functionalism, land tenure, and "the political economy" (whatever that means—I still have no idea), reducing the cacophonous African village, full of life, sweat, laughter, and work—and most importantly, people—to a two-dimensional chart of symbols. The Oxford dons had accomplished the impossible. They made Africa boring.

But while masquerading as a graduate student, I wrote my first newspaper stories for the student rag, the *Cherwell*, practicing my interviewing techniques on some of the folks who dropped by campus—Desmond Tutu, Salman Rushdie, Jeremy Irons, Prince Charles, and the like. I was suddenly so fixated on being a journalist that within a couple of terms I rose from photographer to writer to editor to *the* editor, supposedly the first American to hold that job in years. The last outsider that anyone could remember who had been this deeply sucked into the paper was a plucky Australian business manager back in the 1950s—Rupert Murdoch.

I wrote to Murdoch, asking for a real job, but he never wrote back. So I cast my line deep into American newspaperdom. I made inquiries to the *New York Times*, the *Chicago Sun-Times*, the *Los Angeles Times*, the *Sacramento Bee*, the *Fresno Bee*, the *Arizona Republic*, the *Boston Globe*, the *Lowell Sun* (where Jack Kerouac began, as a sports reporter), typing out cover letters, xeroxing clips, licking the bitter paste of manila envelopes. Not one of those publications wanted anything to do with me, but I kept pushing. I knew if I didn't try as hard as I could to break into journalism, I would regret it for the rest of my life. Few things in this world are as discouraging as unrequited mail, so I was elated to finally get a message on my answering machine from the *St. Petersburg Times*, in central Florida, which turned into the only full-time job offer I got. And when I got it, Bill Stevens, the boss of the area where I would be working, said, "Jeff, this is a good job, a really good job. Actually, it'll be the best fucking job in journalism you'll ever get."

Better not be, I thought. This is just my first stop.

I started out in a small town called Brooksville, in Hernando County, and so my beat was small-town carnage, one-on-one war. Brooksville wasn't Evanston, certainly not Oxford, and I didn't know the first thing about .45-caliber hollow-points or how to talk to parents whose child had just been stabbed to death. No one sat me down and said, This is how violent the richest country in the world really is, how husbands bash their wives' faces with Jim Beam bottles, how the silence and thickness of the woods breed spectacularly sadistic fantasies—how journalism, especially local journalism, is nothing but a history of violence. In my first year, from a town of 7,000, I covered a father and son who nearly killed each other over a meatball, a rodeo rider who punched out a judge, rapes, drownings, fatal car wrecks and murders, including one petrified young mother blown away in front of her kids by an estranged husband while 911 was on the line, listening helplessly.

And people say Africa is violent.

Brooksville was even named after an act of violence. The "Brooks" comes from South Carolina congressman Preston Brooks, who became an instant hero across the South in 1856 after he stormed onto the Senate floor with a metal-headed cane and nearly beat to death Charles Sumner, an abolitionist Massachusetts senator. Since then, Brooksville hadn't changed much. You wouldn't have been a fool to think the municipal flag was the Confederate flag; that's what you saw flying everywhere except in the Sub, short for "Negro Subdivision," its Jim Crow name still in use. The Sub was the most interesting part of town, littered with old Cutlasses and Delta 88s and sinking cabins surrounded by chain-link fences and short-haired fighting dogs. On hot summer nights, it thumped with Tupac and smelled of lighter fluid. The Sub had one old prostitute who the cops told me would lie down for a pack of cigs, and when I pulled over at her corner—I was determined to tell her life story, from birth to the cigs—she eyed me warily.

"Boy," she said, stiffly stepping into my car. Her face was hollow and waxen. She seemed as uncomfortable as I was. "You wanna date?"

I lived in a lemon-yellow duplex. I drove a blue Honda Civic. I met a lot of guys named Junior. I wore Dickies, short-sleeved collared shirts, and a Save the Children tie with smiling, different-colored faces. I was clean-shaven, with shorn hair. If you had spotted me stepping out of my car, you might have thought I was a young door-to-door encyclopedia salesman or a Mormon. My day began at nine. I squatted down in the entryway to the county jail, which smelled of piss and Ajax, put my lips up to a little slot in the armored door, and yelled out: "St. Pete Times!" Eventually someone grumbled and pushed the log through, and I hungrily scanned the offenses column, searching for Murder One, Murder Two, Rape, L & L (lewd and lascivious), and A & B (assault and battery). Then I raced off—to the fire station, the police station, the Hernando County sheriff's office, the courthouse, chasing the morning mist lifting off smooth black roads, chasing the life-changing mistakes people had just made, chasing Africa dreams in citrus groves and the trailer parks off California Street.

What the editors at the *St. Petersburg Times* were trying to teach me was that people didn't want dry copy, some "news item." Boiled-down information is as flavorless as boiled-down vegetables. They wanted a story. St. Pete was the land of the anecdotal lede

(as it is spelled in newsrooms), a technique of backing into an article, whetting the reader's appetite, turning the whole industry-
standard inverse pyramid on its head. Instead of starting off with
all the heavy facts, giving away all the goodies at the top, I learned
how to spool them out, because that's how the best stories are told.

It's not:

BLACK FOREST, GERMANY—Two young children, Han-
sel, 8, and Gretel, 5, were nearly burned to death Friday afternoon after a rather large woman with a wart on her nose lured
them into an oven and . . .

But there were rules.

The trick was to write with a measure of restraint. The editors
were teaching me my third language, newspaperese. Think of it
as eighth-grade English, heavy on verbs, light on adjectives, the
shorter the sentences, the better. The idea is, if you keep out emotions and play it straight, the journalism will be objective or something close to it. There were also the practicalities of deadline. It's
not easy to make art in an hour. But you can write a story.

Yet from the earliest days, I resisted journalism's gospel. I enjoyed
tinkering with ledes, obsessing over the most basic words—should
it be "punched" or "slugged," "ran" or "dashed"?—searching for
the right feel, trying to tuck in a little metaphor here or there.

Less is more, Jeff, less is more. I can't tell you how many times
some dork on the copy desk, the last line of editing before the story
was sent to the printers, felt obliged to tell me that. And I always
wanted to shout back, *No, fuckhead! More is more!*

Every time we sat down at our terminals and stared at that black
screen—we didn't have Internet, or even Windows—the question we really had to answer wasn't who was murdered where, but
Who do I want to be today? Raymond Carver or Gabriel García
Márquez? Long sentences or short? Deadpan or flourish? Rob, another junior reporter, wrote that a bodybuilder who had just been

killed had "arms like sinewy balloons." Cut. I wrote that a boy who said he had been raped lived with a shame "that stained his whole world blue." Cut.

Rob and I became instant allies, the more-is-more insurgents. Rob punched a hole through the back door of our office the minute he picked up the paper and discovered sinewy balloons had been deleted. He vowed in that splintering fury to build a doggie door for the copy editors to crawl through every morning, should he ever become editor. I was convinced that somewhere in our building lay hidden a machine—we had to find it and take it out—called "The Vanillaizer" that the copy desk ran all of our stories through, turning them into pure newspaperese. Without fail, the Vanillaizer would detect my favorite line, and *bleep!* it was gone.

With awe and envy, we worked ourselves up reading the masters of the day, like Rick Bragg of the *New York Times*, who was allowed to lay it on thick. The first female president of the NRA was as "tough as a day-old biscuit." A Florida housing project was "a leaky bucket of a place where dreams seem to run right on through." Bragg wrote in a passionate vernacular about prisoners, the poor, people in trouble, and reading his work made me ask: Why write with your balls cut off? Why be frightened of hearing your own voice?

But not everyone in Brooksville liked the sound of my voice.

To the Editor: I cannot imagine any scenario that would inspire your reporter, Jeffrey Gettleman, to write the type of article that appeared in your paper Oct. 24. Evidently, Mrs. Van Rooyen was gracious enough to grant him an interview, show him through the home she had shared with Mrs. Norton, and even let him look in the refrigerator. He responded by referring to Beth Norton's "veined hands," Mary Van Rooyen's "wrinkled ankle," a "musty bedroom where Jesus posters paper the wall," and the "messy Hershey's bottle." Once I heard a remark made about a certain New York television reporter to the effect that he was the type who would have asked, "Aside from that, Mrs. Lincoln, how did you like the play?" I suspect that Mr. Gettleman fits that description.

Mr. Gettleman didn't give a hoot. He was in the daze of writing stories. The city editor, Mike, gently tried to rein me in. He had seen so many young reporters come and go that the first thing he told any of us was, "When you live in a small town like this, you're going to learn what you like and what you don't like. You're going to learn a lot about journalism and a lot about yourself."

I didn't know what the hell Mike was talking about. I didn't have time for self-reflection.

∞∞∞∞∞

Courtenay came down every month to spend the weekend. She was working for a senator now in Washington, her office in full attack-dog mode, rallying around the man she used to call "a big fat sellout," trying to beat back Newt Gingrich and the Republican uprising. It wasn't easy, after the Monica Lewinsky scandal broke. She and her gang of Senate aides sneaked into the gallery at the impeachment hearings, and I could tell how exciting it was by her voice over the phone each night. We were following our own paths but still together. She was an excellent sport about my new life. The first time she visited, I took her for breakfast at the Hungry Thyme, a diner down the street.

We were sitting in a booth, on the same side, as we always did.

"Is this a joke?" she said as she read the menu, its corners split from all the traffic. "Eggs, toast, *and* hash browns for ninety-nine cents? In Adams Morgan, this would be ten bucks."

There was something now a little sharper about her, more mature, less collegiate, more sophisticated, more judgmental; it was both attractive and disquieting. To me, Adams Morgan sounded like the name of one of my frat brothers. She had her own life now, full of people and places I didn't know.

After breakfast I proposed a canoe ride. We jumped in an old van piloted by a smiley guy in a jumpsuit who drove us several miles through the woods to Silver Lake. There we lowered the canoe into the water and paddled with the current, and soon the world closed beautifully around us. We were on the Withlacoochee—Muskhogean for "crooked river"—slipping slowly through a hushed landscape of live oaks dripping with Spanish moss and half-submerged forests of cypress knees, baby alligators swimming with their little tails wiggling back and forth in the water next to us. That water had a color and quality I'd never seen—so full of tannin it looked like root beer. The air was luxuriant with that tropical smell of irrepressible decay and irrepressible life that Florida breathes, in and out—I could always taste it the minute I landed. It was a secret slice of American wilderness back there, almost as untouched as anything I had seen in Africa.

"This is beautiful," Courtenay said. "How'd you discover it?"

"A homicide."

"Oh."

We bought matching clothes at Brooksville's army surplus store, patronized the beat-up roadside stands that sold flat, greasy pieces of smoked mullet, a bit bony but not bad, played tennis on one of the few courts in town. Courtenay had played recreationally as a kid; she had taken lessons every summer in Saratoga, where her mother had grown up on an apple farm. Her strokes were smooth, racket all the way back and cocked before the ball even hit the ground; she could send it over the net in a line drive as hard as I could with half the effort.

That was the story of our lives. We were from the same line, but she was the superior model. Both of us came from intact families of four, we had the same liberal arts degree from the same college, we had nearly identical Eastern European Jewish family histories that went back hundreds of years, we were branches of the same tree. She just didn't grow up breaking into trailers. She didn't crash into stationary objects (I crumpled my Civic against a fence one night in Brooksville). She wasn't selfish. She didn't have that instinct to always look at things to see how they would advantage or disadvantage her. I didn't know people could be so naturally moral, and if I hadn't met her, I probably would have never known.

She encouraged me to apply to the biggest papers—"What's there to lose?" As we stood at the mailbox, my hands clutching a stack of manila envelopes neatly addressed to the *Boston Globe*, *New York Newsday*, the *Chicago Tribune*, the next step, she'd say: "Fly away, clips, fly! Find the right desk to fall on!"

The months turned to seasons. The seasons to a year. The pain of the coming good-bye became so great, it began to blot out the joy of the entire weekend visit. The bliss of waking up together, of sharing space, of finally being able to sit thigh to thigh again in the back of the Hungry Thyme, cooled into the dreary knowledge that in a few dozen hours, all this was going to end. As Tobias Wolff once wrote, "Happiness is endless happiness, innocent of its own sure passing," but we knew it was about to pass. The pressure of making the most of every minute and being carefree made those weekends anything but. I projected self-confidence about my work, my choices, all that I was chasing, but the way I felt on the morning of our departure made me question everything.

We woke up in the steamy dark of my duplex, and as I slipped on my pseudo-professional costume of tie with no jacket, Courtenay, who hadn't had the heart to pack the night before, sat on my bedroom shag rug, quietly folding her clothes into a black duffel. Our eyes were scratchy red as we motored slowly out of Brooksville, south down Highway 41 through Masaryktown, a soggy hamlet where people brewed their own wine and habituated raccoons.

We clutched each other on the airport curb, her bags at her feet, my Honda still running, her arms around my neck, hugging me so tight, just like that first hug under the pine. It was madness. Anybody and everybody could see it. Once, during this era, we were sitting close to each other in a banquette in a New York restaurant, maybe I was stroking her hair or she had her arm slung around my waist, and a stranger, an older woman, came up to us and said, "I'm sorry to interrupt, but I just have to say it's so nice to see a young couple so clearly in love." What fools we were.

"Don't cry, honey," were Courtenay's parting words. "We'll see each other in two weeks!"

Before those two weeks had a chance to pass, I was sitting in my duplex after work, slumped half-naked in my raggedy living-room armchair, when I heard a knock at the door. I peeked out the window. A blonde in a blue hoodie was standing outside. Bevyn. Bevyn was a friend of one of my neighbors who liked to talk, about what, it didn't matter. She also liked to leave me notes, in exaggerated capital letters, telling me she wanted to work at Blockbuster's and that she had a crush on somebody, but it was a secret. Bevyn was eighteen.

"What's the haps?" she said, leaning against the doorframe. "Out of town again this weekend?"

Bevyn was barefoot, her feet tan and dirty. She was cute, with bright eyes and an earnest face, but nowhere near as attractive as that Ethiopian hooker. This time, though, I started asking the questions—What are the chances Courtenay will find out? What are the odds that tonight will have any bearing on my life? I was in my mid-twenties, living in an outpost town, and I don't think I had fully gotten my head around the idea that I would spend the rest of my life with one woman.

"Hey, Bev," I said. "Come on in."

By her wide eyes I could tell she was impressed by my adult-like existence—the eleven books stacked against my living room wall, the Save the Children tie draped over the chair back, my car keys casually tossed on the floor. To a girl straight out of high school and living in a town where many struggled to make rent, I guess there was some cachet to hooking up with a guy who had an aqua-blue Honda and a j-o-b.

We embraced on my shag carpet and started kissing, wetly. I could feel my face heating up. Part of me wanted to stop right there, but the other part tugged her hoodie over her head and reached around her back and unclasped her bra, tight, on the last hook. I stood there for a second weighing her breasts in each palm. My pulse quickened. No less-is-more bullshit around here.

It wasn't long after Bev that I met a student at the University of Tampa named Julie who asked if I wanted to check out her dorm; then an office manager built like a Dallas Cowboys cheerleader with a little imagination and a couple margaritas, and a divorcee lawyer who solicited my permission to perform certain quite welcome acts—both named Kelly. There were a few others, too, some older and more confident than me. I was energetic going in, slightly remorseful coming out, but I liked the conversation, the backstories, the unpeeling, the tension, the way those nights pointed so cleanly in one direction like the tip of a spear. I liked slowly unbuttoning a girl's shirt and yanking off her jeans. I liked stepping into a new apartment and glancing around at the Ikea dining set or Pier I Papasan chairs and photos hanging on the wall, thinking: Who *are* these people? I was attached to the idea that there was something cleaner about these mini-relationships that had a clear beginning, middle, and end than the interminable void I was stuck in with Courtenay.

Maybe I even wanted to hurt her. Maybe my frustration at not being with her was hardening into anger, anger *at* her.

◇◇◇◇◇◇

I glanced around the trailer and pushed my chair back.

"Willie," I said, "I gotta go."

My deadline was approaching, and I had more than enough material to work with—that I didn't say. While I stood on that rotting porch again, making my last sorry efforts to seem casual, Willie said, perhaps in an attempt to cover any slipups he'd made, "Don't worry, Gee-off, any day now that li'l girl's gonna just pop up."

Pop. Up. That's exactly what the police and the weekend dive crews combing Tampa Bay were waiting for, for Amanda Brown's little seaweed-wrapped body to *pop up.*

I locked the Civic's doors, wrenched the key, pulled out into the road, and stamped down the accelerator. The yellow stripe pulled me faster and faster toward the office. I had a scoop, and I knew that scoops were my ticket out. Only once I was safe in my cubicle did I realize that if I told my editor about Willie's slipup, he'd make me put it in. I wasn't on Willie's side, of course. But I was uncomfortable admitting to myself that my new career, at the heart of it, was about getting people to tell me things they shouldn't. It was beginning to dawn on me that journalism is about using other people, their real lives, and I wasn't sure how I felt about that. Willie had handed me the rope; he'd helped me cinch the knot and place it around his neck. But, I had to believe, it was his rope. And he did the hanging.

The Willie story made it to the front page of Tampa & State, the local news section. When I called him up that next day, it was all *yass sir, no sir* again. He hadn't read my story. He was losing it. The deputies were coming for him, he said.

"Yas sir, the po-lice trying to hang me on my past and I'm breaking apart," he sobbed to me. "I'm going to drive a little ways and then do myself in."

I realized he was in his pickup. I could hear the wind singing through the open window. He was moving, fast.

"I didn't do nothing to that little girl!" he screamed. "I'm gonna die!"

Before the line was cut, I heard pounding, men pounding the windshield, deputies, I could tell by their voices, their commands: *Get out, get out, get your hands up, you fuckin' pervert, get the fuck out.*

It turned out they weren't arresting Willie for Amanda's murder—they still had nothing—but since my story had run and his picture went up on the local news, two more women had come forward and accused him of rape, going back to incidents years before.

I suddenly became the Willie the Crabber guy. That's sometimes how it goes. One day you're an amateur, the next you're the expert—or you're expected to be one, so that's what you try to be. I drew up a tree of the Crain family, tracked down every relative I could, dug up old, handwritten Justice of the Peace orders from the 1960s and attended Pedophiles Anonymous sessions, exchanging pleasantries with men who diddled little boys in the back of Bealls department stores. Most of these guys were extraordinarily friendly, as one must be to reel them in, soundlessly.

I was desperate to understand what motivated Willie, but in the end, I was learning, all you ever really get is the Who, the What, the When, and the Where. Getting at the Why is like trying to untangle the roots of a mangrove.

The closest I ever got to understanding a mind like Willie's was during an interview with one of his relatives in front of the Florida Aquarium, on the Ybor Channel. Sadly, the paper never used a single word of it. That too is often how it goes. The best quotes, the heartfelt, straight-off-the-cuff poetry, those strings of words you won't ever forget until they put you in a box—they just don't fit into newspaperese.

I prepared for my meeting with Willie's ex-brother-in-law the same way as I always did: I read his rap sheet. It was so long it cost me five bucks to copy at the courthouse—armed robbery, battery, resisting arrest, assaulting an LEO.

Out in the sun that day, Ricky was wearing crisply ironed Wranglers, his face clean-shaven, not at all worn out or sun-lined. At first I thought it was the wrong man.

"Ricky?" I mouthed as I pulled up.

He nodded. He had arrived early to our appointment in his Ford F-150 with diamond-tread utility boxes welded in back, like on a fire truck. He was now a successful building contractor.

Once the interview was over—where had he first met Willie, what had Willie been like, who were Willie's friends—I put my spiral away and asked, "Hey, man, got to be honest. I read all this shit about you, but it seems like you're doing really well. What happened?"

This, of course, had nothing to do with anything; some might even call it unprofessional. But I couldn't help myself.

He laid it on me, real simple.

"It took me thirty-five years to figure out which way is up."

"Thirty-five years?"

"Thirty-five fucking years." Ricky kept smiling, as if he held a key to life that nobody else did.

Man, I thought, that sucks. Thirty-five years is an awfully long time.

◇◇◇◇◇◇◇

That summer a little-known terrorist group drove truck bombs into the American embassies in Nairobi and Dar—the only two American embassies I had ever entered. Dar was where Roko and I had been issued new passports after the Kili operation; Nairobi, where I was issued yet another passport after being mugged.

Several American diplomats were killed in the attacks, and more than two hundred Africans died in the avalanche of concrete and rebar. It was the work of Osama bin Laden, and a sign of a danger-ous shift. East Africa's brand of Islam had been tolerant, moderate, and open, but now the angry, radical, and violent Salafist version from Saudi Arabia was infecting it. Some of the operatives who did Osama's bidding were Kenyan and Tanzanian, and, watching the coverage of the bombings on Tampa's evening news, hearing people speak Swahili in the background, seeing all those trees, the lushness, in every shot, I felt something, something that didn't make sense: I felt homesick.

My squadron of manila envelopes was still out there, but it hadn't attracted any attention, so I decided it was time to share my secret. Africa was like an imaginary friend—it existed for me alone, and nobody else would ever understand our magical connection. I hadn't told a soul in the state of Florida that all the hours I was putting in were for one reason and one reason only. But one night, after deadline, not long after those two embassies had been blasted into rubble, I worked up the nerve to ask an editor if the paper might consider sending me to Kenya. It's a big story, I said; I know the area. I can hit the ground running, I have friends there, I can stay the whole time for free. I even speak Swahili.

"Swahili?" the editor said. "You studied Swahili? No fucking kidding."

I had him.

"You're kidding, right? I mean, you got to be kidding?"

I just stood there in front of his terminal, swallowing hard.

He didn't rush me out on the next flight, and I never brought it up again.

◇◇◇◇◇◇◇◇

When Courtenay arrived for her next visit, she should have been the one who detected something different on me, but instead it was I who smelled it on her. I picked her up at Tampa International, right at the gate—you could do this back then, race into short-term parking, blaze through the metal detectors manned by some geezers working for a private "security" company, and run up to the gate just before they flung open the doors and the fat guys in business stomped off.

Of course, Courtenay couldn't have known a thing about Bev, Julie, or the Kellys. But as I closed my eyes and kissed her, I could tell she was thinking about something else. I could *feel* it. She broke off the welcome kiss quickly, making it seem obligatory. When we climbed into my car, she shrank away.

"There's someone in my office," she finally said after we stepped inside my duplex.

"What?" I stammered, fumbling around for the light switch.

"Nothing's happened yet—I thought it was important to see you before I did anything. I wanted to spend this weekend with you, but I think we should take some time off."

Nothing ever leveled me like that. It was like stepping into a dark room and getting hit in the face with a baseball bat.

"You okay?"

"Yeah, yeah," I said, reaching for the arm of my futon. I was actually dizzy.

Another guy? I never saw that coming, and what could I say? At least she had integrity.

"This long-distance isn't working," she said. "I don't want to do it anymore."

"Sweetie, neither do I. Who the fuck is this guy?"

She said his name.

"Jesus Christ. You got to be kidding me. His name is *Jeff*? *Jeff!* That's sick, you know that? Does he know you? Do you know him? How can you do this to me? Look at this place." I hurled a book from the coffee table at the stack on the floor. "You think I chose to be here?"

"I thought you liked it."

"No, it's a fucking act. An act! If there was an easier way to do this"—the "this" was Africa, though it was rarely spoken—"believe me, I'd do it."

"I know, I know," she said. "I just can't be in a long-distance relationship anymore."

Neglect never shouts. It whispers. But I'd been so busy chasing stories and other people behind her back, something she had the decency not to do to me, that I didn't catch what it was trying to say. If life is a question of whom you love and how you love them, I didn't have the answers.

The terror of losing Courtenay evaporated all interest in others. I realized only then I couldn't be myself, or who I wanted to be, without her. The same work that had been so enthralling now seemed stupid. Another guy beaten up? Another fatal on I-75? Another L & L or A & B? Tell me, who really cares? I lobbied her parents, her twin sister, Mavis, her college friends. I sat in the woods and bawled. I became a household name at 1-800-Flowers. *Hello again, Mr. Gettleman. How 'bout another Floral Embrace? Or a Fields of Europe?* I called them in like air strikes.

But Courtenay didn't budge. When she made up her mind, she closed it. Those annoying things she had always insisted on— asking me to lock down weekend plans weeks in advance, to stop whatever I was doing at night and just sit on the couch and talk— suddenly seemed so wise. Courtenay had love's number; she knew how flakey it could be, how you can't glide by on chemistry alone, how love, even genuine, solidly rooted love, requires routine maintenance. She was only twenty-four, and she'd figured that out.

Her absence opened up yawning amounts of time. Without her call, nights were without end. I ate my pasta, washed my bowls, flicked through the newspaper and wandered around the dark corners of my mind. Is she naked and touching him? Could I kick the other Jeff's ass on his way to fetch the morning latte? Does he have a bigger dick? I begged my inner self to let her go, to free myself of her.

I dreaded facing my colleagues in the morning when they asked, in a slightly different way these days, "How's it going?" I just wanted to slip in and out of the office undetected. When weekends finally rolled around, they were even worse. There was no twenty-four-hour news cycle back then; we worked shifts, typically nine to seven, Monday through Friday. When my shift ended, I had nothing to do. I was like a firefighter. I had no homework. I was just waiting for the alarm to ring, but I didn't have any hoses to roll, no reputation as a crucial asset to society to maintain, not even a manly vehicle to wash. For the first time in a while, I didn't know where my life was headed. A plate of delicious food bored me. I began to get smaller.

Making the rounds of all our old places, I'd find myself in the back of a canoe, dipping the paddle into the Withlacoochee. I tried to pretend Courtenay was sitting right there in front of me. But the same landscape we found so serene when we were together now looked desolate and spooky. I swung by the Hungry Thyme and held the dog-eared menu in my hands. Were her fingerprints on this one?

There was a clarity to the feelings I had torturing myself, a tongue returning again and again to the hole of a newly missing tooth. I was learning how impossible it was to make someone love you, even if she'd loved you before. I'd never felt so disconnected from everything, so helplessly lonely, so frustrated at myself.

On Sunday mornings, to take my mind off all of this, there was one errand I could run. It excised two and a half hours from the day. The nearest copy of the *New York Times* was at a Publix supermarket fifty-three miles away. I drove down to Tampa and paced around the parking lot in my flip-flops, staring up at the gulls doing doughnuts in the sky, waiting for the delivery truck. I picked up that five-pound stack of newsprint and flicked right to the Africa stories.

Along with the rise of Islamist militancy on the East African coast, the cave-in of Congo was the big story then, and, standing in the immensity of that Publix parking lot, surrounded by abandoned shopping carts, staring fiercely at those stories about the hundreds of thousands of people squeezed into sprawling refugee camps on the Rwanda border, I began to feel how truly far away Africa had become. Hell, it was beginning to feel like I'd never even been to Africa. The continent was hemorrhaging news. I wanted to write about huge events sweeping across millions of lives, I wanted to be living and working and traveling in a part of the world that meant something to me, but here I was, alone, in a place that had never been part of my plan, writing about meatballs and crabbers.

True, Willie represented the ultimate depths of depravity, and I guess there was some journalistic value in getting down there and showing what that looked like. But my stories were beginning to feel hollow and prurient. I craved standing in a place like Congo, not reading about it but smelling it, feeling it.

◇◇◇◇◇◇◇◇

I don't know what I would have done if Courtenay hadn't finally telephoned me at the end of the summer. She presented me a list of terms I had to accept, along the lines of Appomattox. It was all about The Union.

"I need to know from you that you're committed," she said.

"I am."

"I need to know that from now on, you'll be faithful to *our* dream."

"I will."

"We need to be in the same place for this to work."

"I know, sweetie, I know."

I raced up to DC to see her, and as she opened her apartment's door in a fitted white shirt, everything down to the fraying plaid potholders hanging from little hooks in the kitchen seemed sweet. I stepped through the doorway and told myself I'd never leave. I felt so lucky. We had six, maybe seven good months left before I started being a little weasel again. But during this high-watermark period, I proposed an idea I should have proposed long before.

"Sweetie," I said. "What about Zanzibar?"

We soon found ourselves standing together on that same hunk of coral that I had stood on, solo, years ago, looking out at the night sea. We watched the boys with the moonlit bellies creep around the shallows, hunting for flounder, moving silently as smoke. The tide was out, dhows glued to the sand, their ropes slack and mushy with seaweed, umbilical cords to land. We walked, the soft wet sand oozing between our toes.

The next morning I befriended a fisherman scraping the muck off the bottom of his canoe with something akin to a spatula. He asked if we wanted to go fishing, and without checking with Courtenay, I said "Tuende!" *Let's go!*

We jumped into his tiny canoe and sailed through the bright blue sea, hauling in buckets of rainbow fish. But we hadn't brought any sunscreen with us. And there wasn't a cloud in the sky. We watched the skin on our arms turn red and each other's faces turn scarlet. We didn't even have hats. It was one of the worst sunburns either of us would ever suffer, skin peeling off our ears, in distressingly crispy pieces, for weeks. But Courtenay didn't complain. She usually accepted that side of me, the impulsive part that torpedoed me into new situations and then refused to bail, which probably helped me get my stories, but I'm sure was exasperating to deal with.

The fisherman finally returned us to land, and we sat for a few minutes outside his hut as he unclumped his nets. He had about ten kids, running around in rags, worms of green snot swinging from their noses. I chased a couple and hoisted some of the smaller ones on my shoulders, pretending I was a *mzungu* monster. The adults were always friendly, but the kids had no barriers at all. They rubbed our skin, felt our hair, reached for our hands, and marched down the beach with us in a big parade. I could have played with them for hours.

As soon as we got back to our bungalow, I flopped down on the bed, contentedly exhausted. Courtenay burst into tears.

"They're so poor," she cried. "How can you stand it?"

I didn't know what to say. I couldn't understand what she had seen that was so bad. It was like what was right in front of us was dividing us. She stood above me, impatient for an answer.

"Don't you find it depressing? Didn't you hear those kids coughing? What is it about this place you like so much, anyway?"

"I don't know," I said, and I truly didn't.

I nearly said, "But those kids seemed so happy." But I knew how meaningless that would sound.

◇◇◇◇◇◇◇

The cops eventually found traces of blood on a pair of Willie's underwear, an investigative breakthrough that made me want to vomit. Amanda was tiny, forty-five pounds, and he had apparently forced himself on her. I'm sure he didn't flinch, seeing all that blood flow freely. Amanda Brown was swallowed by an evil so cunning that to this day, nearly two decades later, even with all the technology available, her body hasn't been found, not a bone.

The cops had been tipped off by all the bleach Willie had used to slosh up his bathroom. When the forensic team applied a chemical called Luminol, which can detect where blood has been, the bathroom "lit up," in the words of one investigator. That bathroom was where he most likely sawed Amanda into pieces. They charged him with kidnapping and murder in the first degree.

Since I was the so-called Willie the Crabber expert, the Leeza Gibbons talk show invited me to LA to talk about the case. It was me, Amanda's divorced parents, Kathy and Roy, and the dark star of this whole episode, Willie, via a video link to Tampa's county jail. The three of us who were physically present on the Paramount lot were each given a dressing room with a star on the door and our names written in glittery letters inside it.

I snuck past Roy's room to scope him out. He did body work on trucks and was wearing the jean jacket he always wore, practicing his lines, staring himself down in the mirror: "This ain't about me now . . ."

It was too tragic to be entertainment, but somehow the four of us were seduced. Hollywood is like that. Everyone thinks they can use it for a bigger, better end, but we all (except for Willie) quietly stepped back into our limos, angry at ourselves. Roy never got to say what he wanted, and muttered that Leeza was fake. Kathy was haggard, strung out, like she had just shot up backstage. Willie had a new excuse that made him really look like a psychopath: he said that the blood on his underwear was from one of Amanda's teeth that wiggled loose while they were playing and somehow tumbled down into his balls. I was stiff, a little stupid, offering up some vague descriptions of this or that. I felt dirty for even opening my mouth, but still, I did it.

I had one free day in LA, so I figured what's there to lose and stopped by the *LA Times*, a huge paper of national repute, though it always seemed to be plagued by some crisis. It had just made deep staff cuts, too deep, which meant that it now needed some young, cheap people to fill its pages.

I called Courtenay a couple weeks later.

"Sweetie! You won't believe this. I got it! A full-time job in the San Fernando Valley!"

Silence.

"Sweetie, don't you get it? The *LA Times* actually wants to hire me."

"That's fucking awful."

Courtenay was still in Washington. She had set her sights on becoming a criminal lawyer and had applied to ten law schools around the country.

"I can't believe you did this again. I thought you said you were going to wait to see where I got in before doing anything."

"Sweetie, I did say that. But they came to me."

(A bald-faced lie. The *LA Times* would never have come to me.)

"You mean you want to do more long-distance? How can you do this to us? You're just doing what you want to do, you don't want to do what I want to do. It's been four years since we were in the same place," she said. "This all started when you went to Ethiopia that summer and didn't let me know until I was practically driving you to the airport."

"I know, but we managed."

"Is that what you really want?"

"What?"

"To just manage?"

She won that one. And instead of going to sleep, I stayed up, nursing my anger. I knew she was right, but that didn't stop me from spending the next three hours formulating comebacks.

"You're just trying to hold me back," I said the next evening as soon as we got on the phone.

"What are you talking about?"

"I'm serious." I could feel the resentment building, about to blow. "You're just trying to hold me back. And it's too early to be held back."

"I never said I wanted to hold you back."

"Well, what are you saying, then? You want me to turn down a job at the *LA Times*? One of the biggest papers in the country? With several—did you hear me?—SEVERAL jobs in Africa? Do you think I'm stupid? This is what I've been dreaming about since I met you!"

"Well, you know what?"

"What?"

"I don't give *one shit* about your dream!"

"What'd you just say?"

"You heard me."

So she dumped me again. After all, it was *my* dream, not ours.

"And this time," she shouted over the phone. "Don't bother with 1–800-Flowers! It's pathetic!"

This time, I figured I'd survive. I had friends in LA. And it was LA. That city, even more than New York, exerted a gravitational pull on my set. Roko loved it, and was constantly in and out of Hollywood. He had found an idea for a film that only he could make, about a blind blues singer from San Francisco who had taught himself how to throat-sing like the Central Asian shepherds and then journeyed to Central Asia and won a big throat-singing tournament. The blind American became the Rocky of the throat-singing world, and Roko caught it all on film. At the same time, Roko was helping his dad train for that crazy-ass scheme: rowing solo across the Atlantic. His dad had just rowed Lake Michigan, all three hundred miles—there was the sense he was really going to take on the ocean next. No one was getting in the way of *his* dream.

Chris, from the first Africa trip, was living off Fairfax Avenue, chasing *his* dream, trying to be a filmmaker. We had gotten closer since Africa; he'd been working in London while I was at Oxford, probably my only real friend from those years, and I was always impressed by his determination to stay on one path. He was half British, half American, well read, dapper, very opinionated but somehow not excessively judgmental, and striking looking—strong jaw, broad forehead, manly shoulders, and a crest of blond hair combed straight back. He wore black shirts and fitted blazers. He looked like a Bond villain. Rather than being discouraged by his rejection from film school, he was hot on a new idea for a movie, the story of a guy who loses his short-term memory and tries to solve the murder of his wife by tattooing clues on his body, like little mementos. It sounded complicated. Chris also wanted to tell the story backward—that was very important, he said. I couldn't quite see it, but when you're around someone who does, you start to believe it. "You know," he said, brushing back his blond hair, "the greatest special effect in all of filmmaking is the cut." I believed that too.

Benny had moved to LA as well—he was up in horse country, still trying to crack into acting; to pay the bills, he was working for a shady frozen meat company, selling beef door to door. He was writing plays, auditioning for commercials, taking care of someone's horses, living around the corner from the guy who raised the Benji dogs—I loved Benji as a kid. It was one of those true stereotypes: LA seemed the land of the possible, and if Courtenay couldn't find a law school good enough for her in LA, well, too bad for her.

All my energies had been channeled into getting out of Florida, but, staring out the windows as the jet accelerated upward over Tampa Bay, I started to realize, with a vague and unforeseen unease, that if things worked out, there were going to be many more uprootings. I started to miss the Sub, the spray-painted addresses on trees, those highways and byways and citrus-smelling country roads, those humid nights so soft and luscious you never wanted to see the sun come up. I started to miss that smoked mullet. I knew I'd never have another. I had made myself a promise: Whatever happened from here on out, the road to Africa ran in one direction.

Bill Stevens was right. That job was the best fucking job. It pains me that I will never be able to do it again, return to that same place, that same time, in that same state of mind, eager and uninformed and, best, unformed. Believe me, I had dreamed of bigger papers, major cities, major news. Now I can't imagine any better way to begin a career in journalism than the cop beat in Brooksville, Florida. That job was so elemental. It was rooted in the real world. Newspapers, especially small ones, are like that—they're old-school, they're fact-based, they're pure. The journalism they practice is less adorned than magazine work; it has less spin than radio; it's much deeper than TV. Walt Whitman worked at a small newspaper; so did Gabriel García Márquez. Everybody should work at a small newspaper. The amount of life you take in is staggering.

Mike the city editor was right too. Life in a small town had taught me what I liked and what I didn't. I learned that I loved journalism, the sweaty craziness of it. And I learned that when you really begin to love the sweaty craziness of something, when you're in the daze of it, nothing else matters.

It can't.

◇◇◇◇◇◇◇

Ithaca to Addis. Addis to Oxford. Oxford to Brooksville. Brooksville to Tampa. Tampa to LA. LA to Atlanta. I moved house six times in six years and traveled tens of thousands of miles. By the late summer of 2001, age thirty, I was an *LA Times* national correspondent, based in Atlanta, covering the Deep South. I had turned down a reporting job in Hollywood, which probably would have meant swanky movie premieres and other fringe benefits, because I wanted the freedom of covering a lot of territory. I was a one-man rolling newsroom, pulling into dark little towns shadowed by shuttered textile mills and long-cold smokestacks, checking into roadside motels with a single crunchy towel hanging from the rack.

To file stories, I pulled the cord out of the phone, stuck it into my laptop, and waited eagerly for that *Mwaaaaachhhhh. . . . Meeee-MaaMeeeeeMaa. . . . Kkkkkkkkkkkkkkkkkkk* modem sound. The Internet had arrived to news.

Benny got diagnosed. Dan's journals were published. Courtenay made law review at Michigan Law School and fell for a new guy, ironically some chump named Dan. We had been apart for almost a year. I was now a man alone. I took walks alone, cooked dinner alone, marked my birthday alone, picked out furniture alone, entered restaurants alone, holding up my right index finger and mouthing the most sheepish little word that you can mouth to a hostess: "One."

I discovered there's not a restaurant in the continental United States that sets tables for one. And nothing's more soul-crushing than watching a waiter absentmindedly remove the opposite place settings—the fork, the knife, the spoon, the plate, the place mat, the napkin. I knew Courtenay was The One. I still associated so much discovery with her, big things—sex, love, chopsticks. To use that most romantic measure of hopelessly enduring love, she remained the only woman I had ever farted in front of. She knew all my faults, and still, she had accepted me.

One Tuesday morning I was flying off to North Carolina—alone—for Liddy Dole's announcement that she was running for Senate. The plane took off from Atlanta's Hartsfield airport at 8:30 and I sat in the back, typing up the B-matter—Harvard grad, Phi Beta Kappa, first woman to be in the Cabinet twice, open seat, usually went Republican, etc., etc. It was a mid-grade story for the biggest paper on the West Coast; I did about fifty to seventy-five of these a year.

We landed in Charlotte at 9:30. As I stood up to grab my bags, a big man in front of me flipped open his StarTAC, which had rung right away, and grimaced like someone had just tightened a vise grip on his nuts.

"Wait, what?" He could barely speak into his phone. He looked scared. "The puh . . . puh . . .'"

I stared at his face, standing in the aisle, clutching the handle of my laptop case, impatient to get off the plane, thinking: Just spit it out, brother, spit it out.

"The puh, puh . . . Pentagon? The Twin Towers?"

SIX

MAZAR-I-SHARIF, 2002

I sprinted through the Charlotte airport, in pursuit of what, exactly, it wasn't clear. But I knew whatever I was chasing was going to be big. Since the entire American airspace was suddenly closed, I ran to Hertz and rented the last car on the lot—a brand-new Cadillac de Ville, seventeen feet long, four thousand pounds. Balling it up I-95 for eleven hours straight, I blasted the radio the whole time except for one twenty-five-minute phone call. I ditched the car in a no-parking zone in front of a graffiti-covered school in the Bronx and jumped on the subway—all bridges and tunnels into Manhattan had been sealed off. I spent the next two weeks filing stories from the *LA Times*' New York bureau. It had been impossible for the paper to fly in reinforcements; they needed every word I could give them. I stayed in the city for free, mooching off my sister, now a pediatrician on the Upper East Side, and wearing her husband's clothes. When I got the call for the next assignment and went back up to 238th Street to retrieve the Caddy, I was convinced it would be plastered with tickets, up on blocks. The car was untouched. Luck was with me, or so I thought.

It has become commonplace to say that everything changed after 9/11. For me, it did. The disaster spurred along my career the way no one story, no two hundred stories, no two thousand stories, ever could. "It was the advent of the second plane, sharking in low over the Statue of Liberty: that was the defining moment," Martin Amis wrote. "Until then, America thought she was witnessing nothing more serious than the worst aviation disaster in history; now she had a sense of the fantastic vehemence ranged against her."

Desperate to decode that "fantastic vehemence," American newspapers spent millions of dollars sending scores of inexperienced reporters to places few people had ever considered. War is God's way of teaching Americans geography.

The next airplane I boarded was to Egypt. At the same time I was crossing the Atlantic Ocean, so was Roko's dad. After years of training, studying celestial charts, strapping himself into an erg for hours at a stretch (most people at a gym can't stand that machine for more than ten minutes), Nenad Belic was out on the ocean at last, powering himself on bagel chips and Spam. I gave him a thumbs-up from 35,000 feet.

This was my shot—my long-awaited tryout to be a foreign correspondent. I hit the ground in Cairo, euphoric to be strolling between all those huge old mosques, trying to get a little *eedack!* here and there, though people weren't nearly as generous with the spontaneous high fives as they had been during my Year On. No one wanted to talk about terrorism, and the Egyptians didn't want to own Mohamed Atta or the repressive atmosphere that bred him. I didn't get much. And when things slowed down, I realized how much 9/11 had upset me. During my stint in New York, you couldn't ride the subways without seeing hundreds of faces of missing people staring at you from the subway-station walls. I kept seeing those faces.

The finest piece of practical advice I received as a correspondent that trip was given to me while walking the streets of Khan el-Khalili, looking for a bakery to console myself.

A fellow reporter, a more experienced one, saw me take out my pen to jot down the Arabic word for sugar cookies and watched me drop the cap into one of Cairo's mucky gutters.

"Sport," he said, "lemme tell you something. Get a pen you can use with one hand."

From then on, I went retractable.

I took my anxious energy and new pens to hard-edged Yemen, the poorest country in the Arab world, with more weapons per capita than just about anywhere. I quickly set up base in a hotel in Al Mukalla, a harbor town in Hadhramaut, backed by a wall of flat-topped mountains of red rock. Here I went out to discover Osama's ancestral homeland, but once again, nobody wanted to talk to me, especially about Osama. The only people excited about my arrival were some honey sellers on the side of a mountain. I soon learned I wasn't alone. A legendary reporter from the *Washington Post*, who could find news in a shoebox, came up to me in the hotel lobby looking filthy and wild-eyed. "This place sucks! I haven't seen a fact for a week!"

I went back to my room, tired and irritable. It was then that I checked my e-mail. "Bwan," Roko wrote. "My dad's disappeared." I called Roko right away to find out that his dad had rowed more than 2,500 miles, with only a few hundred left. As he neared the Irish coast, Roko said, a tempest swept in, waves fifty feet high. He had activated his emergency rescue beacon, and the Royal Air Force scrambled aircraft to pluck him out. All they found was the beacon.

Roko's dad could never articulate why he had this passion to row across the ocean. He just shrugged and smiled. I thought I knew how that felt. Six weeks later some Irish fishermen spotted his boat, upside down. They said it looked like a dead whale. To this day, no one has ever found his body. Roko sometimes says that maybe his dad is living it up in Tahiti.

Rare is it that you're presented with such a cautionary tale so intimately. I had known Roko's dad most of my life. I can still see precisely where he was standing at one of our last high school hockey games—left of the scoreboard, high in the stands, by himself, wearing one of his signature 1970s Yugoslavian shirts with ugly stripes. He kept a bristly mustache and had meaty forearms—he looked like a house painter, not a heart doctor. I still don't know what to make of his death. Did Nenad Belic, sixty-two, wait too long to pursue his dream? I'm sure he would have rowed faster had he been a bit younger, and if he had rowed faster, he would have beat those late-summer storms. Or was it that you should constantly integrate adventure and thrills into whatever you're doing, keep steadily feeding those urges with little bites, here and there, but always, so they don't become so voracious they end up devouring you?

Or maybe the lesson was simpler. It wasn't about death. It was about life. It's never long enough. So get it while you can.

Out on the ocean, Nenad didn't get a second chance. I've gotten many.

◇◇◇◇◇◇◇

A few months later, I stepped through the door of the Marriott Hotel in Islamabad, Pakistan. I don't know what it was precisely that tipped me off, the intoxicating waft of sitar music that greeted me, produced by a beautiful old man with a luxuriant white beard sitting in a corner of the lobby, or the loud and self-impressed crowd of diplomats, journalists, spies, aid workers, drivers, translators, and UN people—everybody who draws a paycheck from disaster—who confabulated around the bar, snacking on nuts and drinking glasses of cherry juice, or all that I carried: $18,176 in my front right pocket—mostly crisp Benjamins—two laptops, two satellite phones, a Gore-Tex bivvy sack, a North Face vest, and a new goose-down sleeping bag good to 20 degrees. But now, I thought, I'm traveling with purpose. Walking across the lobby, I nodded casually to some guy talking on two cell phones at once, flattened some rupees on the bar, and ordered one of those glasses of cherry juice. I had worked years for that glass of cherry juice.

Within days I was flying over the Hindu Kush and then the

snow-covered central Asian steppe, swooping in to Mazar-i-Sharif, the largest town in northern Afghanistan and stronghold of the Northern Alliance, a group of warlords allied with the United States. At the time, this whole trip seemed tangential but necessary to getting back to Africa. War is one of those boxes a young journalist must tick if he harbors aspirations of landing his dream job. But Afghanistan ended up being more than that. Even if I had never done anything in the field of journalism after that trip, I would have died a happy journalist—but not, I know now, a happy man.

I stayed in the Farhat, an Afghan guesthouse that occupied the second floor of a small building, above a garage. The minute I walked in, several large bearded men, all dressed in vests and turbans, their pointy elfin shoes lined up against the wall like a fleet of gondolas, rose from the couch to clutch my hand in greeting and offer me nuts and tea and toffee. There were no newspapers here, no refrigerators, no phones. Horse-drawn carts clopped outside through the crisp, fresh snow. I was given a room with a bed as narrow as a diving board and a wood-burning stove.

The Tajik boy who stuffed logs into my stove shadowed me up to the roof and stared with eyes full of amazement as I powered up my sat phone and connected it to my laptop. As I typed, he wiped the falling snowflakes off my screen with a fat fingertip. As soon as I was done, he tugged me downstairs to warm up in the Farhat's TV room, where the big bearded men knelt on the carpet and aimed their bruise-marked foreheads toward Mecca, their lips piously forming around the words of Surat al-Fatihah, the first chapter of the Koran. That was morning. Come evening, those same guys jumped up on the couch and hooked up a TV, which I was surprised to see in that place. I was even more surprised when they somehow tuned it to a Scandinavian porn station. They laughed so hard their eyes watered, watching the tall white people fuck. Mazar was like Brooksville in that way. It wrote its own rules.

The city was contested between four main factions—the Tajiks, the Uzbeks, the Hazaras, and a few Tajik Shias. It was like Berlin after World War II, various powers occupying their own zones, vying to edge out the others. The warlords who ran it slouched on the floor of their dens against low cushions, dispensing great violence from behind heaping bowls of raisins. The slushy streets oozed with their own heavily armed charm. Militiamen of un-known allegiance thundered past in pickup trucks or rode by on horses. All factions favored the same Soviet surplus weaponry and the same functional uniform—baggy pants, long vests, poufy hats, and American high-tops. After dark they hunched with their Ka-lashnikovs behind sandbags or concrete barriers, their checkpoints.

Roll up too fast, you'd spook them, but creep along too slow, raising suspicion, and you might also take one in the chest. At some imperceptible point that the militiamen deemed close enough, they blasted flashlights in our faces, shouldered their AKs, and shouted out, "What is the name of the night!"

The first time I heard it, I tugged the sleeve of my translator, Yama, a wispy Tajik kid who displayed that Afghan miracle of coloring—black hair, bloodred cheeks, bright green eyes, what happens when Alexander the Great rolls through Central Asia.

"Yama," I whispered. "What do they want?"

"Jeff-jan, Jeff-jan," he said, holding his right hand flat, patting it down. *Wait. Wait.*

Yama screwed up all the courage in his 120-pound body.

"Tawoos!" he yelled back toward the sandbags.

"Tawoos?" A mocking voice in the dark. (*Tawoos* means "pea-cock." The warlords liked animal names.)

"Tawoos!" Yama said again, stronger.

The business end of the AKs went down. One of the militiamen cracked a joke. Every night had a name, and Yama, who was quite well connected, always found out the name at dusk. We were clear and free.

Afghanistan grew on me, real fast. I figured, when in Afghanistan, do as the Afghans. I bought a wolf-skin vest, a rabbit-skin vest, a pillbox militia commander hat, and a couple of those shimmering green capes like Hamid Karzai wore. Never once was I turned down for an interview, even if it meant waiting for the warlord to be shaken awake in his icy den and dragged out of bed to sit in his pajamas and socked feet and stare at me like I had just rocketed in from Neptune. Even though Afghanistan was a traditional Muslim country and had had its own struggles with Islamist fascists, the culture here was so much more open than what I had experienced in the Middle East. Many interviews in Mazar ended with bear hugs, my boots kicking in the air; some even ended with a meal. I loved Afghan meals—and when you love the food, you love the place. All those chewy dumplings drizzled in smoky yogurt sauce, the chunks of freshly roasted pumpkin, endless platters of spiced rice and beef kebabs that came one cube of meat, one cube of white fat, all the way up the steel skewer. It made me question contemporary nutritional guidelines. I ate red meat and white fat every day for sixty days straight and never felt better.

I hadn't been this enthused about life, this curious about my surroundings, this connected to strangers, for a long time. I didn't mind being alone. I actually liked it. I got a contact high moving through the market and shaking hands with shopkeepers. If there was one place in the world that was a threat to my love of East Africa, I was now standing in it. Afghanistan was similar to that first trip in one key respect: the contrast between what I had expected and what I found. Afghanistan was hardly all about bombs, misery, terrorists, or war. Afghanistan had that same unexpected warmth as East Africa, that clarity of light, that magic.

I was also dumb lucky. The spring of 2002 was a short-lived interval between conflicts: the Taliban had been momentarily routed, the United States had ceased its bombing, there was even talk of rebuilding. That spring might have been the only time in the past forty years that that beguiling country has tasted peace.

⬦⬦⬦⬦⬦⬦

"Yama," I asked. "Has anyone been to the Valley of Caves?"

"Jeff-jan, I don't think so."

"Is it possible?"

"Yes, no problem. We can do it."

"Is it safe?"

"Well, maybe some Hazara bandits—you know death dance?"

"The what dance?"

"Hazara death dance. They rob you and cut off head and pour boiling oil down your neck and your body dances, just for few minutes." He paused, perplexed. "But I think that's other place, Jeff-jan. I check."

"Yeah," I said. "Check."

The Valley of the Caves was the site of the first battle in the so-called war on terror, and it was the first piece of an assignment that the editors in LA had handed down like a message from Mount Olympus, the very lack of specificities making it so dreamy. Go to Afghanistan. Go to the north. Don't file too much. Go after big game. Hell yeah.

There were no roads in, so we drove through ice-water rivers and, true to the name, slept in caves. One dawn, while I was curled up in my goose-down sleeping bag, I was gently tugged awake by far-off singing. I wiggled over to the mouth of the cave to see a lone man standing on the edge of a cliff, the rising sun silhouetting him. He was singing the clearest, purest, most heartbreaking call to prayer I'd ever heard, without a loudspeaker or microphone, just his lungs and throat cutting that crisp mountain air. With my sleeping bag scrunched around my waist, I just sat there, eyes not moving, transfixed.

When we pulled into the first town, we saw a knot of Northern Alliance guys gathered up ahead, in front of a dilapidated market. I swatted Yama on the leg, thinking, Perfect timing. They were clearly expecting a delegation from Mazar, some warlord, and we were arriving just before the big bearded circus came to town.

"Chetoor hasti?"—*How are you?*—we belted out as we jumped out of our truck.

The village men stood rod-stiff in ripped-up corduroy jackets, their cheeks rubbed raw by the wind.

"What's going on today?" I asked. "Who are you all waiting for?"

The old guys looked at each other sheepishly.

Finally one spoke.

"You," he said.

I was confused.

And then, without another word, the elder put his hand in mine—I could feel how iced his metacarpals were—and began leading me up a white stone path, deeper into the valley.

<><><><><><>

It had all started with a fan plane.

"A fan plane?" I asked Yama, who was sitting cross-legged next to me, translating.

"Yes, Jeff-jan." Yama sighed. "I tell you before, fan plane, helicopter, fan plane, helicopter."

Yama rolled his eyes at me, but I didn't mind. Young Yama was growing on me, like everything else in this country. His scrawny body was packed with that same shaken-soda energy I had when I was twenty—he often jumped me as we were walking up to interviews, squeezing his hands around the top of my bicep like a tightening blood pressure cuff, going "Mock maascil, mock maascil!"—*Make muscle, make muscle!* He once confessed, up on the Farhat roof, that he had never drunk alcohol, never danced with a woman, never had sex. His green eyes glittered when I told him that in America you can do all that—in one night, often in that order.

But Yama knew when to knuckle down. He was as natural a

journalist as I've ever met. Even though he'd never written a story or probably ever held a newspaper in his hands, he possessed the two essential qualities that guide our trade: curiosity and empathy. Empathy is the big one. I like to think we journalists are in the empathy-generation business. If we're doing our jobs well, we're getting people to care about others.

Yama nodded softly in compassion, more vigorously in disbelief, and then violently in utter outrage as the elders of the Valley of the Caves sat with us on the cold floor of a stone house and told us how their lives too had dramatically changed after 9/11.

"Two black fan planes landed in Jacob's Valley . . ."

A big American Special Forces guy—or maybe he was from that extra-covert operational division of the CIA, none of the Americans would ever tell me—stepped out. Call me Baba John, he said, promising the famished villagers that if they helped him fight the Taliban, they would get many wondrous things. A school. A clinic. Roads that wouldn't turn to mud when it rained. Pens. Pencils. Grain.

Baba John never carried a gun and seemed to glide over the black ice coating the valley, laying a warm hand on people's backs, saying "Tashakor, tashakor," *Thank you, thank you*. The villagers fell under his spell. They volunteered to cook for his men, clean the caves, serve as guides to the mountaintops where Baba John's underlings punched numbers into their little blinking things. The Valley of the Caves had been one of the last redoubts that the Taliban couldn't quite conquer, which is why those fan planes landed here. Many locals were killed in the ensuing air raids. The war moved on, and Baba John went with it. Not a single American had come back since he left, the villagers said. They could tell I was having a hard time believing any of this, even through the muffle of translation.

So one suggested in broken English, "Let's go mountain."

So we went mountain. As we climbed, our boots digging through the snow and ice, I could see we were moving through a battlefield. We stepped over sun-bleached bones, broken weapons, and a lot of litter. I bent down and brushed the snow off one colored wrapper: Skittles. Bent down, brushed off another: Pop-Tarts. I found scraps of packaging for Tootsie Rolls, Sara Lee pound cake, and Chiclets. It's difficult to express how strange it was to see the candy wrappers of my youth strewn across the Afghan mountains, but it erased any doubts. My countrymen had been here. These soldiers were the best of the best, starting the war before the war even started, I'm sure Navy SEALs and/or Delta Force, and you would have thought the USG would have had some top-secret hush-hush five-star chow for them, ten-dollar granola bars or something interesting, but no—the best of the best of the best are fed Skittles and Pop-Tarts and Tootsie Rolls. Sugar is good.

I looked off at the faraway hills. The Taliban used to have a bunker up there, one of the commanders said; there might even be some bodies left.

"Bodies?" I asked excitedly.

"Yes," the commander said. "But it might be mined."

"That means we can't go?"

"Well, you're our guest, and if you want to go, we'll go."

I hesitated.

These men were more hospitable than anyone I had ever met, which I appreciated. But just enough of me knew that these dangers were real, though of course I spent the long walk back down the mountain wondering if I had made the right call.

That night I watched the village women bring steaming bowls of thin greenish liquid to their children.

"Grass soup," Yama whispered.

Grass soup? I had a sick feeling in the pit of my stomach, watching the children slowly slurp it. What if the Taliban came back? What if we needed the Valley of the Caves again? I called the American command in Mazar with my sat phone, and an army major swatted away my questions with an infuriating nonchalance.

"I'd imagine Special Forces would say whatever they needed

to, to win cooperation," he said. "That doesn't mean we're going down there." End of interview. Click.

We slogged back to Mazar in silence. We pulled up alongside the Farhat, and I ran up those stairs to the second floor. In the narrow hallway, on my way to my room, I bumped into another reporter, older than I was, who took one look at me and asked, "You got a story?" "Damn right I do," I said over my shoulder. "And I have to write this bastard right now." Once I flipped open my laptop, I didn't hold back. This was a more-is-more job, plain and simple. I won't go as far as Truman Capote, who insisted he didn't need to take notes—taking notes, he claimed, "artificializes the atmosphere of an interview." For me, taking notes is where it all begins. But when it comes to putting things together, it's the flow, the connections, the language, the emotions that matter, and keeping that notebook closed forces you to concentrate, to really try to get down what you feel, the essence, only the good stuff, via a pad of twenty-six black-and-white keys. I'd open my notebook later to check the names, ages, direct quotes. That story raised a question I hadn't considered before, and I don't think many others had, either: How many other people had the US government and its Baba Johns stabbed in the back?

◇◇◇◇◇◇◇

The biggest battle in northern Afghanistan, a few weeks after the Taliban rout in the Valley of the Caves, was at a girls' school in Mazar-i-Sharif, where nearly a thousand young Taliban recruits had been cornered by Northern Alliance militiamen and then bombed by American warplanes. My editors, happy with the caves story, told me to do a "tick-tock" on the girls' school—a minute-by-minute reconstruction. One of the editors suggested a gripping drama, told from three perspectives: the Northern Alliance militiamen closing in on the school; the Americans in their crystal-screened control rooms; and the young Taliban fighters trapped inside, sweaty, terrified, surrounded by thickening doom.

This was the most complicated story I had ever undertaken, so I broke it into pieces.

Step 1: Meet-n-Greet. Yama and I circulated through Mazar's warlord dens, chatting up gregarious killers, eating handfuls of snacks from the plastic snack-wheels that the warlords filled with almonds, raisins, and Turkish delight. One warlord went on and on about how his troops had nearly worked out a surrender with the Taliban fighters holed up in the school—surrenders mean guns, and guns are like coins in Afghanistan. But something broke down while the two sides were haggling. Then the F-18s showed up.

"We had determined the school was an appropriate target," an American army colonel told me. "Our philosophy has been sur-render or die."

"He actually said that—on the record," I told my editor.

"Surrender or die? That's precious. So much for Western en-lightenment. So, when do you think you can file?"

"Can you give me a couple more days? I still need to find some Taliban."

Step 2: Talk to the Bad Guys. The Northern Alliance com-manders had captured some Talibs in the rubble after the bombing, so Yama and I secured the proper permissions (a smile, a bear hug) and drove to a mud-walled prison a couple hours away. The guards hustled us through to eight young Pakistanis. One had a shattered arm, another had a three-inch hole ripped through the center of his face where his nose should have been. "Shrapnel," the young Talib explained. I couldn't stop looking at the pink of his throat, or maybe it was the roof of his mouth, as he spoke. I scribbled every-thing down. But as soon as our guards slunk off to smoke, the boy wiggled his fingers for me to step closer.

"They are lying to you," he whispered in that strange rasp of someone with no nose. "None of us were in the girls' school. We were captured in Kunduz, just a couple weeks ago. Everything we told you was what they told us to tell you."

I clapped my notebook shut and marched into the office of the prison boss.

"Oh, you mean *that* girls' school?" he said. "I'm sorry. I was confused. Actually, all the Taliban there fought to the death. Please"—he swept his hand across a coffee table and smiled—"sit for a while, have some almonds."

"Come on, Yama," I said, right after Yama scooped up an enormous handful—that was our style, stick and move. "Let's go."

I was green, but not that green. The tick-tock was the assignment, but something didn't smell right. Several shopkeepers near the girls' school had been emphatic that after the school was bombed, they saw Talib prisoners being loaded into Northern Alliance trucks. Shopkeepers, in my experience, don't usually lie. Another warlord then gave me a list of names of forty-three Talib fighters who had been captured, but when I asked where I could find them, he looked away and mumbled something about a "road accident."

Yama and I fell back to our secure meeting room—the Farhat's prayer-porn salon—to discuss our next move. We idly picked from a plate of yellow raisins; I'd never eaten so many raisins in my life.

"Man, you guys better be careful," said the other reporter, who had overheard us. He was looking a little more disheveled than when I'd seen him before, using a stick to gouge the mud out from the tread of his boots. The night before I'd heard him on his sat phone, arguing with his wife about when he was going to come home, which expanded a hollowness inside me that I had tried to ignore. Courtenay and I used to argue about when we would see each other next.

"Don't mess with the warlords," he went on. "If they think anything you write will make them look bad, they will kill you. And why wouldn't they? Who's going to punish them? How old are you, anyway?"

"Thirty."

"Shit, man." He laughed, flinging some mud off his stick. "I used to take all kinds of risks when I was thirty. But now that I'm forty, with two kids, I don't do that shit anymore."

◇◇◇◇◇◇

Yama and I kept banging on more sheet-metal gates, inhaling more almonds, bugging more warlords. This was Step 3: Keep Going. The more time I invested in this one story, the more convinced I became that the warlords were hiding something. What they were hiding and why—that I didn't know, but that was all the more reason to press on. Often I had to charm a guy to charm a guy. One afternoon we met a young commander who we had been told knew somebody who knew something. He couldn't have been more than twenty, tall, dark, nice build, walked with the swagger of a college kid—he had just inherited two thousand men from his martyred dad, like a set of cuff links.

"Heard you guys were looking for a prisoner from the girls' school," he said. My heart leaped. "I know where one is."

We jumped into his pickup, plundered from the Taliban, who had tricked it out with monster truck tires and some sweet stripes. We roared past donkey-cart traffic and women in burkas stuffed in the trunks of old Ladas with a stick propping the trunk open. Soon enough we stopped at a dingy little house with a blue gate at the edge of town in an improvised neighborhood called Dasht-i-Shadian, the Desert of Happy People. The young warlord explained that this was the house of a commander for the Northern Alliance, our first proxy force in the war on terrorism.

At first, the guards wouldn't let us see the prisoner. They said he was too frightened, they said their boss was out of town, they said he was scared of foreigners.

"Nonsense," our young warlord friend replied. He glanced at his men, standing behind him with RPGs.

The guards brought out a teenage boy. They sat him down in the middle of a bald little room with concrete walls and a smoking stove that put out a thin circle of heat. Worn and ghost-thin, he was dressed in a filthy *shalwar kameez*, his arms crisscrossed with puffy cuts.

"Don't hurt! Don't hurt!" he screamed when he found out I was American.

I was slow on the uptake.

I pumped him for specifics: Was he a Talib? Yes, sort of. Had he been in the girls' school? Yes, definitely. How many people were inside the school? What time did the bombs fall? What specifically did the Taliban commanders instruct them to do? He spoke haltingly, but I had no doubt he had been inside—everything he told me lined up with what the Americans and warlords had said. He was my third source. I wanted to talk to him for hours. But I didn't have hours. The thugs holding him kept sighing loudly and ostentatiously checking the scratched-up Casios on their hairy wrists.

At one point the boy started to cry, and one of the guards leaned over and stroked a finger across his cheek to catch the tear. Yama tapped my arm gently. Had I seen that?

Of course I had. It was like the Willie the Crabber moment, a tiny slipup that revealed everything. But in this case, it was even creepier. The child was still alive, the crab trap was still empty.

I asked a few more questions, and then one of the guards abruptly declared: "Khalas." *That's it.*

And before the boy rose to his feet and disappeared down a frosty hallway, he looked at me and said: "I have never seen such days as these."

As we drove back to the Farhat, the young warlord shook his head.

"He's a slave."

◇◇◇◇◇◇

Yama and I huddled in my room. There were some guys I didn't recognize in the TV parlor riveted to the Scandinavian porn, so we closed my door, though we could still hear the lusty cries of "Ja, op min rov! Op min rov!"

"I think they're doing things to him," Yama said. "Why else, Jeff-jan, would they be keeping him?"

I looked down at all my notebooks, clothes, chargers, and cords scattered across the floor.

"We should go back," Yama said. "Shouldn't we?"

It took us a few days to track down the helpful warlord again—it wasn't like we could shoot him an e-mail. He was more than happy to pay another visit to the Desert of Happy People. As we drove, I looked off at the fields slipping past. The signs were weak, but they were there. Spring was coming. We weren't wearing our vests anymore; the grass was beginning to turn that shy shade of light green, the sky was bluer. Two months had flown by. This was the longest I had ever worked on a single story.

Expelling loud groans, the guards peeled back the door. The boy emerged, looking more tired, more worn, more scabby. I quickly ran through all the proper Brooksville police-beat questions I had failed to ask before—full name, age, place of birth, father's full name, age, job, location. The boy's name was Bahram, and he was sixteen. When I reached for my camera, his captors stiffened.

"Haram! Haram!" they screamed. *Forbidden!*

But the young commander was watching his men, and his men were watching me, like hawks. I knew their rifles were loaded— I'd heard them chamber up on the way over. I knew they had my back. The room was filled with that static electricity in the air, like right before a fistfight. I snapped away.

I made it an early night, curled up in my diving board bed, look- ing at the images on the back of my digital camera. I zoomed in on a couple. The marks on Bahram's flesh . . . they actually didn't look like cuts . . . they were burns. I started to put together what little Afghan history I knew: the militiamen, especially the ethnic Hazaras, had suffered immensely under the Taliban and would show no mercy to a captured Talib. Before, most of my work had been dailies, and I didn't think too much about the subjects after deadline. But that night I couldn't sleep. It was cold, and I flipped around in my sleeping bag till dawn.

◇◇◇◇◇◇◇◇

The Northwest Frontier Police stopped our car at the bridge, peering into our windows.

We were approaching the Swat Valley, a restricted area of Pakistan where no foreigners were allowed, probably for our own safety, since the Swat Valley was one of Pakistan's most traditional Islamic areas, with close ties to the Taliban. One of the mustached frontier police looked right at me, but I had grown my beard long and woolly, I was wearing a *shalwar kameez*, and if I had learned anything during my trips to Africa, it was how to slap on a checkpoint face, looking disinterested, remote, stone cold, when the cops are staring at you.

The police waved us through.

Soon everything was in Urdu and Arabic, including the slogans scrawled along the cold brick walls.

JIHAD IS A SAINTLY THING TO DO
JIHAD IS NECESSARY
THIS WAY TO PARADISE

It was April now, the planting season. Within the terraced slopes of the valley, the wheat and rice glowed. The snows were melting fast, and the mountain streams sluiced with icy water. I didn't see any adolescents working the fields. I didn't see many people between five and fifty years old. All the women and girls were locked up behind the stone walls; all the young men were gone.

As our truck stumbled up a steep, rutted road, it struck me how easily I had inserted myself into an intricate and dangerous tale. I had crossed thousands of miles for a single story on a single boy. I felt nervous, excited, alert, dangerously sure of myself. It was narcissism, no doubt, pulling me up that road. I firmly believed I was Bahram's last hope. Up ahead, on the right, was a lone house made of stone. A woman waited on the terrace, back to us, gazing out across the hills, a veil over her head, dark hair spilling down her back. As we exited the car, she turned.

So where were we now?

Step 4: Mom. Mom always holds the keys, whether in Brooksville or the Swat Valley. You always learn something from Mom that you couldn't get from anyone else. Why did Bahram join the Taliban? Why did he throw himself into the end of a losing war? What did he want out of life?

Bahram's mom led us into the cool of her home. Poverty had sunk her cheeks and grooved her mocha skin, leaving her face a faint and distant memory of a beauty that had toughened up long ago. There was very little inside her house, but from somewhere she produced a silver pitcher, poured cool spring water into it, and placed it down on a table, on a simple white cloth.

"Here," she said.

The most meager offerings of hospitality are often the greatest.

I showed her the pictures on the back of my camera, and she cried, "Bahram, Bahram," reaching out with her fingers to stroke the air like she was stroking the dark hairs on her son's head.

I took out my notebook, and we began. She told me about the spellbinding mullah who lived a couple of stony towns away, who had recruited boys to fight for the Taliban in Afghanistan. Bahram jumped on one of the mullah's trucks, heading to Mazar, despite his mother's urgings. Bahram's mother knew the Americans had planes; Bahram and the other boys had set off waving swords and sticks.

Bahram's dad had tried to bring him home, walking off in the dead of winter in the heaviest shawl he could find to the border of Afghanistan. But a Pakistani soldier refused to lift the gate. He trudged back, the white teeth of the Hindu Kush shrinking behind him, eventually paying a couple rupees to a card-wallah (his dad was illiterate) to write a fake letter from Bahram to his mom, saying he's fine, he's in Jalalabad, I love you mom, I'll be home soon.

"I did it to save her life," the father said, looking over at his bony wife. Their marriage had been arranged, and public displays of affection are rare in Pashtun culture. But at that moment, the old woman laid a veiny hand on his. The two looked up at me, holding hands. It was only then that I realized what I had been chasing the whole time. "This isn't a war story," I scribbled in my notebook. "It's a love story, between two parents and their son."

The father wiped his face with the sleeve of his *shalwar kameez* and reached into his pocket. He handed me a tiny piece of paper so repeatedly folded and soft, I was afraid that it would crumble into dust if I opened it.

The paper was covered in Urdu writing, with long sequences of scribbled numbers that looked like sat-phone numbers. At the bottom, a circled sum.

I was incredulous.

"Is this a ransom note?"

I asked the father how much Bahram's ransom was.

He looked off into the hills.

"One hundred and twenty-five thousand rupees," he said. "I'm trying to save ten a day."

It was going to take thirty-four years.

Word spread while I was sitting on the floor of the hut, trying to get all this down. Dozens of old men, barely aloft on spindly sticks, mouths full of dull rotten teeth, knocked on the door. They reached out and put their hands on my heart, Pashtun style, then shook my hand. They pressed into my palm the tiniest scrap of paper—a name, a location, an "s/o," and then another name— son of.

"There are a hundred Bahrams here," one man said.

Many were being held for ransom in "private jails" across northern Afghanistan. War creates ideal economic conditions for scumbags. I had stumbled onto a full-fledged human-trafficking ring, run by American allies, involving hundreds, maybe even thousands, of teenage boys, captured thanks to American bombs. My pockets were soon stuffed with crinkled pieces of paper, just like those from the first trip to Malawi, and again I was overwhelmed. I didn't have the capacity to absorb all that was being asked of me, nor the courage to tell these men who were putting their hand on my heart the truth. I wasn't a conduit to a just world. I was simply a reporter.

I kept digging, because that's what reporters do when they're not quite ready to sit down and write. Soon the edge of my shovel hit something I hadn't been expecting and didn't want to find. A man named Jamshade, who was in his late twenties or early thirties, said that he had been captured by the Northern Alliance as well.

"The soldiers do things to you that make you want to kill yourself," Jamshade said. "They have this game—they think they are so clever for thinking it up—called *keel* [nail]. They start with the youngest prisoners and ask them their age. If a boy says thirteen, they send thirteen soldiers to him. If he says sixteen, the boy gets sixteen.

"They take them to an underground room and hold the boys down, and the whole house fills with screaming, and the soldiers yell louder than the screaming, like they are mad or crazy or have turned into wild animals: '*Keel! Keel!*' Hit the *keel* on the head."

"Sometimes," Jamshade said, his voice shrinking, "I still hear them."

◇◇◇◇◇◇◇

I called up my editor in LA.

"I just found out he's being raped. Can we spring him?"

"How much do they want?"

"Less than three grand. I still have that with me, I got it right here in my pocket, I can give it to the dad . . ."

My editor listened to everything I said.

"You make a damn good case," he told me. "Let me consult and call you back tomorrow."

I was giddy when the sat phone rang. I was standing outside on Bahram's stone terrace, looking off at the snowy peaks of the Hindu Kush.

"I'm sorry, Jeff," my editor said. "The verdict is that we should bear witness on this one."

I wanted to smash the phone on a rock. Bear witness to whom? To God? To the reading public? To my bosses on the *LA Times* foreign desk, subsection Middle East–South Central Asia? Is this what journalism is?

I forget what I muttered back. Whatever I said, it must have provoked him, because he came back at me with "remaining objective" and "staying neutral." This was just the same old keep-your-emotions-out-of-it, less-is-more garbage. But less was not more in this case. Less was just less. Objective, sure, I aspired to that. But neutral? Really? Did I want to be neutral in anything I did? That wasn't me. I didn't want to be the eye that watches without trying to help. I didn't want to be the helicopter circling above.

What if I thought I could change things? What if I *knew* I could change things?

◇◇◇◇◇◇◇

As soon as we drove out of Bahram's village, I saw a black truck parked alongside the river. Six men with black berets and submachine guns were walking slowly up the hill toward us. I shut my eyes, hoping they would disappear.

The men in black berets arrested me at gunpoint. They called themselves the Local Force. They said I was breaking the law by being in a restricted area, and they took me to jail. I told the Local Force that I was an Australian journalist, working for the *Sydney Daily Times*, a paper that didn't even exist, but I didn't know any better and I wasn't taking any chances. The American military had killed many people in this valley, and Daniel Pearl had just been beheaded in Pakistan. From the moment I left the international airport in Islamabad, I had been concealing my identity. My stomach balled into a fist when a little mullah walked into the room where I was being interrogated and started speaking English as well as I did. With a gnomish beard down to his chest and a knowing glint in his eye, he asked: "Where exactly in Sydney do you live?"

By the harbor, I told him.

Right when the jig was about to be up, a top commander called in from Peshawar, spoke to me over the phone, and said I needed to leave the area, at once.

Step 5: The Close Call. It's part of every good story, like nearly breaking a leg while skiing down a beautifully open back bowl knee-deep in fresh powder, no tracks but your own. It's the only way to know you've pushed yourself as far as you can possibly go. But as you reach journalism's higher slopes, it gets easier and easier to take a fall from which you will not get up.

If you've forgotten at this point that I was still just a junior national reporter in Atlanta, well, so had I. Until a few days later, when I found myself back in Georgia, the magnolias in full bloom, filling my whole neighborhood with a sharp and enticing scent weirdly similar to Lemon Fresh Pledge.

I had worked nearly three months on this story in Afghanistan and Pakistan, and now the final words would be pecked out in my dining room in Atlanta, a plate of once-limp spaghetti cooling into a hardened thicket of carbohydrates. The national desk was eager for me to get back to work for them, and suggested I cover a dispute that was heating up in Mississippi over frozen catfish fillets. Frozen catfish fillets? Are you serious? I turned off my cell phone, yanked the phone line out of the wall, and for several days I was "sick."

Two more months passed. I started to deeply regret my inaction; I could have given Bahram's dad the ransom money when I was in Pakistan, but I had been too chickenshit to disobey a direct order. I was obsessed with pleasing the foreign desk. They had enormous power over me. Every day I thought about Africa, even as the Bahram story morphed into more shapes than an amoeba. I was passed from editor to editor, my odyssey ending with one of the editing legends at the *LA Times*, a man whose palate was more Hemingway than Faulkner. We kept sending drafts back and forth via e-mail. I kept putting in adjectives, he kept taking them out; I'd load up the sentences with metaphors, he'd run the *LA Times*' version of the Vanillaizer over the story and expunge them. This was Step 6: Final Negotiations. Sometimes it's unbelievably hard not to write garbage. But writing is like traveling. Often you have to pass through a bunch of places you don't want to visit in order to arrive where you do. While Papa Hemingway and I kept haggling over things like a stove that put out a "thin *circle* of heat" versus a "thin *coat* of heat," Bahram's captors kept playing *keel*.

Finally some balance was struck. The story was published on July 21, 2002, the day before my thirty-first birthday. Bahram's watery brown eyes stared out from the front page of over a million newspapers. Man, did that feel good—I couldn't imagine any more exuberant feeling than seeing it all there, my byline, my picture, and this story that I'd spent so many months on. What could be better?

I logged on to my e-mail that morning. I'd usually have five messages or so. Now there were twenty, all with the single-word subject heading "Bahram." By the next day, fifty. By the end of the week, 117, and this was an era when people didn't e-mail each other over every little event as momentous as an ingrown hair. Everyone was asking the same thing: How can I help? What can we possibly do? A former Miss Afghanistan; an organizer of gay athletic events; some "Red Princess" lady; an executive at the RAND Corporation; a woman from the FAA; a researcher working on fungal genetics; a man who had just lost his own son. Obviously, not everyone was content to bear witness.

But again the editors instructed me to keep "professional distance." I had to grovel for permission from a company lawyer simply to deputize one of the readers to take charge—the corporate discomfort in dealing with this may have had something to do with the fact that the culprits in this case were American allies, and we were still in that intensely jingoistic early post-9/11 phase. Within weeks the readers united into a group called the BLF—the Bahram Liberation Fund—collected several thousand dollars, and wired it to Pakistan. Of course there were real questions about whether this might simply fuel additional child trafficking or make it more expensive to free the other Bahrams already in captivity. But the BLF figured that just because there are always a million questions about what exactly you should do, that doesn't mean you shouldn't do anything. For a couple days, we didn't know what was happening—the money seemed to vanish between LA and the Swat Valley; the Northern Alliance captors, sensing that Bahram's dad was suddenly flush, jacked up the price; the dad himself disappeared into the misty mountains, presumed dead. Then I received a glorious e-mail.

"He's Out!!!"

◇◇◇◇◇◇◇

It wasn't easy going back to reporting on frozen catfish fillets after that. My solution to the letdown was to move around as much as possible, eat my meals standing up, run a lot, pump iron a lot, and blast the music in my car like the idiots I used to see in LA. Now I got it. If you turn the radio up loud enough, you don't have to think.

My first real assignment back on the Dixie beat was about a brawny geezer on trial for blowing up a church full of black people in 1963. Nothing got the editors all hot like the unrepentant South. Newspapers always say they don't like stereotypes, but it's stereotypes we eagerly color in all the time because it's easy—and we're usually on deadline. I walked into the Birmingham courtroom wearing black pants, a black jacket, and looking like John Walker Lindh (I'd refused to shave my beard since returning from Afghanistan, and my hair was nearly dreaded up). I must have been quite a sight, but as I stepped over a few legs and tried to subtly take a seat at the back of the courtroom, all the other reporters were craning their necks to get a better view of the front.

"You see who that is?"

Who?

"Howell Raines," someone breathed, like he had just witnessed the second coming.

Howell Raines, the new executive editor of the *New York Times*, sat in the front row in a dapper suit with a polka-dotted pocket square, dutifully taking notes on a legal pad, next to a big guy with hunks of back fat sticking out of his tight jacket, who must have been his limo driver.

A Birmingham native and the product of Alabama schools, Howell was loaded with journalistic gifts. Not only was he equipped with a bloodhound's nose for the big political story, but he could write like a dream, a rare combination, and he wasn't afraid to write about the things that meant the most to him.

"It is difficult to describe—or even to keep alive in our

memories—worlds that cease to exist," he wrote at the beginning of an essay that was more a confession on a childhood friendship with his family's young black maid in segregated Birmingham. "Usually we think of vanished worlds as having to do with far-off places or with ways of life, like that of the Western frontier, that are remote from us in time. But I grew up in a place that disappeared, and it was here in this country and not so long ago."

A second burst of excited whispers revealed that Howell's limo driver was no limo driver. That's Bragg, Rick Bragg! During a recess in the trial, I worked up the courage to introduce myself to Bragg, and in his easy, folksy manner, he threw a fleshy arm over my shoulder and said, "Howell, got a young fella here I want you to meet."

These two men were waging the more-is-more battle at the highest levels of our trade. They wrote about strong feelings in warm, earthy, deeply intuitive language. I was aware that their talents and independence had engendered enemies. But still, I wanted in.

I was shocked how easy it was to scamper up the ladder once I had my feet on those lower rungs. I guess there's no momentum like momentum. After all those years of my writing samples floating aimlessly around America—"Fly away, clips, fly! Find the right desk to fall on!"—all it took was one stamp and one envelope addressed to Howell Raines, New York Times, 229 West 43rd Street. Soon I was walking through the revolving door at that very address, wearing my own new dapper suit, about to interview at the greatest newspaper in history.

When the editors at the LA Times found out, they dangled in front of me one of the two jobs that could keep me at the paper. "What about South Africa?" my boss said. "The Johannesburg bureau, you cover Malawi, Mozambique, Zimbabwe, the whole region, even Madagascar. It's all yours—if you stay." I had my heart set on East Africa, the Nairobi bureau, but damn. Madagascar? I spent the next week racked with indecision.

Suddenly things crystallized: If I move 10,000 miles away, with Courtenay and me still split up, we're finished. Africa can wait. I couldn't believe I said that to myself, but I did. I even muttered it out loud while getting dressed, to make it seem true. This was unprecedented. I could finally see an opportunity as a choice, and I made it with Courtenay in mind. She was still doubtful about our long-term prospects, and as instructed I had laid off the Floral Embraces, but I continued to hope she would come around. The score was still lopsided, but it was no longer a shutout: it was something like Africa 3, Courtenay 1.

I went with the *New York Times*—and where did they post me? Down the hall. It was literally a lateral move: I squatted behind my one big metal filing cabinet stuffed with expense reports, road maps, and yellowed newspaper clippings that covered everything from coroners' reports to a New Year's Eve "possum drop" in Brasstown, North Carolina, and pushed it like a bobsled seventy feet across the corridor's flesh-colored carpet from the *LA Times* Atlanta office to the *New York Times* Atlanta office—same building, same floor.

I inherited a Grand Prix as a company car, deeply disappointed in its aged condition until I found out that it was Bragg's old load. A few months after I'd sat in it for the first time (pulling up the seat several inches), Courtenay was riding shotgun, coming in from the airport for her first visit in more than a year. No promises. No intimacy. No kissing, even. But she had agreed to at least discuss the possibility of getting back together, for the fourth time.

It'd all started the night of 9/11. From my cell phone somewhere on I-95, I called her, breaking nearly a year of silence. Her voice, deeper than most women's, was so soothing, and she actually sounded happy to hear from me. I think we were both desperate for comfort after being snatched awake from the collective daydream we all had been living in, otherwise known as the 1990s. We couldn't have been the only couple in the world that those nineteen hijackers brought back together. That day caused a lot of books to be written, a lot of carry-on suitcases to be pawed through, and a lot of relationships to be reexamined. Our twenty-five-minute conversation that night led to more calls and the second epistolary buildup, this time electronically.

"Oh Jeffrey, I don't know what I think about your calling," she e-mailed me while I was still in Afghanistan—nothing like a little danger to resurrect a romance. "I looked at your pictures again today—I wish I could see the steppe and feel the cold air, believe it or not."

I did believe it. I believed it with all my heart.

Howell liked me. How much, I'll never know, but that's not what mattered. I soon discovered that the *New York Times*, perhaps like any big company, is run not so dissimilarly from an African dictatorship. The key thing is not how much the Big Man actually likes you but how much other people *think* the Big Man likes you. Apparently, when I was hired, other people thought the Big Man liked me a lot.

My first story in the *New York Times* was on two young women fussing over who was Miss North Carolina. I bashed it out in about an hour. It ran A1. I made the mistake of musing out loud how it might be nice to get a few spare copies for my folks, and, lo and behold, I came into work a few days later to find, sitting on my chair, wrapped like a Christmas present, the actual steel plate from the printing press. I was feeling like the Golden Child. I bet another reporter that I could get the word *doofus* on the front page, no quotes. I was cruising.

By January 2003, before I'd even been at the paper six months, the national editor asked me what post I would like next—not how it usually goes. The *New York Times* is like the Marine Corps—you go where they tell you. I had just enough humility to know the foreign desk was still out of reach, so I gathered some intel from reliable sources and asked for Miami, a dream job usually reserved for much more senior people. The national editor told me to start working on my base tan.

"Miami!" Courtenay pulled the covers over us in delight. We were cuddled up side by side in my bed in Atlanta, under a quilt embroidered with dime-size mirrors that I had bartered hard for in Islamabad, a sunny Saturday afternoon outside, just one of many such days in the South during the winter. We were now fully back together. "I can't believe it's finally going to work out."

I was tracing gentle circles on the inside of her arm, like I used to. Some of the freckles had faded, but her arms were still beautiful. Her lush raven hair now had a few silvery threads.

This time I wasn't making a decision for myself and then trying to recast it as "ours." Courtenay had been one of my reliable sources; I had asked her about Miami before uttering a word to the bosses. That was big for me. She had refused to follow me to Brooksville, to LA, to Atlanta, not simply because of job prospects but because she hadn't wanted me "to win," as she put it, to think I could go anywhere and she'd trot along after me. Now we were making these decisions together. Besides prestige and Bragg's old Pontiac, the *New York Times* had given me something real: the confidence and security to prioritize our relationship. And that's sexier than all the far-flung datelines and bylines in the world.

"Do you think we could buy a little house on the water?"

"Yes."

"Would you help me study for the bar down there?"

"Of course."

"I can't wait," Courtenay said, curling up next to me.

"Neither can I," I said. "Now, where's the best place to live in Miami?"

We never found out.

SEVEN

⬥⬥⬥⬥⬥

BAGHDAD, 2004

The Palestine Hotel was like Rick's. Everybody went there—
four-star American generals, Arab sheikhs, tattooed contractors,
bearded journalists, plump-bellied members of the Iraqi governing
council, tall Sudanese prostitutes, harried aid workers, even Iraqi
oil painters and musicians. At a bar on the ground floor, journalists
who had just polished off a story and their second beers joked with
former sergeants turned Halliburton project managers making two
hundred and fifty grand a year. Newly appointed council members
licked their date-smeared fingers while speaking in hushed voices
to placid-faced sheikhs. Nondescript Western men in suits or nondescript Arab men in traditional robes made multimillion-dollar
decisions over bowls of garlicky hummus. They studied everything
that parted the glass doors. Located on the banks of the Tigris in
central Baghdad, the Palestine hosted an orgy of ambition. It was
also where other orgies took place—newly made and soon-to-be-
separated couples full of war-zone lust, trashing their marriages in
a room, up on the rooftop, or out by the overchlorinated pool.

In Pakistan I had first come into contact with this world-
within-a-war-zone, this big party at the edge of the world. But
the Palestine, with its past splendor and present status as a site for
speculations about the future, made the Islamabad Marriott seem

like an Econo Lodge in Indianapolis. Every war has its hotel where noncombatants gather—like the Florida in Madrid, where Hemingway, Martha Gellhorn, John Dos Passos, and Robert Capa shacked up during the Spanish Civil War—but in the twenty-first century that cast of characters had swelled, bloated to the point of obesity. No matter what two sides fight an actual war, there is a parallel battle being waged, with some overlap, between the profiteers. This place, with its honeycombed balconies studded with satellite dishes, its 420 rooms costing from $90 to $300 a night—cash only, please—was the incubator for and the emblem of the opportunities that war offers to those in a position to exploit them.

That's why I was there. Journalists need material, and there was more material here than any of us knew what to do with. In Afghanistan I had worked with exactly one other journalist—Yama—and come across only a handful of others, like the forty-year-old guy digging mud out of his boots with a stick. Here there were hundreds of us—the *LA Times*, AP, Reuters, the *Guardian*, BBC, Al Jazeera, *Le Monde*, *Corriere della Sera*. This was the biggest story in the world.

And it was America's show, complete with its very own showrunner. A familiar sound above the Palestine was the loud thumping of the Black Hawk that ferried around L. Paul Bremer III, who issued his directives from on high. With coiffed hair that appeared to have been snapped on like a piece of Lego, a thousand-dollar suit, and suede desert boots, Bremer was the primary architect of the American occupation, which had begun days before I was about to take the Miami job. He was the one who issued Coalition Provisional Authority Order No. 2, the decision to lay off the entire Iraqi army for the crime of having served under Saddam Hussein. He swaggered around Iraq the way a quarterback wends his way through the hallways of his Texas high school on game day. Bremer possessed an air of confidence that was so absolute it could have only derived from a profound ignorance. Or sociopathy.

I pulled up to the Palestine for my nightly reprieve of partying in the back of an armored Bimmer that cost a quarter of a million dollars. When I walked in, many people knew who I was, having read my dispatch from the day before. One guy even quoted a line of it back to me. I went around with an Amstel in my right hand, wearing Iraqi madras shirts and ripped cords, pockets bulging with Iraqi dinars, crumpled $100 bills, two cell phones, and five retractable pens.

"Hey, Jeff, meet Richard," a freelance photojournalist said. I'd done a story or two with him, though we usually used a different photographer, a young woman. "Jeff, what's up? I'm at Reuters," the clean-shaven guy said. "Who do you work for?" I dropped it on him like a mortar shell—it was important to me to let my new fraternity of journalists know who they were dealing with. "Me? I look like steerage, don't I? But I work for the *New York Times*."

After I finished my Amstel, I sidled up to the bar. It was Tim from a British paper and Keith from the *LA Times*. "Yeah, I was in Karbala today, that suicide bomb," Tim said. "Heard about that one," replied Keith. I didn't join in, or say where or what I'd been covering—Hilla, south of Baghdad, a cluster bomb nearly took off a kid's face. The boy had been playing in a pasture littered with unexploded American bomblets, a cow kicked one, and *boom!* the thing sprayed shrapnel into the boy's eyes and cheeks, leaving hundreds of ugly blue freckles across his face that looked like pencil stabs. During the interview, his father, who had a shoe-polish-black mustache that didn't quite jibe with the white hair at his temples, bawled the whole time. But I didn't say a word about this to Keith or Tim. My mind had quickly jumped to something else, and I didn't have much time to execute. "How many dead?" Keith asked Tim, about the bombing in Karbala. "Oh, not too bad," Tim said. "Twenty. But a lot of wounded women and children. I got good color." "I bet," Keith said. I have to get out of here, I thought.

I patted them on the back, left the bar, and walked toward the elevator bank. My hands shook as I pressed 15 on the panel. The doors closed, and the car jerked to life. When the doors reopened,

I stepped briskly out, eyes locked on the garish green-and-brown-striped carpeting that pointed down the corridor like a highway center line. I paused midway. I could still turn around, head back to my room at the bureau, polish up my story, maybe even get some sleep. I knocked on the door.

"Oh, shit, he's here!" I heard from the other side of the door. "Gotta go! Call ya back!"

The door flung open. Elizabeth stood there, cell phone in hand, wearing a black abaya. We locked mouths immediately, all that pent-up tension mashing into itself, and I set to work on the zipper—the only reason she was wearing a head-to-toe gown in the privacy of her hotel room was so I could remove it. I unzipped her from neck to knees, pushed the abaya back from her shoulders, watched the black fabric hit the floor.

Think of Courtenay, think of Courtenay. I could hear those words while we were in bed, beyond the breathing, beyond the sounds of someone right underneath me, skin against mine. The memory of Courtenay was a device, a powerful aid, not necessarily inconvenient. When I thought of her, it made me feel guilty—but not too guilty. It took me out of the moment and prolonged the act and thereby gave us both more pleasure, allowing us to remain in our little desirous escape world as the one around us lit up with RPG fire. I even shared this with Elizabeth, who said, "That's twisted." But twisted fit the mood and the times. And she didn't seem to mind.

We never lay there for more than a couple minutes—we squeezed in our trysts between web and print deadlines, between mortar barrages and rocket attacks. There's not a lot of cuddling in battlefield affairs—at least not in my limited experience. Everything's so rushed, you're seeking survival through momentary contact. It's a way to keep the war close and simultaneously at bay. For me, it worked surprisingly well, lying in a strange bed in a strange room in a strange hotel in a strange, cursed city, leaving a wet spot on the sheets as blood settled into pools out on the streets; a machine gun (*buh-buh, buh-buh-buh-buh*) cracking in the near distance; an Iraqi down there trying to get as far away from another Iraqi as possible, snuffing out his life, while we two Americans had just gotten as physically close as humanly possible.

Elizabeth jumped out of bed before me, and I followed her lead, dressing quickly. I heard a chopper whumping above the hotel; maybe it was even Bremer's.

"I better go file," I said, grabbing my phone from the floor.

"No problem," she said. "See you at the house."

◇◇◇◇◇◇

It began with a suicide bomb.

I was the rookie. She was the veteran. I had just arrived in country. She had been here for months. Elizabeth Nichols was thirty years old; she hailed from Philadelphia; she had covered the Taliban and Mexican drug lords. She had ducked rockets in Kunduz and driven the Khyber Pass. She was on a first-name basis with photo editors at the widest-circulating magazines. She was like a Dan Eldon filled out and all grown up. She was tall, dark, intelligent, and gutsy and loved Tootsie Rolls and chocolate-chip cookies. In February 2004 the two of us were assigned to cover a suicide bombing in the Kurdish city of Erbil. It was my first big one. We sped up the northern highway for five hours, the desert rising into mountains, a sheet of ice on the ground by the time we stepped out. A man with a bomb hidden in his jacket had walked into the headquarters of the Kurdistan Democratic Party, where scores of people—including children—had been exchanging greetings, eating chocolates, and paying respect to Kurdish leaders on the first day of Eid al-Adha, the Feast of the Sacrifice.

As we walked up, Elizabeth looked at me.

"You good?"

The building was large, plain, one story. A cold drizzle fell on the front step. Two *pesh merga* guards stood at the entrance, smoking cigarettes. Elizabeth didn't pause. She walked straight through the door. The guards nearly tripped over their own slushy boots trying to step aside. I fell in, happy for her to show me the ropes.

The blast had curled the ceiling fan blades, scorched the wallpaper off the walls, and smeared clumps of yellow fat across the floor. I could smell burned hair; I looked up and saw tufts of it sticking to the ceiling. Chunks of glass crunched under our feet, but sometimes we stepped on something softer, wetter. Scores of people had been blown apart in that room, so much coagulating blood on the floor that I started thinking that human beings are just bags of fluid, waiting to be stuck. I could get down only a few notes with my shaking hands before I had to stop and wipe the tears from my eyes. Elizabeth clicked away, sometimes holding her camera down by her shoes and angling it up—she was so good she didn't even have to look through the viewfinder, the camera was like a sixth sense for her. There was nobody to interview; all the witnesses had been in this room. Elizabeth stopped shooting for a moment and pointed at something on the floor. "Oh my God," she said. It was an eyeball, and out of its socket, it looked much bigger than either of us would have ever guessed. I felt a bubble of vomit creeping up my throat.

That night I was useless; I had suddenly forgotten all my newspaperese. I was by myself, working—or trying to. We each had our own room. This was before anything had happened, while we were still shadowboxing, a casual touch on the arm here, a lingering hand on the shoulder there, carefully measuring each other's interest through gestures that could be easily dismissed as mere collegiality, if necessary. I stared out the windows at the mountains barely visible through the scrim of mist and rain. ERBIL, IRAQ—More than 50 people were killed in a *fiery* suicide bomb, no, *massive* suicide bomb, no, *deafening* suicide bomb . . . When you're struggling with adjectives, you know you're in trouble.

That's how it went in Iraq; there was always wonderful access to see things you should never see. You were never too late, nobody ever said no, the police or soldiers or militiamen would always do the same thing when we arrived—step aside. My first job in Brooksville had been ideal training for this. Iraq was murder more than it was war. But there was no police tape here, nothing between me and the madness. In Iraq, I was wiping it off my shoes.

I can't count how many bombings I covered. Too many, clearly. After that first one, I couldn't stop looking at people's eyeballs, including my colleagues', wondering how far back they really went. Soon I didn't flinch anymore when the translator grimaced at the ceiling and said, "Meat, meat, meat." I just looked up and made notes. I stepped into dark burning buildings, piercing screams rending the air, crowds of the instantly dispossessed surrounding me, shaking their fists at me, often the lone American—"You did this! You did this!" even if it had been a suicide bomb. I started to think of shredded human beings as man-slaw. Many days that's all we did, go looking for man-slaw. We'd drive around the back streets, pressing cell phones to our ears, trying to raise a fixer in this or that corner of Baghdad, trying to locate the source of a column of smoke uncoiling in the distance. Where there was smoke, there was meat. "Infijar, infijar, wein infijar?" Elizabeth shouted. *Where's the bomb?* We were bomb chasers.

Late one morning, my tolerance for death and dismemberment at a high point, we zoomed through western Baghdad, knifing through canyons of blown-up buildings. The city soon dissolved in a haze of dust. The road opened up into a six-lane highway, Ramadi seventy-five miles away. Ten Marines had just been killed in Ramadi. We passed small homes made out of mud, walled villages, date palms covered in coppery powder. There wasn't a cloud in the sky, but there was nothing glorious about the sunshine here. The sky shone like sheet metal.

"Are they going to even let us get close?" Elizabeth asked.

"I don't know—hopefully they didn't close all the roads yet."

"The marines always mess up my shots."

She was amped, nervous, futzing with the zipper on her abaya, which she wore every day, her cover, a steel plate from a flak jacket carefully concealed underneath. American forces were always much stricter about photographs; the access was not wonderful. Our driver Walid, and Khalid, our translator, chatted in the front in Arabic, about what, I don't know. The road began to curve.

"You'll get something," I said. "You always manage to get something. Don't be stressed. You can always get a shot of Ramadi."

"If I never take another picture of—"

A blue van shot across the highway and screeched to a halt fifty feet in front of us, cutting us off. The van's doors flew open. Walid slammed on the brakes. We careened off the tarmac. By the time we'd come to a halt, dust all around us, we were surrounded by armed masked men.

"We're dead! We're dead!" Elizabeth screamed.

Dozens more flooded into the road, carrying machine guns and grenade launchers. Our car was bulletproof, but not that bulletproof. I slumped down in my seat, as if that made a difference.

The insurgents ripped open the front doors and grabbed Walid and Khalid and threw them onto the ground. Then they surged toward me. My door was locked. They banged their guns on my window. These were the men Paul Bremer had laid off.

"Don't get out! Don't get out!" Elizabeth said, grabbing my arm. "They'll kill you."

Instantly I thought of Danny Pearl. When twenty guys with guns are running toward you, all you can think of is how exactly this will end. Will they shoot you or saw off your head? Burn you alive? Who will find your body? We were only a few miles up the road from where four American contractors had just been ambushed and killed, their charred bodies gleefully strung up from a bridge. There was no flight-or-fight. Choice was an illusion, which created its own strange sense of calm, at least initially.

I stepped out.

A masked man hoisted a belt-fed PKM machine gun up to his shoulder and leveled it at my chest.

Click.

The safety off, he closed one eye and squinted down the barrel; the other gunmen near me scattered away. I didn't even bother to put up my hands.

I didn't feel my pulse hammering in my neck anymore. I didn't feel anything: total numbness. I had no thoughts. That moment was the still point of my life.

I looked beyond the gunman up at the sheet-metal sky. I was about to die.

I don't remember how, but two guys pounced on me, shoved me into a van, Elizabeth tossed in beside me. It looked like Khalid and Walid were in another van, but I wasn't sure. Where were they going to take us? Back to their base, where it was easier to dump my body and gang-rape Elizabeth? She looked at me, abject terror widening her eyes. The insurgents starting arguing—insurgents argue too—apparently about who was going to ride shotgun. While they were snapping at each other, I reached deep into my front pocket, got my fingers around my passport, and slipped it to Elizabeth, who without any instruction stuffed it down the front of her jeans. We were so stupid those days, carrying our American passports everywhere we went; occasionally we'd need to flash them to get into a Green Zone press conference, as if that dose of propaganda was worth the risk of being in the situation I was in right now. September 11 had eliminated any illusions of journalistic privilege. The insurgents had taken the same tack as George Bush—you were with them or against them. I was praying the terrorists would still have some manners and not frisk her, at least not there.

We raced through a little town, insurgents everywhere. That line the American generals in Baghdad kept feeding us—that *maybe* 5 percent of Iraqis were against the occupation—was Vietnam-size horseshit. I nearly lost control of my bowels as we pulled up to a garage surrounded by a mob. Welding equipment, jugs of propane, artillery shells, and coils of brass wire were heaped in messy piles on the floor, along with a fully rigged rocket launcher. I tried not to stare. I still had twenty masked men with the muzzles of their rifles three inches from my face, shouting questions in a mixture of Arabic and broken English.

"American?"

"No," I said.

"Where from?"

"I'm Greek."

"Greck?"

"Yes." I repeated it with a little more confidence. "Greck."

"Greck" was my way of imitating how some Arabs pronounce *Greek*, and I could tell I stumped them on that one. I saw one insurgent screw up his face, looking at me like I was speaking Greck.

I couldn't use the Sydney harbor one anymore, nor could I say I was a Brit, a Spaniard, an Italian, a Pole, a Dane, a Kiwi, or a Bulgarian—all those countries, along with, for some reason, Mongolia and Tonga and Nicaragua, had joined the Coalition of the Willing. French wouldn't have worked either. Even though France had wisely stayed out of Iraq, everywhere somebody speaks French—except for me, and knowing my luck, one of those gunmen might have taken some French classes at a university before most of them were shut. This is why I went with Greck. The Grecks also had a pretty good soccer team, and Iraqis loved soccer.

Elizabeth sat still and silent next to me in the van, but the men seemed agnostic toward her. It was me they were after, me they wanted to kill before moving on to the next battle, but they still had some bizarre respect for human life and weren't so wanton as to make an irredeemable move.

"Greck! What are you doing here?"

"Greck! Who do you work for?"

"Greck! How do we know you're not a spy?"

I answered the questions with words that didn't feel my own, as if my mouth were now operating independently.

Finally, the bulging-eyed underlings parted for a man whose face was uncovered. He wore a pair of silver-rimmed aviators. Just like Baba John, he didn't carry a weapon; he didn't need to. He was like the captain of a ship with no radio: in total control. All the other insurgents shrank away as he stepped toward me. He asked more questions, then stared at my face. He barked something out in Arabic, and someone ran up to him with something shiny. It was a metal bowl of water, which he held for a moment.

"Drink," he said.

My mouth was so parched from fear, no sip had ever tasted so wet. I handed back the bowl, trying to see what was behind the aviators.

"Now," he said, "you're our friends."

Aviators gestured for us to leave the van, but right as we stepped out, there was a bright white flash. *Hoosh! Hoosh!* A series of rockets flew west, toward the nearest marine base, blasting up clouds of sulfuric smoke with a fast, clean sound. *Hoosh!* The men cheered, pumping their fists in the air, yelling "Viva mujahideen! Viva mujahideen!" and for a few seconds, though I knew it was fleeting, the attention swung away from us. I heard Khalid, who had gone colorless during my interrogation, shout "Viva mujahideen!" Khalid's cheering on the insurgents?

"Woo-hoo!" I yelled as I stood in the street, slugging that smoky sky as hard as I could with my fist. "Woo-hoo! Viva mujahideen, viva mujahideen!" I yelled, though I was also whispering "You muthafuckas" under my breath. "Woo-hoo! Woo-hoo! (You fucking muthafuckas.) Viva mujahideen!"

As soon as those rockets disappeared into the bright sky, the men looked at us again. I lowered my head, resigned to being a captive. The show was over.

We were marched into a house with bars on the windows. Up the stairs, up the stairs, they ordered. Khalid could barely lift his big feet; my shoes dumbly followed. It wasn't even noon, and I was spectacularly enervated. Two women, faces covered, came into our room and pointed at Elizabeth. They took her away.

We didn't eat. We didn't drink. We didn't talk. Nobody offered us anything. Now, clearly, we were *not* friends. I could hear the women chatting in high birdsong in the next room. What are they doing to her in there? What are they saying?

If we spent the night, they'd surely pass us up to more sophisticated insurgents. If they did that, then we would be strip-searched, and they'd find my passport in Elizabeth's underpants or make me draw a map of Greece, which I couldn't. I sat silently, for hours that felt like days, itchy with stress. There were two insurgents in our room, two more right outside the door, several by the gate, hundreds in the street.

Around sunset, a man with a neatly cropped beard and Kalashnikov came in. There was no law in this town, just more men with guns.

"Passport?" the bearded man asked. He sat down, and his eyes swept the room, distractedly—he and I both knew that the marines were suiting up, probably waiting for the cover of darkness to launch their counterattack. My focus, so sharp in the beginning, was now waning. One of the most exhausting activities in the world is lying repeatedly with firearms in your face.

"My passport?" I muttered.

"Yes," he said. "Your passport. Where is your passport?"

I looked him right in the eyes.

"At the Palestine."

The bearded man stood up, took the rifle he had propped up by the door, and walked out. There wasn't an adult in Iraq who hadn't heard of the Palestine.

The guards around us started talking fast. The energy in the room had suddenly changed. They motioned for us to stand and put on our shoes and ushered us outside. The sun was going down fast. Elizabeth reappeared. Were we free? I was so drained, so tense from all the ups and downs, I wouldn't allow myself to feel anything. We climbed quietly into the car. Walid turned the key. Khalid closed his eyes. I looked out at the desert.

"Be careful," one of the insurgents said, completely seriously, leaning on our window, as if we were old buds. "The road back to Baghdad can be dangerous."

When we pulled up to the bureau, the entire Iraqi staff was standing on the lawn, waiting for us. One after the other, the mustached guards, the cooks, the other drivers and translators, around two dozen people, most who usually resisted cracking a smile, hugged me so tight, eyes closed, jiggling with sobs. Everyone back in Baghdad had thought we were gone. When I finally walked back up into my room, alone, I felt tremendously empty.

◇◇◇◇◇◇◇

"Don't you think it's time to come home?" Courtenay asked me that night.

"Sweetie, come on. Don't tell me to come home."

I was suppressing my feelings automatically. That's what Iraq was for me. Extreme experiences. Intense suppression. And a lot of lies, which fit the tune of the day. Colin Powell had lied to the nation about WMDs. The American generals were lying about the insurgency. The Iraqis were lying to the Americans. Elizabeth had a boyfriend back in Paris and was lying to him. I was lying to Courtenay. We were all lying. Iraq was the new Bright Shining Lie.

"It was just bad luck, that's all, that road was supposed to be clear, they didn't hurt us, I'll never do anything like that again," I told her, knowing that it wasn't true. "I'm exhausted, so exhausted, you have no idea how exhausted, tell me how you've been, tell me where we'll go when I get out of here, just talk, please, honey, just talk."

More and more, I said less and less. Courtenay and I had been doing relatively well before, but Iraq quickly accentuated the dickhead in me. Want, want, want. Take, take, take. Me, me, me. I guess I always had a selfish streak. But living alone for so many years, usually far from friends and family, people who would have been more than happy to call me on my faults, and constantly trying to do whatever it took to inch up the journalism ladder had amplified my self-centeredness to a new level that now seems almost hard to recognize. When Courtenay phoned to tell me how she had just visited a college friend in Seattle and how nice it would be to live there, I shot back: *Seattle? I can't believe you're talking to me about Seattle. What kind of job do you expect me to get in Seattle?* Courtenay never had a deep hankering to live in Seattle. But, staying with her friend, she had glimpsed another life: marriage, kids, a car in the garage, morning walks to the coffee house, *being together.* And here I was in a war zone—with another woman.

I regret Iraq. It was the low point of my adult life. It was the low point for the United States. It was the height of misguided self-interest. It was bad news. But I couldn't see it that way at the time. The way I saw it, the way I had to see it, was that this was part of my dream.

Afghanistan?

Check.

Iraq?

Check.

I had just been kidnapped, almost shot in the face, and even closer to shitting myself, sure, but that's what the job was about. I finally understood why Dan had blundered his way into the depths of Mogadishu that day. The more war you get, the more war you want. It's an addiction.

I didn't know jack about Iraq, but now my services were in high demand. I was writing for the front page, I was in big-time magazines, I was interviewed frequently on live television news shows. I loved live TV, it made *me* feel live: suicide bombs blowing up around the corner, American troops taking over towns, buildings burning, guns, guns, guns, guns of all types blasting, billions of dollars circulating through that crushed city, insurgents blowing things up. I could speak about any of it. How many other reporters had been captured by masked men in the heart of insurgent territory and talked their way out of it?

The imperial hubris, that swagger of the American troops strutting around with their SAW machine guns slung over their shoulders exactly the same way my frat brothers used to strut up the driveway, lacrosse sticks slung over their shoulders, that conviction that everything was going exactly according to plan, that's how I felt. I knew many soldiers didn't believe in what they were doing. I knew it was a mask, but it fit me too. You would have never guessed how terrified I was on a daily basis; fear gripped my gut the instant the hood of our car broke the plane of the bureau's gates in the morning, and it stayed with me until we pulled in again in the evening. There were no front lines in Iraq. No place was safe. One sunny Saturday afternoon a friend of mine, Marla, a vivacious young woman from San Francisco who was trying to help Iraqi children, was driving on the airport road when her convoy was hit by a suicide bomber. She was thrown from the car, badly burned. The American soldiers who responded to the scene stepped right over her, thinking she was dead. Her last words were true for only one more short moment: "I'm alive."

When I needed an escape, I'd allow Nairobi's soapy cumulus clouds to float through my mind. This often happened when I was up on the bureau's rooftop, doing push-ups in the hundred-degree heat with a bulletproof vest on for extra resistance, cranking up the *Rocky* soundtrack—if there was ever a guy who lived more-is-more, who never settled for subtleties, it was Rock. (And say whatever you want about Sylvester Stallone, I've heard it all before, but he wrote that script, insisted on starring in the title role, held on to his dream about a dream, and even slugged it out with the most chiseled man ever to grace the silver screen, Apollo Creed.) Elizabeth would often be up there with me, listening to her iPod and doing her own workouts.

"Did you see what happened with me and that police officer?" I asked her between a set of push-ups.

"No, I was shooting down the street."

"Oh shit, I could've sworn you were there. I was standing in the rubble interviewing some people, and this police officer kept tapping me on the back, saying, 'Mista, mista' . . ."

"Yeah?"

"He was bugging the hell out of me, and finally I turn around and he's holding up this gray droopy thing, and he says, 'Hey, mista, foot, foot.'"

"Jesus," Elizabeth said.

"Jesus is right. I'd say it was about size nine."

That was our currency—suicide bombers, insurgents, pieces of people. We were pieces of people. Elizabeth knew how badly I wanted to be a full-time foreign correspondent. As we were driving back from another street filled with man-slaw, the vegetable carts flipped over, a gash five feet deep where the asphalt had been blown apart, she turned to me and said, apropos of nothing: "I'll make introductions for you. I'll get us work. I'd love to go to Africa." But that fantasy, like my sanity, was possible only through intense suppression. When Elizabeth and I laced up our gym shoes and went jogging by the Tigris, I couldn't help but think of the very deliberate way Courtenay used to lace up her gym shoes before we went running on the beach in Florida. The specter of our relationship was always there, no matter how delicately or recklessly I tried to push it away.

Elizabeth was laughing about something or other the morning we climbed into a truck packed with seventeen marines, all young and skinny, revved up on instant coffee and government-issued Skittles. They were dressed in full battle-rattle—helmets, flak jackets, boots, gloves, ammo vests, and Kevlar groin guards—a twenty-first-century suit of armor that covered nearly every inch of their flesh. The mission was essentially 'Nam-style search and destroy, but it had been given a different name, befitting the new era of euphemism: movement to contact.

Our convoy of trucks rolled through an agricultural area of orange groves and small houses—we had been persuaded to return to the scene of our kidnapping, a town called Karma, of all things. In every stretch of Karma the insurgents made the grievous mistake of squeezing off a poorly chosen potshot to ambush us. The marines leaped to their feet, raised their M-16s to their cheeks, and lit up everything in sight, right down to one white-bearded man driving an ancient pickup who failed to understand the obscure hand signals American marines use to mean stop. I watched the Marines open up on him, leaving him slumped over the steering wheel, a constellation of white stars on the windshield. Killing him was totally optional—and they shot him full of holes.

That old man was the war. An inexorable road pulling him toward us. All those rifles rising in one smooth motion. The spat-out copper casings hitting the back of my hands, the pungent gunpowder on the tip of my tongue, the smell of split-open oranges. As I looked back, plumes of black smoke boiled up from the bulrushes, wattle houses burned, and cattle lay on their sides. It looked like a biblical landscape. And we were the eleventh plague.

The road ended in Fallujah. The marines quickly took a swath of the city, leaving insurgents on their backs in the middle of the streets, faces bearded with flies. Live insurgents were still everywhere, though, and we sprinted across every open intersection to make sure that we didn't get shot. As it grew dark, the marines invited us to spend the night in a house they had just commandeered, whose inhabitants had either fled or been killed. The marines had excellent intuition and were quite gentlemanly (to fellow Americans). Without Elizabeth and my uttering a word, they insisted we share a room at the top of the stairs.

"Just stay away from the windows," a gunnery sergeant warned. "These guys are about to attack."

As soon as the door closed, we started kissing, the steel plates of our flaks knocking together. We were only getting more cavalier and addled as the war heated up. I had a story to file, Elizabeth had pictures to edit, I'm pretty sure what we were about to do was not allowed within the American military's embed rules, and the marines were pounding up and down the stairs on the other side of our door. Stress is the highest-octane fuel you can pour on lust. The bedroom was so strange—I've never felt like such an intruder—a velvet bedspread pulled taut, the couple's clothes hanging in the closet, little pictures of their children on the bedside tables. As we tumbled into the bed, a firefight erupted, blasts of gunfire so close I couldn't decipher their direction, the deafening growl of a Gatling gun from above, huge explosions making the windows shiver, the marines firing three-round bursts from our roof. *Bap-bap-bap. Bap-bap-bap.* We didn't stop. We were keeping the war at bay, for a few more minutes.

I stepped back into the Baghdad newsroom feeling as if I had just emerged from the war's smoking, gooey plasma. Sometimes I was giddy about my exploits. Other times, increasingly, I felt intense pangs of guilt and betrayal. Their tendrils stayed wrapped around me for days. It was the opposite of what I would have expected. As my time in Iraq stretched into months, I became less skilled at applying a tourniquet to my own emotions, more aware of the absurdity of my own life. I'd wake up each morning to a glass of freshly squeezed OJ and a detailed body count from the night before. All Khalid and the other translators wanted to know was: What was the style of death? That's how Khalid said it, meaning, Was the guy axed in the head or burned by acid or shot or blown up or strangled or drowned in a bucket of goat manure or drilled in the face and thighs with Makita power tools?

Evening time. The whisper of a breeze. The sad sooty trees in front of the bureau suddenly thickened with hundreds of sparrows that had disappeared during the hot hours of the day. As the sun set, the birds started chittering madly, as if they were witnessing the miracle of dawn. The lifting of that brutal, leaden heat was a miracle. After sunset we could move again.

I filed the Web version of my dispatch—the Web was my first deadline; the editors were increasingly pushy about driving traffic to our website. I showered and walked outside, smelling of Speed Stick. I nodded to the young guard who stood at the edge of our compound. He unlatched the gate. I stepped briefly into sniper range, slipped between a pair of blast walls, jogged for a quarter mile through a dim concrete canyon until it opened up and a tall brown building rose in front of me. The Palestine. It was just down the street from our bureau, on the same side of the Tigris. I took the jumpy elevator up to the fifteenth floor and followed that long hallway illuminated by chandeliers that looked like kryptonite. This time I nearly turned around.

Afterward, as I was buttoning up my shirt, a white flash lit up the room. A split second later, a deafening crack. Mortars. I walked to the window and looked out at the Green Zone and saw the red glow of a spreading fire. I grabbed my phone and punched in the numbers and was about to hit SEND when Elizabeth said to me:

"This could be our life. You know that, don't you?"

There was something about the way she said it that made me feel uneasy. I did want this life, needed it, I was good at it, had worked years to finally get a taste of it, but there was something frightening about it becoming a reality in a way that I hadn't envisioned. Elizabeth could sense my ambivalence.

"You two are never really going to break up, are you?"

The phone was still in my hand. I was still standing by the window. I hit SEND as she started in again.

"You met at a sorority dance, how cute."

"Hey, Jeffrey here, from the NYT." I turned away from her and spoke into the phone. "What's going on over there? Any casualties?"

"I don't know," said the voice on the other end. "What do you mean?"

"I don't know," Elizabeth said. "Maybe I got you wrong."

"I'm watching you guys get lit up by mortars."

"I don't see anything."

"You don't *see* anything? I'm looking right at it! There's a roof on fire. I'm at the Palestine. *I* can see it!"

Wham! Another shell slammed in.

"Yeah, sorry. I'm in a bunker. I don't have any info."

Elizabeth watched me as I talked and watched me leave. Outside, the Tigris gleamed black and glossy like a strip of wet asphalt. The wind was swirling, undecided. I was back in the bureau, at my computer, fifteen minutes later. By that point, the fire was out.

EIGHT

⬨⬨⬨⬨⬨⬨

ZANZIBAR, 2004

Courtenay found a hotel on the east coast of Zanzibar, along a wide, deserted beach. The last time we had visited Zanzibar was six years before. Now I was a mess. I jumped every time a door closed too loudly, I scanned every road for garbage bombs. I swatted mosquitoes against the wall, thinking: I've seen *people* smeared like that.

Our mornings were quiet and slow. We ate our papaya and mango salad on a shaded veranda where the waiters called me *ndugu*, brother—I insisted, and you can do that in East Africa, call everyone brother and, even better, be called brother. We paddled around the salty sea and walked back during the heat of the day to our bungalow that wore a little hat of thatch. We kissed a little, but not much more than that. It felt strange touching her, stranger than it had with a stranger.

Elizabeth had scrambled me. I could never really picture the two of us together outside Iraq, and our affair had lasted barely two months. But now I couldn't imagine being a foreign correspondent without a like-minded partner right next to me. The problem was, Courtenay didn't have the war bug, she wasn't a journalist, she was a lawyer, she had never expressed interest in any of this. We were still in love, I'd never been in love with anyone else, I'd illicitly tested our love and realized that she might be the only one I could ever trust. But maybe we had grown too different. Maybe we had never even wanted the same thing to begin with.

There was no easy way to begin unloading the weight Iraq had put on me, all those styles of death. People listening to those stories never say the right thing. There is no right thing. If you were there, you got it; otherwise, you didn't. At night, when Courtenay and I should have been at least attempting to talk about what we couldn't talk about, we both could feel the odd space growing between us. We ate our dinner quietly, swallowed our chalky malaria pills, retreated back to the bungalow for another chaste kiss, and then lay flat on our backs, staring at the ceiling fan wobble.

"Did you meet someone else out there?" Courtenay finally asked.

"No," I said with a sigh. "Don't worry."

"What do you mean, 'Don't worry'? Don't give me that. Was there someone else or not?"

I watched the fan blades stir the soupy tropical air. I could hear waves crashing against the reef a few hundred yards from the shore. It made me think back to the Zanzibar of years ago, when having a half-naked woman lying next to me, the bottom of her feet dusted with sand, her skin still warm from the sun, was the stuff of fantasy. Back then I hadn't hurt anyone—I was clean, I could have built any kind of life possible.

"No, sweetie, there was no one. Like I said, you have nothing to worry about."

I felt like a little shit.

For the next week, I was determined to stick as closely as possible to a vacation routine—breakfast, swim, read, lunch, rest, swim, exercise a little, dinner. Everything was so slow, so measured, the lapping of the Indian Ocean, the rustling of palms, the rhythmic scratching sound each morning of someone sweeping up the leaves from the dirt paths with a reed broom. Gradually, my body began to uncoil. When Courtenay and I walked through the village, we were two slow-moving figures, not talking much, softly disconnected from what was happening around us. Women thumped grain in pestles, toddlers sucked on fuzzy mango pits, fishermen sat cross-legged in the sand, fixing the holes in their nets so their kids could eat. We followed a sandy track through the palms, and often old men rode past us on rickety bicycles, their pedals creaking long after they disappeared around a bend. It made me realize that long after those pedals have fallen off, or the spokes snap, or the frame cracks, these people will keep going. Flesh rejuvenates. It's stronger than steel, despite what I saw in Iraq. You have to believe that. You have to believe that we're put on this planet to endure, not to be summarily vanished.

Finally, I brought up a problem, what I saw as *the* fundamental problem of our relationship.

"Sweetie," I said one afternoon while we were looking for shells on the beach. "What do you *really* think of this place?"

"What do you mean? Zanzibar? It's beautiful."

"No, I was thinking about Africa. I know, it's probably years away, if it even comes through at all. But could you live here? Does it excite you? Scare you?"

She kept walking a few steps.

"Be honest," I said.

"Let's sit down. I will be honest."

We sat on the beach, looking out at the waves, and she began to pour sand over my feet.

"I've known you for thirteen years, and I don't think *you've* changed."

I shook my head and opened my mouth.

"But maybe I have." Courtenay kept pouring the sand over my feet. "I actually think it could be really great. Yeah, why not?" She lifted her head. "I think it would be fun to move to Africa with you. I'm sure I could find something interesting to do."

"Are you serious?"

"Listen," she said. "You don't give me enough credit. I was

sleeping on the banks of the Volga and shitting in holes the summer after sophomore year. You didn't forget that I went to Russia,
twice, did you? I'd wanted to see the world long before you came
along."

I *had* sold her so short, and I *had* failed to realize that Courtenay
never had any great antipathy toward my Africa dream per se, she
just resented the idea when it drove us apart. If we could do Africa
together, well, that was a whole other story. She could be my like-
minded partner, what Whitman called a camerado. I leaned in and
hugged her.

That evening I came in from a long swim. The sun slanted
through the slats. The light was growing soft. A faint breeze lifted
off the ocean. It was one of those calming denouements to a day
that seemed specially designed for reconciliation.

Courtenay was standing by the window. I stepped toward her.
She turned. Her kiss filled my mouth. I broke it only to taste her
neck, the sun, the salt. A bead of sweat trickled down her tem-
ple. I kissed that too. I could hear the wind stirring the palms,
their fronds brushing together lightly, making a sound like rain. I
wanted to stop time.

I peeled off her bathing suit and wiggled out of my trunks and
we lay down, slowly. Her skin smelled irresistible, earthy and gently burned, and her face, freckles, eyes, were unbelievably beautiful. Parts of her body felt so firm; others exquisitely soft. I was a
teenage boy all over again. My attraction was instant and 100 percent involuntary. It had always been. I had to listen to that. I had to
never forget it. I could never, ever, let anything confuse that again.
Things are usually so much simpler than they seem.

Afterward we just lay there, feeling the fan blow over our bodies. I knew this was the time to come clean. I should start with
Elizabeth and work my way backward. I could see the moon rising
through our window.

But as I turned to look into Courtenay's eyes, six inches away
from mine, I suddenly realized that a discernible future—one I had

always dreamed of—was on the line. I didn't know what her reaction would be; she saw the world in black and white. I mumbled that I needed her more than ever and left it at that. We showered together, I wrapped her in a towel, we slathered on our bug spray and headed over to the restaurant. After dinner we walked along the beach, the sand cool and silvery under the moonlight. She was talkative, wondering what it would be like if we ever did live in East Africa and were able to visit Zanzibar whenever we wanted. I was quiet, knowing that it was only weakness, smallness, that had kept me from doing what I should have done. This was the beginning of a period of fear. I didn't see how we could stay close and she wouldn't find out, somehow, some way.

I was sent back to Iraq for another three-month tour. Elizabeth was sent back as well. We worked on a couple stories together, but we weren't sleeping with each other anymore. Eventually she was reassigned somewhere else in the Middle East. Everything else was the same, though. The bombs were the same, the Palestine was the same, the styles were just as numerous.

I couldn't have fully appreciated what the United States had done to Iraq had I not been there. Saddam Hussein had gassed Kurds, machine-gunned Shias, held an entire pivotal nation in a sadistic thrall, but it was the American invasion that unleashed a violence so horrific and random and multivectored that nearly every day some Iraqi children somewhere were being blown apart. The whole society was morphing into hollow-eyed insomniacs, lying in bed at night rigid as corpses, wincing at the shudders of the bombs, staring up at the widening cracks in the ceiling, indulging in the darkest fantasies of their own personal doom. The Iraqis I worked with didn't necessarily see me as the embodiment of American aggression, but still, I was in that house for one reason: my country invaded theirs. As I poured my bowl of muesli at the breakfast table and reached for the milk, I sometimes looked up to see a pair of exhausted eyes blankly staring at me. Other times I'd get one of those wan, gray fuck-you smiles.

I wasn't the only one who wanted out.

I was racing through a story one night about an American marine, Wassef Ali Hassoun, a corporal of Lebanese descent, who had walked off the job in suspicious circumstances, most likely a desertion. I hastily scanned one of the e-mail feeds from another reporter to grab a quote from a cousin in Salt Lake City who had said that in a recent call home Corporal Hassoun had admitted he was depressed. But I didn't bother to include the second useless part of the quote, where the cousin had said, "But I'm sure he didn't run away." How the hell would you know, cuz?

The story was published the next morning, and I didn't think much more about it. That afternoon New York had the gall to interrupt my daily workout with the *Rocky* soundtrack to tell me the family was upset. Too bad, I told the subeditor, and resumed my push-ups.

The phone rang again a couple hours later. I was cruising around in a carload of people, and the clerk on the foreign desk said, "Please hold for Bill Keller."

Bill Keller! I didn't want to hold for Bill Keller! Just hearing his name made me stutter. While I had been in Iraq, a bloody insurgency had erupted at the *New York Times*, set in motion by a young, mendacious reporter, Jayson Blair. Howell took the first bullet, fired as executive editor and replaced by Bill Keller, a former managing editor. My in-house idol/rabbi, Bragg, of the world's lushest newspaper prose, also went down, quitting in a dustup over datelines that probably would have passed unnoticed had the Blair scandal not set off a period of intense self-directed scrutiny. Bill Keller hadn't hired me, I didn't know where I stood with him; we had had few direct interactions. He had been an esteemed Africa correspondent and could give me my shot or deny it forever. He jumped on the phone and came charging at me.

"Don't you ever do that again! Shaving people's quotes—we don't do that!"

"I-I," I stammered back, "I was just trying to be selective. Don't we always reject ten times of what we write down?"

"Did you hear me?" he snapped. "You changed the meaning when you did what you did. People may not like what we write, but they should think it's fair."

"I won't do it again," I said.

◇◇◇◇◇◇◇

I've committed those seven words I cut—"But I'm sure he didn't run away"—to memory, because they ended my run. Maybe if I had been on firmer ground, I could have swerved. But I was still new at the paper. I had had an unusual trajectory, skipping over local news and going straight to national and foreign, which was not how the Gray Lady typically liked it. My career took a U-turn.

Keller pulled me out of Baghdad, kicked me off the foreign rotation, and sentenced me to Metro: I would do my time in Newark, in an office in a basement that Keller had visited exactly once, though it was only a short train ride from headquarters. Newark felt like the desolate edge of our empire. The office was small and messy, furnished with a stinky carpet, a toilet that barely worked, and an eight-and-a-half-by-eleven sheet of white typing paper taped to the window that read "The New York Times." For a prick like me, that basement was a special hell.

"That's the problem with the *New York Times*," Courtenay said, shaking her head. "It swoops people up and then spits them out."

I couldn't believe it. The biggest story of our generation was raging in the Fertile Crescent, and where do they send me? The Jersey Gulag?

But I'm burying the lede. Courtenay was a public defender in Newark. She worked literally around the corner from the *Times*'s outpost. There were now ninety-seven steps between us.

The rest just flowed. We moved to Hoboken. We opened a joint checking account. We bought a mattress at Sleepy's. I stopped cheating. I still hadn't found the right time or right way to come clean, but some days I let myself think that it didn't matter anymore. That was another life. Despite all that had happened, or maybe even because of it, I felt welded to her. As the months passed, I realized I was happier than I had been in years, probably since college. Courtenay and I did everything together. Where you saw one of us, you saw the other. We were like Hoboken's Tom and Dom.

We swam laps together at the Y. We ate cannoli together on Washington Street. We dragged sacks of laundry together to the Laundromat on Saturdays, making me realize you can have it all, just not at the same time. Come Monday, we commuted into Newark together on the rustiest highway in America, Route 1/9, and I was always a little sheepish picking Courtenay up for lunch, the doorway of her building crowded with large young adult males in puffy jackets and cornrows, mouthfuls of gold teeth. Every time I parted through them, I felt like a white dwarf.

"Don't be scared." She'd laugh. "They're just my clients."

Many of her clients didn't know Courtenay's name. She was just another face in the blurry mishmash of judges, prosecutors, probation officers, cops, and government-appointed whatever-you-call-thems. But she loved it. If there was anything she believed in, it was justice. And if there was anyone in America who needed justice, it was these kids. They had so much arrayed against them, their downward spiraling lives the distillate of all of the very deliberate decisions our society has made about public education, urban planning, poverty, punishment, resource distribution, and race. One boy told the guards at Newark's Youth House—the juvenile jail—that he needed to see his attorney.

"What's the lady look like?" the guard asked.

"You know," the boy said, offhandedly, "the one who's half Puerto Rican, half something else."

I loved nesting with that woman who looked half Puerto Rican, half something else. But while we were eating Chinese leftovers in our little kitchen and riding the PATH train into Manhattan to catch the latest art-house flicks, the war was still out there, getting manlier and hairier still: more dead Americans, more head cutters, more shaped charges that melted holes through armored Humvees like lava, more meat. And though I had been benched, I knew the foreign desk was desperate, so I wasn't surprised at all when the call finally came: Jeff, want to go back, just for a few weeks? Iraq was about to hold its first democratic elections—time for real mayhem.

But this time, for the first time, I didn't want to go. I was happy; the thought of Iraq made me unhappy. But Courtenay was the one who said, "Do it, it'll help. Just please come home as soon as you can."

I started having night sweats as soon as I arrived. I chalked it up to jet lag, then to stress. I'd wake up in the middle of the night sweating so much I felt individual droplets like jujubes slowly rolling down my ribs. It was as if I were having a physical reaction to Iraq. I stripped the bed and balled up the wet sheets and then collapsed back on the uncovered mattress. I just wanted to go home. I tried my usual antidote: working out. But the day after I did one measly set of pull-ups in the garden, next to the soot-choked fig tree that no longer sprouted fruit, I couldn't straighten my arms.

I was always cold. I drifted through the bureau's drab corridors constantly shivering, teeth chattering, looking forward from the minute I pulled myself out of bed to the hot bath I was going to lower myself into that night. Baghdad was different now, so much of the city off-limits. Even the Palestine was deserted—the insurgents had bombed it several times, the floor of Aladdin's bar covered in crushed glass. I started getting headaches. I asked Jane, the wife of a more senior correspondent who lived with us and played the role of house mom, for cold medicine, then some aspirin, then something more powerful than aspirin.

Gone was that Rocky Balboa soundtrack in my head, the unending power of the universe flowing through my veins, that feeling I was hurtling through space toward something worthy and custom-built. I felt like dog shit. I didn't even bother to set my alarm, didn't have to. The terrifying blast of a man's last stand—a suicide bomb—shook our entire house each morning at seven thirty or eight, rush hour, maximum damage. Crack! Dozens were dead before I even rolled over. Now I had to wade through it. I was nauseated as I sat up and clutched the damp sheets and tried to hug Courtenay, but she was seven thousand miles away.

I trudged downstairs. Jane looked at me. Jane grew up in Rhodesia (now Zimbabwe).

"Jeff, have you considered malaria?"

Malaria? Here?

"Yeah, malaria. You should get it checked out."

I stumbled into the Green Zone hospital. One of the nurses at the reception desk looked me over.

"I think I have malaria," I said.

"No way. You'd be running a high fever."

She stuck a digital thermometer in my ear, the first one I'd ever seen.

"Holy shit!" She jumped back. "See this?"

It read 104.4.

I was on my back within minutes, skimming the surface of consciousness. Nurses banged in and out of my room all night, their combat boots on the cement floor sounding like struck anvils. I felt their jarring steps in my teeth. They jabbed that newfangled thermometer in one ear, then the other. Then they stomped out. I was just coherent enough not to complain. I was getting treated for free, and all around me were nineteen-year-olds taking their last breaths sixty years before they should have.

The same. Worse now. I was up to 105.

My nurse stepped out into the hallway.

"Sarge!" she yelled. "What should I give this guy?"

I was so hot, constantly turning the pillow over, looking for somewhere cool to rest my cheek.

A very kind army doctor, a major, came into my room at dawn. He looked down at me with old watery eyes and more concern than just about anyone else I had seen in that entire country. He had been an army doc for years but had never treated a case of malaria.

He brought me a rectangular glass slide—which I hadn't seen since biology class—smeared with my own thickening blood.

"This is really interesting," he said. "It's definitely malaria. But it's not the usual suspects, *falciparum* or *vivax*. It's something else I've never heard of. It's called *plasmodium malariae*. We checked it out in a book." He held his fleshy hand up to the light, admiring the slide. "It's a very rare strain."

I couldn't even lift my head to look. I needed to get home.

◇◇◇◇◇◇

I landed at JFK, no memory whatsoever of crawling into a cab, let alone the thirteen-hour flight I'd just endured. Strange, bright, malaria-induced fever dreams sluiced through my head as my eyes fluttered closed in the backseat. I crossed bridges and rivers. Manhattan's skyscrapers slid past. It seemed like the instant I rang the buzzer, Courtenay materialized at the door. She hugged me tight, and I felt my biscuit-weight bones about to crack apart in her arms.

The disease reared up, attacked, retreated, then attacked again. The Italians originally thought malaria was caused by smelly swamp fumes. Bad air, they named the fever, "mal aria." It wasn't until the nineteenth century that scientists pinpointed the culprit: the female Anopheles mosquito, which carries a microscopic, jelly-bean-shaped parasite in its stomach. It's demoralizing to be felled by a mosquito. There are several varieties of malaria—unfortunately the one that invaded my bloodstream can linger for decades, and I'm still not sure where I was infected. Tanzania? Iraq? Who knows?

Courtenay tried to nurse me back to health. She stirred molasses into my drinks, for extra iron. She stacked blankets on top of me to take the edge off the chills. She fried me grilled cheese sandwiches and sawed off the crusts.

While I lay there, for two full months, I concocted a new plan.

I brought it to fruition one chilly night in Newark after I got on my feet again. We were out to dinner, at one of the fancier joints in town, a place called Maize.

We sat down. Water was poured. Menus were placed in our hands. Courtenay began perusing the options: "Oh, honey, look at this! They have a green apple and goat cheese salad."

I looked.

"Yummy!"

It actually did sound yummy, but I was distracted.

"Courtenay," I said, hoarse actually, "I have something for you." And I brought out the first jewelry box. She opened it and said, "Oh my God. It's beautiful. Is it real?"

(It was *not* real, it was an heirloom necklace with a huge rhinestone in it. But this was part of the plan. I knew she'd say that.)

Then, right as I was pulling out the other, smaller box and bringing it softly to the table, about to propose to the only woman I have ever loved with the line "No, but this one is . . . ," the bread dude showed up.

"So, what we have here is: cracked wheat, parmesan-crusted rolls, some really nice foe-koch . . ."

He spotted those two little boxes and stopped mid-*focaccia*.

"Oops," he said, hightailing it away.

"Courtenay—" I cracked open the little box. My tongue felt thick. The rock shone. I was terrified. "Will you marry me?"

Her eyes filled up, and the moment we had delayed, denied, and nearly lost several times finally arrived with the clatter of someone's fork behind me.

∞∞∞∞∞

On our wedding day Courtenay looked especially stunning, ivory dress, muslin covering her arms, white rose in her hair. But I'll just have to remember it: in an effort to save some coin we asked my dad's brother, Uncle Larry, to shoot the pictures, and Uncle Larry, a mad scientist trapped in the body of an ordinary-looking suburban dentist, prides himself on using ancient gear. That day his Mamiyaflex camera, which he had kept on life support with paper clips and chewing gum for several decades, conked out. As a result, we have a stack of photos where all you can see are some shadows and maybe a glimpse of a muslin arm.

We exchanged our vows, and Courtenay kissed me long, hard, and eager, and she's usually stingy with the French kiss—she calls it a "snake kiss." I'll sweetly remember that part too.

It was so strange, and at the same time so comforting, to look out at that disparate group of people from all stages of life, half relatives, half friends, the people we are and the people we had chosen to be.

Benny gave the funniest speech. I say "gave," but he was nearly paralyzed so he typed it out on a computer that he operated with his eyeball and had a friend read it aloud. Benny could still giggle, though; ALS never muffled that.

At the end of the night, Roko chauffeured us across the Tappan Zee Bridge in a Chrysler minivan decked out with streamers and Campbell's soup cans banging from the bumper, back to the house with steep steps on River Road. Courtenay and I spent our first night as husband and wife in her attic, on that same sofa bed where I whipped out the expired red-and-blue Malawi specials and the whole great adventure began in earnest.

I began actively, and of course self-servingly, to cleave my life into two separate chapters, before marriage and after. I focused on the after chapter as much as possible, and the fear of her discovering the before chapter's full contents began to fade. We had a life to build now, I kept telling myself, and so we did. We voted in the elementary school gym. We got to know the guys at the parking garage. We took strolls out by the Hudson and stared across the water at Manhattan's lights. Slammed doors no longer made me jump. Cheesy TV commercials, though, those would still make me tear up.

I usually went to work early, before the other reporters, so Courtenay and I could drive in together. I was sitting by myself one morning in the basement when I received an e-mail that the Nairobi job had just opened up. I had written probably a thousand stories by now, my ticket all filled out, and there was nothing more I could do—or not do. A more experienced couple was up for the job, and I knew that while this group of editors appreciated that I spoke Swahili and had visited the region many times, that wasn't going to move anyone's needle. If the more experienced couple wanted it, it was theirs.

I sent in a memo with my qualifications and a couple of story ideas, then waited weeks.

I was summoned into the foreign editor's office, which was crammed with books, many on Japan, where she had worked years ago. She shut the door.

I called Courtenay at a legal conference ten minutes later. I could barely speak.

NINE

NAIROBI, 2006

Anthropologists have a theory that every *mzungu* who arrives in Africa eager to make his mark falls into one of the three classic "roles"—though "holes" would probably be more apt—that the first white men on the continent occupied: the Mercenary, the Missionary, and the Misfit. Alliteration usually carries the day for these sorts of things.

The Mercenary comes to exploit Africa's weakness for personal gain. Some of the most celebrated Victorian-age explorers, like Henry Morton Stanley, blasted their way across the continent, stepping over dead Africans, in the service of a powerful boss—in Stanley's case, King Leopold II of Belgium, who was obsessed with the idea of swallowing Congo. The Congolese called Stanley Bula Matari, "Breaker of Rocks," such was his penchant for destruction. These days, there are still plenty of white men laying wastage across Africa. I meet them all the time. Some are quite affable—just don't ask what they did in the Comoros in 1995 or Somalia in 2011.

Then there's the Missionary who brings the gospel. It could be the gospel of the Good Book or the gospel of aid work or even the gospel of Coca-Cola—any alien belief system foisted on the unsuspecting, for their own betterment, of course. I tried to play this role once, in Ethiopia, when I didn't know what my What was.

The Misfit, well, he didn't fit in back home, so he escaped and ran off to Africa. As the fidgety young man pulling up to the *jua kalis* or trying to scale Mount Kilimanjaro on a diet of cream wafers with white athletic socks on his hands, I'd played this role as well. I was a natural.

But now, as our 747 began its initial descent through the night sky, I wasn't sure what my role was. The well-worn story of the white man with a bad case of *le mal d'Afrique* was now my story. I was thirty-four years old, married, working for a big company, and about to touch down at Jomo Kenyatta International Airport. It was July 2006. What would be my M?

◇◇◇◇◇◇◇

The rush of nervous excitement intensified as Courtenay and I swung out of the airport onto Mombasa Road. I associated this part of the world with so much—youth, wonder, discovery. I credited it with making me who I was. And I wasn't returning to see anyone specific or do anything in particular that I used to do; I just wanted to tap into the spirit of this place and feel how I used to feel. That, I think anyone would agree, is dangerous.

As we drove north toward the glass towers of downtown Nairobi, the boulevards of my dreams were reassuringly as dark, deserted, and slightly menacing as they had always been. The streetlights still didn't work. A screen of dust and smoke hung in the air, making our headlights seem weak. Nothing had changed. I couldn't help but think of Dan as we skirted the bushy turnoff to his old place. I looked down his road and missed him. If I had never met him that summer, my life would have turned out so differently. When we passed a certain patch of grass along Uhuru Highway, I squeezed Courtenay's hand and blurted out, "Hey, honey, look, look!" I was so hopelessly emotional, I pointed out the place where Roko and I had been mugged by a gang of eight like I had spotted an old friend.

Sure, I wasn't that floppy-headed backpacker anymore. That guy had spirit. I was so tempered and practical compared to him, so adult. I even had proper suitcases now—with goddamned wheels. But as we turned this way and that, the streets narrowing, the walls getting higher, beautiful dark, flowering trees hanging over the road, their crepe-paper petals collecting along the curb, I was almost dumbstruck by the fact that I was finally here. I'd made it—*we'd* made it.

As soon as we stepped into our new house, Courtenay's mouth dropped open.

"This is all ours?"

"Yes," said Marc, the *Times* correspondent I was replacing, as he walked in with us. "All yours. We've even left you some nice furniture." He grinned and swept his hand toward a worn-out couch with a swirly floral pattern and an enormous circular wooden table with a lazy Susan in the middle, like at a Chinese restaurant.

It was a five-bedroom house far bigger than either of us had grown up in. "What are we going to do with all these rooms?" Courtenay whispered as we trailed around after Marc. "I don't know," I whispered back. "What about a gym?" "Sure." "An office?" "Sure." "A guest room?" "Sure." "Can we have two guest rooms?" All the rooms were large, ceilings high, inlaid wood everywhere. The yard was just as impressive: a palm tree, blooming jasmine bushes, an herb garden with more rosemary and basil than we could ever eat, and a grove of banana trees. Along the side hedge that was about ten feet tall ran a nice straightaway of grass, perfect for Frisbee.

After showing us around the compound, Marc and his wife turned to us and said they had arranged to stay with friends and that from now on, this was our house.

"Five years," said Marc's wife, Omaira, referring to the standard tour of duty. "It's over too fast."

We heard their car leave the driveway. Courtenay and I wandered around our palatial dwelling a bunch more times and then crawled into bed. I could hear the sounds of the nightjar bird and trilling insects and little frogs. I could even smell some wood smoke, as you often can on a cool night in Nairobi. As I began to drift off to sleep, I caught a few melodic chords of *lingala* music. An *askari* was out there somewhere, listening to a small radio, maybe even his phone.

◇◇◇◇◇◇◇

We needed work permits, furniture, driver's licenses, sheets, curtains, mosquito nets, padlocks, press IDs, alien cards, car insurance, a phone line, and flatware. We needed a dog. We needed friends. We needed to figure out how to interact with the Kenyans around us. Because labor costs were absurdly cheap, most *mzungus*—and wealthy Kenyans, for that matter—employed a team of helpers. For a hundred bucks a week you could have your house cleaned spotlessly on a daily basis, your clothes washed and ironed, a hot meal waiting for you in the evening, and a driver waiting for you in the morning. Of course, we were this fabulously wealthy only here. I don't think many Kenyans realized we could never live like this in our own country.

The moment Marc walked out the door, I became the mini-commander of a small unit: Madline the cook; Alfred the gardener; Hanson the bureau manager; Hannah the bureau assistant; Richard the driver; and two night watchmen from a private security service. I had never been the boss of anyone, save Benny, who stopped listening to me and routinely flipped me off, even before we promoted him to crew chief. Some expats still used the term "servants" to describe their domestic operations; most of us, by 2006, preferred "staff." Behind our house sat a somewhat drab, low-slung building, the appendage to any large Nairobi house: the SQ.

The whole system was colonial and excessive, and I wanted to stay true to my values. But laying people off wasn't the answer—these jobs in our house supported a chain of relatives stretching from our front door to little green villages hundreds of miles away. So I had to figure out a way to delicately walk along the new lines that sketched out my new world.

When being driven by Richard, should I sit shotgun or in the backseat? Did we insist to Madline that she use the front door, or pretend there was nothing Jim Crow weird about her using only the back? Did I speak Swahili with Dominic and Mecha, the night watchmen, even if they spoke my native language much better than I spoke theirs? What about salaries, presents, tips? All the stuff, as an academic friend of mine says, that makes up the micropolitics of navigating social hierarchies, of playing one of those three classic *mzungu* roles.

But the most pressing question, since I had the sense I would be dealing with the vestiges of colonialism for as long as we lived here, was what the hell to write about. This was my self-declared dream job, after all, so: (a) I'd better like this job, and (b) I'd better be good at it.

This wasn't Hernando County. I now covered Kenya, Tanzania, Uganda, Rwanda, Burundi, Congo, Djibouti, Somalia, Sudan, Ethiopia, Eritrea, and the Seychelles, which sweep up more than 400 million people and 3.3 million square miles—and that is only one-third of the continent. I know this because at one point I didn't, but few Americans appreciate how vast the whole of Africa is: the Lower 48, China, Japan, India, and Europe can all fit comfortably here. The week I showed up, my region was bursting with news. Islamist rebels were blasting their way into southern Somalia, Darfurian rebels were blowing up police stations, Congolese rebels were tying women to trees, and the Lord's Resistance Army, made up of Ugandan rebels, was slicing, clubbing, and raping its way across central Africa like two thousand Willie Crains. Did I mention rebels? So many of the countries I covered were fragile and poorly governed, ripe for the taking. As Rick Bragg used to say, "The best stories in the newspaper are about people in trouble." By our standards, most people in East Africa were in trouble. I had no idea where to start.

"Just remember," one of the foreign editors back in New York had warned me before I left, "let's not get too *ooga-booga* out there."

"Excuse me?"

"Oog-gah. Boog-gah," he said deliberately, as if repeating the name of a delicate dish to a first-day-on-the-job waiter. "You know, the stereotypes, the platitudes, Africa as primitive and violent."

I was kind of shocked there was even a term like this. But I knew I'd better play along.

"Oh, I see, um, like those old black-and-white movies where there'd be a scene of some tribesmen in loincloths stamping up and down in a jungle with a huge smoking pot barking, *Ooga-booga, ooga-booga?*"

"Bingo," the editor said, his eyes disappearing back into his screen. "Now I see why you got the job."

During a later lunch, a former Africa hand, a man no longer in the mix but who had done some brave work back in the day, a more-is-more guy, if I had to hazard a guess, said with a long, thin, conspiratorial smile, "Whatever you do, Jeff . . ."

"Uh-huh."

"Don't forget the *ooga-booga*. It's what makes Africa Africa."

The *ooga-booga* tug-of-war looked unwinnable. That would be the trick of the job, walking that line, not sanitizing the extremes but not pandering to types. I don't think any other region of the world has this problem to this extent. *Ooga-booga* is not a pretty term. It can be seen as the crudest shorthand for everything primitive. You don't hear people call anything in China or the Amazon or the Middle East *ooga-booga*. Yes, of course, there are concerns about looking down at any foreign culture from the position of white privilege. But what other part of the world has been so laden with stereotypes about power and race as Africa? Is it even possible for an outsider to look at Africa, to see it as it really is, without eyes jaundiced by all that we have read and heard about it?

The Kenyan writer Binyavanga Wainaina best nailed down what plagues the prose of whites writing about Africa in his wickedly sarcastic short story "How to Write about Africa":

> Never have a picture of a well-adjusted African on the cover of your book, or in it, unless that African has won the Nobel Prize. An AK-47, prominent ribs, naked breasts: use these. . . . In your text, treat Africa as if it were one country. It is hot and dusty with rolling grasslands and huge herds of animals and tall, thin people who are starving. Or it is hot and steamy with very short people who eat primates. . . . Make sure you show that you are able to eat such food without flinching, and describe how you learn to enjoy it—because you care. . . . Avoid having the African characters laugh, or struggle to educate their kids, or just make do. . . . Animals, on the other hand, must be treated as well rounded, complex characters. . . . Elephants are caring, and are good feminists or dignified patriarchs. So are gorillas. Never, ever say anything negative about an elephant or a gorilla.

For my first big story, I tried to steer clear of *ooga-booga*, and elephants and gorillas, for that matter. I chose something much more familiar, much less troublesome. I picked a good murder. In this business, you can never really go wrong with a good murder.

◇◇◇◇◇◇◇

The Honorable Thomas Patrick Gilbert Cholmondeley stood six foot six. He was blond, broad, and balding. He lived in Kenya's fertile Rift Valley on 50,000 acres of gorgeous land. He had attended Eton and his father was in the House of Lords. Dressed in cravat and riding boots, he was said to terrorize the squatters who lived in the shacks on the outskirts of his family's estate. He had the luxury of being a Misfit because his great-grandfather had been a Mercenary: those 50,000 acres had been dubiously acquired at the turn of the twentieth century from illiterate Maasai, one of Kenya's most traditional tribes, who herd animals on the Rift Valley plains.

Shortly before Courtenay and I landed in Nairobi, Cholmondeley (pronounced for some silly British reason CHUM-lee) got down on one knee, raised a colonial-era Lee-Enfield rifle, and shot to death a fleeing African man who had trespassed on his ranch with a poached antelope slung over his shoulder. The year before, Cholmondeley had done the same thing, killing another black Kenyan. That time, no charges were filed—no formal investigation was even opened—and protests exploded. Highways were barricaded, tires set alight, young Maasai men clashed with the police. The case tapped into a sore subject in Africa: the lingering suspicion that colonialism had never really ended. Many black Kenyans feared that Cholmondeley's white skin—and his blue blood—allowed him to literally get away with murder.

But many *mzungus*—surprise, surprise—felt differently. They were protective of Cholmondeley, whom they saw as a champion of wildlife and someone who felt genuinely threatened on his enormous plot of land. They believed he had been unfairly blamed for a simple case of self-defense in the first shooting, and that Kenyan politicians were stirring up trouble because they had their eyes on the Delamere land—entirely possible in Kenya. But after the second killing, Cholmondeley was booked on murder, and for Kenyans, it was sexy to have a *mzungu* on trial for murder, especially this *mzungu*. It turned the tables. The all-powerful was now powerless. Cholmondeley wasn't riding around on a fine steed with a silk cravat cinched smartly around his neck. He was locked up in Kamiti Maximum Security Prison wearing a striped shorts set, like all the other inmates, made of coarse cloth.

Any newspaper story north of a thousand words should either

try to help a living creature achieve a less painful life or scrape away at some deeper truth. It needs to have a moral, a lesson, a point. I gravitated toward the Honorable Killer's story because it turned on what I was struggling with during our early days in Kenya: how to occupy a position of privilege in a very poor place, how to live as a white man in an African country. Or, more accurately, how *not* to live as a white man in an African country.

One of the first white men to leave his mark on Kenya was Hugh Cholmondeley, Tom's great-grandfather, the third Baron Delamere. When he came galloping over a hill in Kenya's Rift Valley during a lion-hunting safari in 1897, he was stunned by what he found: cool, misty highlands in the middle of equatorial Africa. This land, he pronounced, was white man's country.

With livestock imported from Cheshire and aristocrats imported from Mayfair, Delamere sent Kenya down a special path. Kenya (the country is named for Mount Kenya, which in turn derives its name from the Kikuyu, Embu, and Kamba words for "God's resting place") wasn't going to be an African colony of industrial import like South Africa or Rhodesia; it was going to be a land of gentleman farmers, a *mzungu* Sybaris. By the 1920s Kenya had become the place in the British Empire—and this was when the Brits were at their absolute peak, ruling a quarter of humanity—where you could hunt "lion" (never plural), throw gin-soaked parties, pal around with aristocrats, and cheat on your wife. At the time there was a common expression among colonial officers: "Are you married, or do you live in Kenya?"

Delamere and his ilk were so skilled at grand iconography that even to this day many people think of Kenya's Africa, with its rolling green hills and galloping zebra and red-roofed manor houses surrounded by veldt, as *the* Africa. But the Africans weren't so enthused by this Africa. Eventually they rebelled—the Mau Mau Uprising of the 1950s—and it wasn't pretty. Mau Mau fighters killed thirty-two white settlers and in return, the British incarcerated tens of thousands of black Kenyans and hanged more than 1,000.

At no other time or in no other place were as many subjects hanged by the Crown. Ten years later, Kenya won its hard-fought independence. Still, the Delameres' 50,000 acres remained untouched.

◇◇◇◇◇◇

We set off on the drive into the Rift Valley looking for answers, Courtenay and I. She was riding shotgun, but this wasn't take-your-spouse-to-work day. Times were changing, for us and the newspaper industry. Just as I was promoted to East Africa bureau chief, the *Times* opened its first video production unit to create unique content for our website, which was rapidly becoming the core of our business. "Know anyone in Nairobi who could travel around with you and shoot some video?" the head of the new video department had asked. "Yeah," I said. "As a matter of fact, I do."

This by itself was the greatest wonder of these early days: working with my camerado. Courtenay had investigated some legal jobs here, but she soon found out she wasn't even allowed to practice in Kenya. Kenya has a much different legal system than the one in the United States, and she would have to spend a long time retraining. So she decided to take a break, and the video department was more than happy to train her on how to shoot and edit, which she picked up quite fast. As the road to the Rift Valley threaded along a mountain ridge, with a vertiginous drop-off that afforded views for miles and miles, Courtenay gazed out the window, a new video camera on her lap. The oceanic savannah, a blanket of tan with a few green patches at this time of year, stretched to the horizon. Tiny, far-off zebras nibbled on the grass. Baboons barked in the trees. I've been on a lot of roads in a lot of places, but I can't think of many more spectacular than the one leading out of Nairobi into the Rift Valley, the same road where Dom stopped during my Year On to get that stunning view. It was about twenty-five minutes from our house.

The first town we hit was Naivasha, anchor of Kenya's flower industry. When I had rumbled through here with Tom and Dom, it was a dusty crossroads, a few shacks and a few Coke signs. Now it was a voracious sprawl crawling up the hillsides. Crowds of destitute kids drifted through the streets, plastic shoes scraping the gravel, glassy eyes trying to catch ours. But there was still that energy that reminded me of the *jua kali* days with Dan. Everywhere we looked, people were working hard: selling tubs of yogurt on the side of the road, fixing flats, carrying cords of wood on their backs for what I knew was very little pay. As we drove past one young man, he turned to us and asked hopefully through the open window: "Una kazi?" *You have any work?*

We weren't allowed onto Cholmondeley's farm, but a photographer friend of mine, an old buddy of Dan's, had persuaded one of Cholmondeley's friends to talk to us. Grant was his name. He was waiting for us on his veranda, on a nearby farm, dressed in khaki shirt, trim khaki shorts, and safari boots, his muscular legs planted on the deck, cut-glass tumbler in hand. It was almost sunset.

As we stepped out of our car, he asked, "G and T?"

We sank into heavy log chairs on his veranda, and the gin instantly loosened my shoulders and warmed my stomach, smoothly rolling together all the elements in front of me—the sun sinking behind the hills, the warthogs mowing Grant's endless acreage, the bright white birds hanging effortlessly in the air. A little alcohol had clarified why these guys were holding on. What they owned was far more impressive than a SoHo loft or a sleek yacht. They owned nature.

"Grant," I said. "This place is incredible."

He took a long drink from his tumbler, crunched a piece of ice in his teeth, and glanced at the sky. The light was fading fast, as it does when you're sitting on the equator.

"Africa"—Grant scowled—"is a different place at night."

He stood up.

"Why don't we go inside?"

Slipping off our shoes by the veranda door, we padded into the living room, full of wonderfully cool stuff: animal bones, shells, maps, ancient books, Maasai jewelry, grainy pictures of ancestors kneeling next to felled beasts—all the bric-a-brac I would see time and again on display in old white Kenyan families' homes. Grant was a KC, a Kenyan cowboy, a white man born and raised here, descended from settler stock. Even though we were all *mzungus*, there were subtribal rivalries within Kenya's *mzungus*, just as there were within the Abu Luhya, the Somalis, the Kalenjin, and other ethnic groups in East Africa. Many KCs still farmed tea, like the first settlers, and ran safari companies and wore fading T-shirts that read "I'd Rather Be Pushing My Land Rover Than Driving Your Toyota." Some still consulted *Up-Country Swahili for the Soldier, Settler, Miner, Merchant, and Their Wives and for All Who Deal with Up-Country Natives*, a slim tome published in 1936, perfect for translating all those handy phrases like "Boy! My razor's spoilt! I can tell you've used it. It's still dirty with your black hairs!"

We all sat down. I pulled out my notebook. Grant looked at me down the end of his nose. So Cholmondeley had said the poacher threatened him with his pack of hunting dogs? Grant nodded, while his own underloved snorting terrier kept licking my hands as I was trying to write.

"Aw, just throw her off, throw her off," Grant said in a scolding voice.

We talked for forty-five minutes before Grant stood up again—he was beginning to seem restless. "Come on," he said gruffly. "Let me show you something."

We walked down a hallway to a big steel door, which Grant wrenched open with a grunt.

"This is my Keep." He glanced dismissively toward Courtenay and the camera in her hands. "No pictures." We all squeezed in— the Keep was the size of a walk-in closet, and Grant ran his fingers along the metalwork on all sides. "Double grilles here, here, and here." He rapped the door. "Bulletproof."

It closed with a satisfying *thunk*, like an expensive product of the

German auto industry. Inside stood an arsenal: semi-automatic rifles, shotguns, high-powered pistols, stacks of ammo boxes. It was
as if the Mau Mau Uprising had never ended.

"Grant, man, looks like you're preparing for the end of the
world," I tried to joke. "I didn't know people were allowed to have
this many guns in Kenya."

"Yes, the white man has always occupied a privileged position
in this country. Why? Because he doesn't get in trouble. He doesn't
act like a fool."

"Wasn't it a little foolish for Tom to be walking around with a
gun that second time?"

Grant stared at me. "I'll give you that. It was dumb. But I want
you to know something," he said. "I like the Africans. I live with
them, I work with them. I'm not a racialist."

Courtenay and I shot each other a quick look.

"We all realize that we have to make their lives better—we just
don't make a bloody fuss about it, like the NGOs. At some point
things will calm down, but let's be realistic—this is the third world,
it's Africa, man."

When I didn't say anything back, he seemed irritated.

"Let me tell you something, okay? This isn't New York, okay? If
something happens, you can't call the police. What if they're rent-
ing out their guns for a hundred shilingi an hour? That's what I've
heard. Look what happened to Joan Root. Or my friend Martin
Palmer. Martin drowned in his own blood."

He shook his head. "Why am I telling you all this? They told
me about your background before you came. You were running
around with Dan Eldon. Look what happened to him."

He hit the lights. As he felt around for the lock, we stood in the
dark for a second, close to each other. I could feel him breathing
heavily. Grant knew this place a lot better than we did and was
clearly afraid of what was out there. How afraid were we supposed
to be? He cranked open the door and stepped into the hallway. We
followed. It felt immeasurably cooler.

"It's getting late," he said.

I checked my watch: not even eight.

"If I were you, I'd hit the road."

As I crouched on the veranda, lacing up my shoes, I couldn't help myself.

"Grant, why do you even stay here?"

"I can't tell you why. I love this place, that's why."

And then he stepped toward me and bent down, his face inches from mine. I could smell the gin on his breath.

"And fuck," he whispered in my ear. "I'll shoot somebody. Just like Tom. I will, I swear I will."

◇◇◇◇◇◇◇

Crime was the *mzungu* obsession. It was what bonded us together and filled in the cracks in conversations at cocktail parties. In the summer of 2006, it was the favorite topic in Nairobi, and from what I've gathered, it's been like that since public safety began to crumble in the late 1970s. "Did you hear about Lizzie getting stuffed in the trunk of her car?" "What about those blokes who came to the lady's house for yoga with rolled-up mats under their arms and robbed her blind?" "What's the best kind of wall to build these days?" "What kind of Keep?" "Any movement on firearm licenses?"

I tried to reassure Courtenay that many *mzungus* had been living here either too long or not long enough and were paranoid, but the facts didn't always cooperate. A few days after I treated myself to an expensive coffee table, allegedly made from a Zanzibari or Lamu shutter, I forget which, that we had bought from an Indian saleswoman who was very pretty, very stylish, and ran a very successful furniture business not far from our house, I was sitting in the kitchen with Courtenay, having breakfast. We were drinking freshly squeezed passion fruit juice, Madline the cook was at the stove, and the two of us were trying to act as if there was nothing unusual about having a six-foot-tall African woman dressed in a crisp white chef's outfit flipping eggs for us in our own kitchen. Kenya's two leading daily newspapers, the *Nation* and the *Standard*, both among the best in sub-Saharan Africa, were spread out in front of us. Courtenay pushed over the *Nation*.

"See this?"

It was a picture of a pretty Indian woman, eyes lined with kohl. She was in her late thirties or early forties, face staring out from the "Promotion to Glory" section of the paper, the obits.

The woman who had just sold us the coffee table had been shot in the stomach in a botched carjacking around the corner from where we lived and bled to death on the way to the hospital.

"Is this how it's going to be out here?" Courtenay said. "We meet someone, and then they die?"

If you believe in Max Weber's concept of a state as maintaining a monopoly on violence, well, Kenya wasn't a very strong state then. Everyone with means hired an *askari* with a club or a machete to guard his property. They were everywhere—in front of our house, the *Times* bureau, the grocery store, the bank, the school, standing vigilant in a deserted parking lot.

There's no good reason why Kenya, one of Africa's most developed nations, has to be the land of *askaris*. Just about all of Kenya's neighbors are much poorer and also much safer. It stems from a corrupt and dysfunctional police service and the inequality built into Kenya's charter myth. This society has always maintained unusually well fortified divisions between the classes, races, and tribes. As *mzungus*, we felt like targets. We were unbelievably rich—most Kenyans lived on a couple dollars a day—and it wasn't like we blended in.

◇◇◇◇◇◇◇

Courtenay and I flashed our new press credentials at the checkpoint outside the courthouse. I loved that press credential—one little plastic card that displayed the three things that took forever to unite: my name, "the Newyork Times" (spelled as two words), and "The Republic of Kenya." The cops barely looked and shooed us through.

When the courtroom's side doors swung open, all the wooden benches creaked. Everyone jumped to their feet, instantly turning their heads in the same direction, like a school of fish. Tom Cholmondeley shuffled past us, wearing a rumpled khaki suit, blue shirt, paisley tie, and cowboy boots, shackles clanging.

I had searched the files in the bureau to see if a *mzungu* had ever been charged with murder before. Nothing. So I consulted the *Daily Nation*'s archives and found a few sheets of yellowing newsprint on Frank Sundstrom, a nice-looking American sailor who had passed through Mombasa in 1980 on a goodwill mission. He had picked up a prostitute—"an African girl" was how the *Daily Nation* referred to her—got her drunk and high, had sex with her a couple times, then smashed a beer bottle across her face, punching a two-inch hole in her windpipe. Monica Njeri had also drowned in her own blood. Frank Sundstrom pleaded guilty to manslaughter, as if dispatching with a woman like a goat had been an accident. He was fined seventy bucks.

I scoured the Sundstrom files—it had been years since I had handled old newsprint like that. One tragedy of the Internet age is that search engines take you to exactly where you want and only where you want—or where they *think* you want—and you miss all the fascinating miscellany. Right above the story on the Sundstrom trial was an item about Kenya's former president, Daniel arap Moi, shutting down a union for "over-indulgence in politics"—an echo back to the Cold War dictator days. Next to that was an ad for Saudia Airlines' "Direct flights to Mogadishu," when a visit to Somalia wasn't suicidal. If you're looking back in time, that miscellany provides helpful context. This part of Africa was a much different place in the 1980s.

"My Lord!" began the prosecutor, a short black man wearing

a long blond wig—some things apparently hadn't changed. "We shall introduce witnesses to prove: One, that the gunshots were fired by the accused. Two, the gunshots were fired from a high-caliber rifle meant for game hunting. Three . . ."

The prosecutor paused for effect. I looked over at Cholmondeley, who, if he was found guilty, could be hanged. He was sitting on a bench on the side of the courtroom, his back and head against the wall. He seemed vaguely amused.

". . . the deceased was running away. Four . . ."

When Cholmondeley's lawyer, Fred Ojiambo, took the floor (he was also wearing a colonial-style wig), he raised problems with the ballistics, problems with the witness statements, problems with the management of the crime scene, all sorts of problems. He even implied it was one of Cholmondeley's buddies, a rally car driver named Flash, who had actually shot the poacher.

"Hon," Courtenay whispered to me, "Flash didn't shoot the poacher. Tom signed a confession saying it was an accident. How on earth does this guy plan to argue Tom didn't shoot the guy?"

I checked my watch. I was about to give Courtenay the "let's scoot" look, but when I glanced over at her, she was looking wistfully at the defense attorney. I could tell she missed it. She loved the courtroom's clarity, the mental combat, serving as an advocate for someone whose back was literally against the wall. That was her dream.

◇◇◇◇◇◇◇

Justice, like getting a hamburger or a phone line connected, takes a little more time in East Africa. The Cholmondeley trial took nearly three years. In the meantime, we continued our adjustment process of playing house in a foreign land.

My feeling is you don't really know a place until you drive it, so early on we forced ourselves to get behind the wheel, which, by the way, is mounted on the other side here, though that was the least of our problems. Nairobi possessed no working traffic lights. Busy intersections were a philosophical study, game theory, a Kenyan version of the prisoner's dilemma, four cars staring at each other, traffic backing up behind them, an endless combination of altruistic or selfish moves. It wasn't like the police were any help. If anything, they were a menace. They erected checkpoints all over the city, often at night, placing a blinding flare in the middle of the road next to a set of gnarly metal spikes. They were armed with assault rifles, and you had to slowly weave around them, giving them time to peer into your car.

"What on earth are they looking for?" Courtenay asked.

I'd soon learn the answer: *kitu kidogo*, which in Swahili means "a little something," the euphemistic code for a bribe. I was stopped countless times—for allegedly speeding, for not having an emergency triangle, for changing lanes in a roundabout. I always paid a little something and was allowed to go on my way.

And then there were the *matatus*.

Matatus are Kenya's public transport, "Nairobi's subway," as Dan put it, the weathered army of hundreds of minibuses that circulated commuters around the city. Their drivers were paid for each passenger and therefore drove as close to death as possible, cutting off other vehicles, zooming by on the shoulder, plunging headlong into traffic on the wrong side of the road to snatch up a single fare, aspirational names decaled on the windshield or airbrushed on the backside: Sniper, Slayer, Prince of Peace, I Feel Nothing, Paragon the Road Veteran, and one plain white van with the typical yellow *matatu* stripe that blasted 1980s house music while flitting through traffic like a flea on methamphetamines, Laptop. I can't tell you how many times I was cut off by Laptop.

The roads themselves were shambolic, the asphalt so crumbled, the potholes so deep and numerous, that you had to constantly weave back and forth to avoid breaking an axle. The joke in Nairobi was that only the drunks drove straight.

One night as Courtenay and I were shuddering through a forest on a dark, blown-out road, I spotted a single light shining from the shoulder. It was odd, but I kept going.

"Wait," Courtenay said. "Did you see that? Was that a person lying there?"

A single thought flashed across my mind: Ambush.

"Maybe he's playing dead," I said.

"I don't think so. And we can't just leave someone lying next to the road, can we?"

I swung around to get a better look, driving slowly but making sure not to stop. That's a cardinal rule in Nairobi: Never stop. Especially at night. Especially in a forest. I flashed the high beams, illuminating a man sprawled on his back, flashlight by his side. I turned around again, headed back in our original direction.

"What should we do?" Courtenay asked. "We have to stop."

I drove another hundred yards and turned us around again. We pulled up to a green Mercedes that had also stopped not far from the silhouette of the man. I got out of our car, and a young Kenyan woman stepped out of hers, a few passengers in the backseat. When she and I approached each other, she whispered in English: "You check him."

"I don't even know first aid," I said.

"Still," she said.

In the glare of the headlights, I started to walk toward the man on the ground but stopped several feet short, to make sure he wasn't about to leap up and grab me. He didn't. I edged closer. He just lay there.

His eyes were half-open, wet and yellowish. There were no outward signs of trauma except a dab of blood on his bottom lip. I fumbled around to unbutton his shirt. I'd seen a lot of dead people, but I'd never touched a still person before.

I slipped my hand inside his shirt and ran it across the smooth skin of his chest. It was tight as a drum. Here lay a man cut from the old cloth, who had never eaten too much in his entire life. He must have been about fifty. His skin was cold. I felt for his heart.

"Amekufa?" the woman asked me, switching into Swahili.

I stood up, brushed the red dirt from my knees.

"Amekufa," I proclaimed, with what I think was the appropriate amount of gravitas. *He's dead.* It was obviously a hit-and-run. "It must have just happened," I added, "otherwise that flashlight wouldn't be here."

"I'm glad you checked him," the woman said, in English, as we walked back—me to my Mitsubishi, she to her Mercedes. "If we'd have gone to the police, they would've accused us of killing him. But you can go, you can tell them. They'll believe *you.*"

I'm not so sure the police would have believed me. They could have easily turned this into an opportunity for *kitu kidogo,* a lot of it. The woman in the Mercedes was wealthier than we were, a native-born Kenyan, flawless English, and I knew what she had been thinking. Even with a British aristocrat rotting away in jail, she simply assumed that we *mzungus* were still untouchable. It was Kenyan racial profiling, benign in our case, but just as rigid. It's unsettling to be ascribed privileges and powers that don't feel deserved. It might sound nice or even flattering, but it only creates distance, makes you feel like a phony.

I ended up finding two neighborhood *askaris* who were standing outside a gate and asking them if they could wave down the next police patrol that passed. The dead man probably had a family now frantically looking for him, but there was little we could do. Courtenay and I turned around and drove home, the only car on the road.

TEN

◇◇◇◇◇◇

SOMALIA, 2006

When the Moroccan traveler Ibn Battuta disembarked in Mogadishu in 1331, on his way back from Mecca, he was greeted by a eunuch bearing a bottle of Damascus rosewater and brought to a house that was "decorated with carpets and contained everything needful." Mogadishu was a thriving mercantile city, one of the most important on the East African coast. Ibn Battuta couldn't believe how big it was: "The people have very many camels, and slaughter many hundreds every day. They have also many sheep."

When I touched down 675 years later, ten men with AK-47s looked at me with dark, unblinking eyes—or eye, in one case—and ushered me and my translator, Bakis, into a gun truck. The city was in ruins. Everywhere I looked, there were heaps of bullet-pocked rubble, with people living in them. My welcome delegation wore chains of bullets over their bony backs and the standard African combat footwear: flip-flops. Each guard was paid ten dollars a day, nothing compared to what they could get by kidnapping me. A contact of mine in Nairobi had helped line this up, saying he knew an elder who knew the guards' boss, and there was nothing to worry about; honor still meant a lot here. Still, as the gun truck's doors slammed and the wheels began to roll, I couldn't help but wonder just how strong the transitive property of trust really was.

It was September, but summer never ends in Somalia—our whole entourage, especially me, were sweating through our shirts.

This was my first big story outside of Kenya, and ever since Dan was murdered here, I'd harbored a dangerous fascination with this city. Mogadishu. Mog. That one little word summoned up all the nastiness Africa could quite possibly produce—famine, ruin, anarchy, war, misery, hopelessness.

We cruised away from the airport, passing women wrapped in black gowns, backs bent, taking a lashing from the sun. Every building was riddled with holes, huge cactuses exploding out the glassless windows. Cartoon drawings of meat, car parts, and pills were painted on the walls of the few operational stores, advertising for the illiterate—Somalia instituted its first written language in 1972. The *Times* video desk didn't share my fascination with Mog and wouldn't let Courtenay near it, so our plans of continental conquest had been put on hold. Courtenay was game to take risks with me, but the video guys were still new to the *Times* operation. They were reluctant to endanger anyone's life for a story.

The story here was that an Islamist movement had just defeated a band of warlords and taken over much of the country. For the first time since 1991, Mog was under one rule. What that rule was—that was the big question. Diplomats and UN people back in Nairobi had dubbed the new administration the "African Taliban" partly because of suspected links between the Islamists and al-Qaeda. But from what I could tell those first few days, that wasn't accurate. I covered community cleanups in which dozens of volunteers worked with the clerics to scoop out years of built-up garbage and silt from the streets. We saw boys—and girls—in school, and one of the first things the Taliban had done when they seized power in Afghanistan was to close down girls' schools. We saw young couples strolling by the shot-up seaside. I didn't hear a single gunshot, the peace secured by young men who patrolled the ruins with struggling beards on their chins, young men who spoke little, wore green prayer caps, and abstained from khat, the bitter, addictive leaf many Somalis chewed. They had done something that nobody else, including 25,000 American soldiers, had been able to accomplish: for the first time in fifteen years, they had brought a semblance of stability to Mogadishu. The populace seemed to respect them. They simply called them the Youth, but they used the Arabic word, al-Shabaab.

I was staying at the Sahafi Hotel, Dan's last address. A couple times I went up to the roof and gazed across the crenulated rooftops of the city and tried to channel him, but it was beginning to feel artificial. There's no doubt that I thought about him often— something would inevitably trigger it, chicken tikka, a good blast of reggae rap, passing an old Land Rover chugging up a hill in a cloud of black smoke. But it was beginning to occur to me that I had spent a chunk of my life following in the footsteps of a boy, and now that I was finally living in this part of the world, I'd better start looking at it through my own eyes.

My last evening in Mog, the Sahafi's manager came to my room. I was packing and opened the door, thinking he was coming to settle the bill, but he remained silent in the doorway in a way that caught me off guard. I looked up from my bag.

"Abu Mansoor's looking for you."

"Abu Mansoor?"

"Abu Mansoor."

"Me?"

"You."

In this town, you didn't want Abu Mansoor looking for you. He was one of the leaders of al-Shabaab; people spoke of him in hushed tones that conveyed reverence and fear. It would be much better if Abu Mansoor didn't know who you were. Or where you were staying.

He stood waiting for me in the Sahafi's meeting room, flanked by two boy soldiers with rather large guns. He had a prayer bruise on his forehead, something you get only by banging your head against a prayer mat thousands of times. He wore a long shirt and short pants that stopped above the ankle—like Capri pants, a Salafist interpretation of a cryptic clause in the Koran that says "Whoever trails his garment on the ground out of pride, Allah will not look at him on Judgment Day." He had bright eyes with long eyelashes and motioned toward a table where two bottles of orange Fanta sat, apparently one for him and one for me. The boy soldiers watched me closely.

"Please," Abu Mansoor said.

I sat down and took a quick, nervous sip, the soda tasting sweeter because of the circumstances. I'll admit it: I derived a slight thrill from sharing a Fanta with a real militant.

"I heard you were asking a lot of questions about the Islamists," Abu Mansoor said.

Before I could answer, he reached down under the table—which made me uneasy. I was relieved when he came up with a black plastic bag.

"So I got this for you in the Bakara market." He handed me the bag and nodded for me to open it.

What I pulled out was smoothly covered and relatively slender but heavy as a brick.

"It's in English," he said. "Will you read it?"

I didn't know what to say. It was the most beautiful Koran I'd ever seen. He leaned toward me and grabbed my hand.

"Ever since I was fifteen, I've been dreaming of sharia. And now . . ." He was so choked up, he couldn't even finish his sentence. We spoke about the Islamist movement, its goals, and how Somalia had been waiting for this moment for decades.

"We don't have a problem with Americans," he said. "Look at you, you're here, we've been protecting you all week—maybe you didn't even know it. We want peace, we crave it more than you could ever understand, to get out of this darkness, to stop killing each other, to stop being the laughingstock of the world."

He looked me squarely in the eyes, as had many of the other

Islamists I'd met that week. There was this painful earnestness, an almost awkwardly sincere effort to connect.

He took one last swig of Fanta, killing it, and stood up.

"See you soon, inshallah."

◇◇◇◇◇◇

When I returned to Nairobi, I was at a loss about how to frame this. The African Taliban story was a damn good one; when I'd pitched it, New York liked it immediately. There was just one problem: it wasn't true. The Taliban wouldn't have bought me a Fanta and held my hand. There were a few similarities, but the differences were more telling.

"Don't listen to anybody else," Courtenay said. "Write it the way you want."

"I know, but you know how it is these days with terrorism stories. I don't want to look naive. Maybe there are some al-Qaeda guys creeping around."

I figured the American embassy must know something. It was just up the street from where we lived, a steel-girded fortress, so I stopped by to speak to a couple of political officers in the Somalia section. We hadn't had an embassy in Mogadishu for years, and all matters Somalia were run from two places: Nairobi and Langley, Virginia.

"We're in a swamp," one of the diplomats told me. "The guys in control of the capital aren't the internationally recognized government, and the internationally recognized government is too weak to set foot in the capital."

"Well, wait," I said. "Who do you think *should* be the government? Those Islamist guys have accomplished more than—"

"But you can't just take over a country by force. That's a no-no. There's an internationally recognized government for Somalia, and it ain't them."

"You mean the warlords?"

The other guy looked at me.

"Pal, we prefer the term 'clan elders.'"

The diplomats told me the Islamists needed to hand over three al-Qaeda terrorists who had been hiding out in Mog; when I asked what evidence they had of active support, they just looked at each other and said, "That's classified."

"Now, this is on background," one guy would say—meaning I couldn't attribute it to him—before proceeding to tell me something I already knew. "Wait, now this is off the record," the other guy would say, before uttering something useless. "Okay, now we're back on," the first one would say, then uttering something *really* useless.

When I asked about a rumor that Ethiopian troops were covertly slipping into the country, preparing to attack the Islamists, both vigorously shook their heads. I knew it wasn't just plausible; it was highly likely. And these guys had to know. Though the United States abruptly disengaged from many African countries as soon as the Cold War ended, it returned in the early 2000s to use African militaries as a proxy in the new war. Ethiopia was perfect for this, a Christian-led country that had its own worries about Muslim extremists. Each passing year, Ethiopia was drawing closer and closer to the United States, getting millions of dollars in American military training, prized intelligence, and other support.

But the diplomats were dismissive.

"We're not supporting the Ethiopians as a proxy force, as some people suggest," one said.

"Uh-uh," said the other. "It's just going to cause more trouble. The fighting ends up protracted and long. We're telling them to stay out."

"And you know what?" his partner chimed in. "And this is on deep background. What we really support is peace and development."

I never got those forty-seven minutes of my life back. When the third and final set of bulletproof doors clanked behind me, I realized I was a bit light-headed. When it comes to Somalia, I was thinking as I walked off from the embassy, my government is dangerously stupid. But I shouldn't have been that surprised; if we could break Iraq, just imagine what we could do to a really poor place where few were watching.

Maybe I would get something from Louis, my buddy the French diplomat. Louis always seemed to know something.

"Ah, *les Américains*," he said, leaning back to blow a perfect smoke ring. "They have no idea what they're about to get into."

Louis knew Somalia. He knew the sheikhs, the clans, the constantly shifting alliances, where the weapons came from and which regions produced, on a per annum basis, the most sheep, goats, camels, sorghum, and gum arabic. He even spoke some Somali, along with French, Spanish, Italian, English, German, and Dutch. Somalia was a big part of my beat, so Louis ended up playing the same role for me that Jose Lorenzo, the condom guy, had in Ethiopia.

"I can't remember any time the Americans have delivered a worse mess than this. You know what they're doing?"

He bent forward and dropped his voice to a whisper—that's what I loved about Louis, life was a Le Carré novel to him.

"They're still backing the warlords. The CIA never cut the assistance, even after the clerics kicked the warlords' ass, despite all those briefcases of cash. You know the assholes the CIA was backing? Qanyare? Abdi Qeybdiid? Hussein Aidid? They were the same assholes who shot down your helicopters during Black Hawk Down. You Americans"—he waved his lit cigarette at me—"you're so tragic at history."

We were sitting on the balcony at Trattoria, Louis's favorite restaurant. "Mangia, mangia," he said, motioning to me impatiently. I hadn't touched my food. I was hungry, no doubt, but Louis was streaming, and this was some good juice.

"It's always military instead of politics, there's no information sharing, it's all terrorism, terrorism, terrorism. This is *bool sheet, bool sheet*!" Louis suddenly calmed down. "Who knows?" he said, and shrugged. "The Islamists will just wait it out."

"For how long?"

"Long, man, long. Remember when you were young? Every summer like an ocean? Like you were high on acid, the details that rich, so much seeming to happen?"

I knew what Louis was talking about. I was feeling it right now. Looking out at Nairobi's streets, seeing people flow past in suits, hijabs, and traditional Maasai blankets, hearing swatches of different languages mixing in the air, I realized these days were probably as rich as any I'd ever have. Time felt longer, like I could pack more in.

"That's how the Islamists are," Louis went on. "They keep changing and changing, but they'll never give up on their goal to rule the world. They have a totally different concept of time."

◇◇◇◇◇◇◇

The specter of war hung over Somalia for the next three months. The Islamists kept taking towns; the Ethiopians kept deploying troops, covertly, or at least that was what I kept hearing. By December the Islamists were turning out enormous rallies in Mog, where they paraded fresh recruits around a crumbling soccer stadium. I went back one more time and saw Abu Mansoor at one of these rallies. He was sitting up in the stands, with some of his Shabaab friends, watching ten-year-olds march around the field with AK-47s half as long as they were. Abu Mansoor saw me looking at him and nodded. I nodded back. It was the last time I ever saw him.

European diplomats, Louis among them, shuttled back and forth between Mog and Baidoa, a market town in central Somalia that served as the base of the feeble, corrupt, and internationally recognized Transitional Federal Government of Somalia. The TFG, as it was known, was an entity so reviled by the people of Somalia that it couldn't even set foot in its own capital. In private, most Western diplomats conceded that the TFG was nothing more than a band of geriatric warlords. But the urgency now was to craft a power-sharing agreement between these warlords, who had the international recognition, and the Islamists, who had the real power and support, to avert an all-out war: the last time Somalia descended into all-out war, in the 1990s, hundreds of thousands died.

On December 24, four days into our Christmas vacation in Zanzibar, which my parents had flown in for, their first visit to Africa, I got a call. Or more accurately, eleven calls—in thirty-eight minutes. I'd missed them all because I was on vacation, swimming in the Indian Ocean with my dad, off one of my favorite beaches in the world. This was the downside to my new job. News could break anywhere, at any time, no matter where I was, and knowing that that possibility always existed, even if it didn't always happen, made it difficult to ever truly relax. I made myself call Bakis, my translator, back. He answered in half a ring.

"Jaffar," he said. "It's started."

Ethiopians were pouring across the border, attacking Somalia from three different directions, unleashing everything they had—tanks, artillery, gunships, MiGs, infantry divisions—Ethiopia may be one of the most impoverished countries in the world, but it sure can wage war. A once-in-a-decade, full-scale invasion was under way, and here I was, standing in a bathing suit in a beach town, on an island, with two parents sadly staring at me. For stories like this, all that matters is how fast you move.

"Be careful," my dad said, folding a pair of ancient Fruit of the Loom tightie-whities and frowning into his suitcase as our vacation was cut short. "I don't want to get another call from Bill Keller, like I did when you were kidnapped."

Courtenay and I hugged them good-bye and jumped on a plane back to Nairobi. We ran around our house like a pair of looters, snatching laptops, cameras, tape recorders, and handfuls of money along with sunscreen, toothpaste, jeans, T-shirts, and birth control. The video desk was suddenly interested. We won't risk anyone's life for A13. But for A1? Send in the whole team.

We barely made the next flight to Addis. Up in the skies, Courtenay was anxious. "Will it be safe? Do you have a plan? Isn't this a crazy time to try to get into Mogadishu?"

"It'll be fine," I said. "The Ethiopians like me. You'll see."

Actually, I was right. The Ethiopians were happy to help—this was less than six months before Courtenay and I would be declared enemies of the state, but none of us had any inkling that was about to happen. The Ethiopians were like the Americans back in Iraq, full of noblesse oblige. You want to go in with our troops? *Minem chegger yellem*, no problem, we'll arrange. They knew this was going to be a rout. They also liked the fact that this *mzungu* still remembered some phrases in Amharic from that wet, lonely summer a decade before.

We climbed on board a troop transport plane to Kismayo loaded with so many red-tipped artillery shells that had we crashed, it wouldn't have hurt at all. I looked over at the man strapped in next to me, a stone-faced sniper. "Kas bu kas, enkulal begru yehedal," I said. The guy just started cracking up. For some reason, hearing a *mzungu* recite that proverb—*Slowly, slowly, the egg will walk*, their version of "Rome wasn't built in a day"—always cracks Ethiopians up.

Kismayo, a forlorn port town in southern Somalia, wasn't where I was supposed to be. I was supposed to be in Mog, where the Islamists were gearing up for one last stand, but the Ethiopians said Mog was "too hot" to bring us in. For a journalist, that's about the worst thing you can hear. *Too hot?* That's an oxymoron. A huge story unfolding without you causes a prickly discomfort that won't go away until you get there or the story ends (and that could take days, weeks, even years). We constantly dream up apocalyptic scenarios in which the news breaks, and we're the only reporter able to get in and cover it. I may have been in Somalia, but I was in a quiet town where nothing was happening, and I couldn't even find a fixer to help me make phone calls. Kismayo had plenty of local journalists, but none wanted to work with us. I later found out the reason was that some jerk in Nairobi (a guy who had applied for my job before I got it) told his fixer that I was Jewish, a dangerous and quite sinister disclosure in that land.

Exactly one fixer agreed to help us. He was a surly junior radio reporter, about twenty-five years old, who acted as if he were doing us an enormous favor by accepting $200 a day, twice the going rate.

Nasteh Dahir Farah, whom we would soon call Nasty, cut quite a dashing figure. He was tall, immaculately dressed in business slacks and Polo shirts, always carried three pens in his pocket, and, it turned out, was extremely well connected. His uncle was one of Kismayo's warlords, which imbued Nasty with a sense of entitlement— he walked with his back very straight. He was not starry-eyed at all about *mzungus*. He was also one of those fixers who seemed to enjoy giving the man he worked for bad news.

"Jaffar," he said, "there are no flights to Mogadishu. The only way—which I wouldn't recommend—is by road."

I could tell Courtenay didn't like that.

"How bad do you want to get there?" she asked me.

I stared at the ground.

"That bad?"

That afternoon Nasty said we might be able to meet his uncle, Yusuf the Bald. He took us to the center of town where we stopped in front of a shot-up building. Various gunmen lounged on the steps, crushed water bottles and crinkled biscuit wrappers scattered everywhere. A dozen older women sat on the ground a respectful distance from the door. Their heads swiveled toward us as we approached. Without seeming to sense all the people staring at us, Nasty cut through the crowd. He led us into a room with little light. Yusuf the Bald sat behind a vast, virtually empty desk, the velvet curtains drawn behind him. My eyes adjusted and I began to make out his features. He was a dead ringer for a black Lenin— clean head, triangular goatee, high cheekbones. His voice was deep and husky.

"So, my friends, you need my help?"

Courtenay and I humbly nodded.

Nasty spoke a slew of Somali to him, Yusuf the Bald grunted, and we said good-bye.

As we trotted down the steps, Nasty turned to me and said with the tiniest hint of excitement in his voice: "There may be a solution."

He broke down the expenses on the back of a Yemeni biscuit wrapper: 1 gun truck; 18 gunmen; 6 sacks of rice; 4 flats of water; 2 kilos of goat meat; petrol; ammo; engine oil; a couple cases of Pepsi; and a couple kilos of khat. "Chewing khat is probably the best way of dealing with life in Somalia," Dan had written in the last journal he had ever made. "It reduces your appetite, keeps you alert, and makes you feel invincible. After nine hours of chewing, you are ready to fight anyone."

"It's gonna cost you three," Nasty said—Somalis never bother with the word *thousand*.

"Three?"

"I wouldn't skimp on the gunmen," he said. "Or the khat."

Three. I'll always associate Nasty with that number. Three thousand dollars for the gunmen. Three pens in his pocket. We spent exactly three days with him. A year later, Nasty was shot to death in Kismayo, most likely because of his work as a journalist. Maybe I remember him better than I should because of the way he died, walking out of an Internet café one evening after finishing his work, headed back home to see his pregnant wife, taking several slugs in the chest and stomach. The memories of those who die violently are always the sharpest.

◇◇◇◇◇◇◇

The road to Mog was more than three hundred miles long. "Don't worry," Nasty reassured us. "It'll take about eight hours. We'll be there by nightfall."

By nightfall, we were nowhere. We chugged through mangrove

bushes and largely forgotten wastes. We passed Jilib, Bu'ale, Bar-
awa, Merca, all towns of the enemy clan. Each was barricaded with
logs and oil drums placed in the middle of the road, primitive for-
tifications. We blasted through. After we ran over a particularly big
one, I heard a sudden *thum-thum-thum*. This was no engine knock.

"Seriously?" Courtenay said.

We stopped, got out, and watched an adolescent "gunman" wig-
gle under the chassis and pry something loose from the back right
tire, which was flat. I shone my flashlight on it. A flip-flop, studded
with nails.

It was then that my sat phone rang. The foreign desk. Awesome.

"Jeff, you close to Mog?"

It was an editor.

"Yeah, um, just, uh, a couple hours."

"Good, good, because AP and Eddie Sanders of the *LA Times*
are already there."

Eddie Sanders was a damn good reporter who lived in Nairobi,
not far from me, though I rarely saw him. He was too busy scoop-
ing me.

"You hear we got Americans involved?"

"What?"

"Airstrikes. When you think you can file?"

I told him that his guess was as good as mine. I looked at the
teenage guards scratching their heads, staring at the flip-flop like it
was an artifact from outer space. The bushes thrummed with bug
life. In every direction stretched pulling darkness. There were clan
armies all around us. Somalia may be one of the most homogenous
nations—same language, same religion, same culture, same ethnicity, for practically all of its ten million people. But in Somalia, it's
all about the clan. From long ago, the Somalis have divided themselves into a dizzying number of rival clans, sub-clans, sub-sub-
clans, as a way to protect themselves, through kinship and blood
money, in the depths of the desert. The men guarding us hailed

from a much smaller sub-clan than the enemy sub-clans where we happened to break down. If we didn't fix that flat by sunup, we were dead.

◇◇◇◇◇◇◇◇

When we pulled into the Sahafi twenty-six hours later, all of us were covered in fine orange dust.

"Nasty, we made it, we made it!"

I wanted to hug him for getting us there, but he just extended a cool hand.

I peeled out a fistful of Benjamins. Nasty stuffed the wad in his pocket. Holding his good-looking head high, he walked off, back straight, disappearing behind a beaded curtain, the entrance to a café that smelled vaguely of freshly roasted goat. That was the last I ever saw him.

I looked around. The city was a pigsty. Papers, plastic bottles, ripped-up posters of a man claiming to be Somalia's new prime minister, and all sorts of other junk blew through the streets. The Ethiopians, backed by the Americans, had crushed the Islamic militias in about five days. But Somalia's great moment of liberation was nothing more than a continuation of the national nightmare. The reviled warlords, the same ones who had razed this city and Somalia's future, had returned, plump, graying figures sitting atop the turrets of Ethiopian tanks. They would be Ethiopia's stooges, and everyone knew it. Courtenay and I jumped into one of their technicals, Somalia's contribution to modern warfare, a pickup truck with a cannon riveted to the back. We cruised Mog's crushed streets, covering disingenuous disarmament exercises, in which the warlords turned in their oldest, rustiest weapons, which probably didn't even work, and made grandiose speeches about "the new Somalia." I felt like I was betraying my instincts by even attending these ceremonies, but that was all that was going on. The fighting had stopped, allowing the warlords to get back to business.

"Tell me, you live in Nairobi?" Abdi Rashid, a potbellied war-lord, asked me as soon as we sat down. "You know a guy named Dave?"

"Who's Dave?"

"Dave owes me a million dollars. He works for the CIA. He was one of the guys who came last year and told us to buy weapons to fight al-Shabaab, and he said he'd pay us back. I got his e-mail right here."

Abdi Rashid opened up a diary. I leaned across his desk. And there it was: no_email_today@yahoo.com, an address that only a Baba John could have created.

(That was my last visit with Abdi Rashid. A few years later, the Shabaab bombed his hotel, and as he crawled carefully down the stairs to see what had happened, the Shabaab blasted him into the afterworld.)

That first evening, Courtenay and I retreated to our room on the Sahafi's second floor. She sat cross-legged on the bed, wearing headphones that looked like earmuffs, transcoding her footage while I settled in at the little desk by the TV that didn't work and wrote my dispatch. When it came time to record a voice-over for Courtenay's video, we crawled under a leaden bedspread that smelled of tropical sweat. Hiding under a bedspread was a little trick to get clean sound. We were two big lumps under the covers in a dark and steamy hotel room two degrees north of the equator.

Courtenay held the mic to my mouth, and I read the text on her laptop screen.

"You're popping your *p*'s," she said. "Don't spit so much."

"I'm trying not to, but it's hot as balls under here!"

"Okay, honey, okay. Let's do it again. Just take a deep breath. Start from 'I passed the blackened shell' . . ."

While we were in the middle of the blackened shell, someone started pounding on the door.

"Fucking hell," Courtenay said.

"Don't worry. Just pause it."

I whipped off the bedspread, feeling a surge of relatively cool air, and flung open the door to find the Sahafi's old waiter, known as Camel Rib, standing sheepishly in the corridor. We talked briefly. I ducked back in the room to find my wallet.

"What's Camel Rib want?"

"Oh, just some money."

"I thought you already paid him."

"Yeah, yeah, it's fine. He just needed a little more."

The next day I pulled back the curtains and peered out the dirty window, down into the Sahafi's courtyard. A dozen men sat in white plastic chairs, sipping thimble-size glasses of sugar tea. Some wore the same light purple scarves that my Islamist security detail used to wear when I was here with Abu Mansoor. Their beards were dyed red, and they sat off by themselves, talking quietly, heads together.

When Courtenay and I walked down to get dinner, I let her open the door. "You didn't," she said. Garlands of bougainvillea blossoms hung from the ceiling, along with pink and blue balloons. The table was sprinkled with flower petals and laid with barbequed lobster split down the middle, grilled calamari, a pyramid of glistening chips, sliced tomatoes, bananas, camel steaks, and a half gallon of sugary grapefruit juice. It was as if we'd stepped back into the Ibn Battuta days; some of his juiciest recollections from that fourteenth-century visit were of the opulent feasts he ate: stews of chicken, meat, and fish; curdled milk with peppercorns and saffron; carefully sliced mango pickles.

As soon as we sat down, I poured two glasses of grapefruit juice. We clinked.

"To thirty-four years," I said. "Happy birthday." We even stole a quick kiss—when Camel Rib ran back to grab some ketchup; PDA is forbidden in Somalia.

After we picked the lobster clean and decimated that mountain of chips, Camel Rib reappeared with a cake. It was slathered in pink icing, with yellow and green stripes, Courtenay's name spelled correctly, and Yemeni biscuits glued to the sides, like port-holes. There were even birthday candles. I didn't know Mog had birthday candles; it was so different from what I had expected, everything was. We crawled into bed and fell asleep, full and fast. Our reverie was soon shattered by automatic gunfire. *Kuh-kuh, kuh-kuh.*

"What's that?" Courtenay said, clutching me.

"I don't know."

I slipped out of bed, feeling around for my headlamp. The Sahafi always cut the power in the middle of the night. Just as I got my hands on it, *kuh-kuh* rang out again. Return shots were coming from right outside the gate, so close I could hear the empties clinking to the pavement. I stood absolutely still, halted breath, my body tense.

"What should we do?" Courtenay asked. "Get under the bed?"

"Get your camera," I said. "Just remember, they're shooting, but they're not shooting at us."

She pulled on a shirt and grabbed her camera. We crept out into the hallway, barefoot, bent at the waist, staying low. We could smell gunpowder in the air. We scampered up to the roof, carefully peering over the edge. It was so dark we couldn't see a thing. Another burst of gunfire rang out. We yanked our heads back down. It triggered a quick flashback of playing paintball with Roko and Chris on the outskirts of LA at a place called Fields of Fire that was frequented by skinheads and kids from Watts. Those days at Fields of Fire were the best combat training I ever received, not the $5,000 "hostile environment" course the paper paid for.

America's decision to green-light Ethiopia's invasion of Somalia and overthrow a popular, grassroots, and surprisingly effective Islamist administration led, over the next five years, to the ex-plosion of chaos, high-seas piracy, terrorism spreading across East Africa, and ultimately the next Somali famine, in which more than 250,000 people died. That policy decision was one of the most questionable in recent history—right behind Bremer's Coalition Provisional Authority Order No. 2, if measured in lives lost, although I'm not sure what else you'd measure it in.

That night, Courtenay's first birthday in Africa, was the beginning of al-Shabaab's insurgency. The Islamists weren't going quietly into the night—they weren't then, and they haven't now.

ELEVEN

⬦⬦⬦⬦⬦⬦

EAST AND CENTRAL AFRICA, 2007

We traveled by bus, by car, by dump truck, by big plane and tiny plane, by motorcycle, rickshaw, technical, helicopter, bicycle, foot, horse, donkey cart, camel, ferry, steam train, speedboat, dhow, and dugout canoe.

We swiped away the mosquito net at 5:00 a.m., silently pulling on our clothes in our dark bedroom, throwing our gear into the truck in our driveway, the *Times*'s driver, Richard, already in his seat, radio tuned to BBC, slipping down Nairobi's lampless streets to the airport as thousands of Kenyans streamed up both sides of the road, marching to work. Hope can be a trite concept, but there is no better word for what was powering people up the shoulders of those roads, clouds of breath coming out of their mouths in the predawn chill. Visitors always say, "Wow, there's so many people *walking* here," and those early-morning airport runs helped me gain a greater appreciation of Kenya's unrelenting hustle.

We had no financial burdens, no opposing schedules, no kids, though we were trying now, knowing that Nairobi would be a wonderful place to start a family. I had no idea what people meant by a "work-life balance." My life, right then, was perfectly balanced. The casual conversations at cocktail parties over samosas and South African rosé flowed into leads, the leads flowed into story ideas, the story ideas flowed into journeys, my wife my travel partner. We moved through the airport as one, me in that tacky Madras shirt in which I survived the Fallujah mob, she in a flannel and those nylon "sexy pants" that made the distinct swishing sound. We didn't even have to tell each other what to do. She ran over to the immigration desk and filled out the yellow disembarkation cards; I kicked our bags closer to the front of the line. We'd reunite at the check-in counter.

"These are the good old days, Jeff," Boris, an old photographer friend from LA, wrote to me one day. "Enjoy them."

Of course I couldn't appreciate how great my life was, even when someone was kind enough to take the time to remind me. It's impossible to know when you're in the thick of it—that's the definition of *it*. There was one Friday night in Brooksville when I was lonely and depressed—this was right after Courtenay first dumped me—and I found myself sitting at a high school football game, just twenty-six years old but already feeling that yawning distance from youth, and I remember the clock about to run out, and the coach desperately calling one last time-out, and the players sprinting to the sideline and ripping off their steaming helmets, everyone taking a knee and all those bright, alert eyes burning with the unswerving belief that nothing was more important in the entire universe than advancing that piece of pigskin 72 inches. I gazed out at the clarity of the lines painted on that field and at all those terribly earnest faces, thinking: Fellas, it just doesn't get any better than this. You might not make fourth and two, but you're as alive as you'll ever be.

◇◇◇◇◇◇

The Djiboutian Air Force plane buzzed over the desert, casting a black dot of a shadow like a flea crawling across a rock. I could feel the heat lancing through the aircraft's aluminum skin. Down below, there were no trees, no grass, no huts, no roads, nothing to draw the likes of man, just miles of trackless sand.

Courtenay stepped out on the landing strip, an indistinguishable spot in the desert marked only by a flaccid windsock. She wore a red bandanna around her neck, her top lip beaded with tiny droplets of sweat. "Don't laugh," she said. "It's my biology." She looked tough and somehow adorable at the same time. The Eritreans had just crossed the border, and Djiboutians were checking them at the top of a hill overlooking Bab-el-Mandeb, the Gateway of Tears, the narrowest point of the Red Sea, where Africa and Arabia nearly touch. We drove in Humvees to the base of the hill, got out, and began walking.

A Djiboutian officer looked over at me. "It's an interesting front line," he said.

That was an understatement. The two armies were dug into the top of the hill right next to each other, several hundred opposing soldiers hunched over their rifles, blankly staring right into each other's sweating faces, maybe three feet apart tops. There was no cushion, no no-man's-land. The slightest spark would rip across that line like a fuse. As we approached, an Eritrean infantryman, who was wearing a rag on his head, started waving his weapon at us and yelling.

So many of Africa's borders aren't merely senseless. They're vague. The Eritreans said the hill was theirs; the Djiboutians said it wasn't. The colonial-era documents back in Rome and Paris were unhelpful, and I had no idea who was right. But as we peeked out from behind a wall of Djiboutian soldiers, I realized how quaint the idea of neutrality really is. We're always taking a side. That's how you cover a war, whether in Iraq or Afghanistan or the Horn of Africa; you go in with one side. The Djiboutians, feeling aggressed, had invited us up here. Djibouti had been a French colony until the 1970s, one of the last to shrug off the cloying *mzungu* hand. It still maintained a mutual defense pact with France, and all its soldiers were smartly equipped, carrying the latest offerings of the Kalashnikov product line and wearing CamelBaks. That morning, we had been served fresh croissants in the officers' mess.

The Eritreans, on the other hand, looked homeless. They were skinny and sandy, with unruly Afros and scratched-up guns. They didn't even wear boots, just cheap black plastic sandals. Eritrea is a very poor, very proud country, having fought decades for its independence from Ethiopia and then shunning foreign aid. The Eritreans said they were going to go their own way, and they have. In the capital, Asmara, stands a statue of a pair of black plastic sandals, the symbol of Eritrean resistance.

"Eritreans kneel on only two occasions," the information minister had told me. "When we pray, and when we shoot."

The Eritrean soldier with the rag on his head shouted at us what I am 99.99 percent sure were curses and stomped off. He wore a small plastic cross around his neck, and his chest was sweating. We walked carefully past where he had been standing, past soldiers in foxholes and machine-gun pits. Courtenay held the camera to her face, slowly panning. We could see the bright blue water of the Red Sea from the top of the hill. The sun beat down. As we headed back to where we had started, Courtenay pointed to a small tight plastic bag of cooked rice sitting on one of the rocks separating the soldiers. We kept walking. She stuck out her right pinkie again. Another small tight bag, beaded from steam. It looked like a man-of-war, ready to pop.

"Excusez-moi, monsieur," I said to one of the Djiboutian officers (that's as far as my French goes). I saw a single droplet of sweat roll down the back of his neck. It wasn't even nine in the morning, and already triple digits. "What's going on?"

"We're feeding them," he said.

"Why aren't they taking it?"

"Because"—he dropped his voice lower—"they're too proud."

Courtenay paused to shoot the rice.

"That's the one act of mercy out here," she said, and then turned off her camera.

Two of Africa's smallest countries were about to go war over a heap of sand, "David versus David," as I put it in my story, thinking at the time this conflict was kind of cute—this was before the Eritreans sprang, killing dozens. By the standards of the region, this war was barely fit for print. There were much bigger ones in each direction from where we were standing. But finding a story in Djibouti, a country that the paper rarely wrote about, was part of a grander plan. Courtenay and I had a sense this wasn't going to last forever. She still wanted to return to law, and we wanted to raise a family, and who knew how long the video department would last. One top editor in New York had cautioned me that the whole video push was "an experiment." So Courtenay and I vowed to visit all twelve of "our" countries in our first year, to see them together while we could.

We got back to our hotel, on Djibouti's main square, in the midafternoon stillness, when men lie under trees. We rested for a couple hours in our room, and I awoke to see Courtenay rooting around in her backpack, emerging with a perfectly clean shirt and a tube of lipstick. It never ceased to amaze me how she packed, bags within bags, everything neatly sorted, pens in a plastic case, shirts rolled up to minimize wrinkles, underwear segregated in one gallon-size Ziploc bag, socks in another. We showered and stepped into the evening air.

Downtown Djibouti, called Centre Ville, was safe back then, before al-Shabaab started rolling grenades into discos. It was how I imagined Africa fifty years ago. The buildings were old and columned, paint flaking off. There was no traffic. Women in diaphanous scarves floated through the graceful archways like something out of Raphael's *School of Athens*, leaving a trail of incense and perfume. The aroma of fresh baguettes wafted above the briny smell of the sloshing sea. It was like I was back in my Year On, hitting the streets of a strange land, senses at full capacity, discovering a place I had barely imagined.

"This looks great!" Courtenay said as we walked into a small restaurant near the souk called the Seven Brothers. It specialized in traditional Yemeni barbeque that uses a tubular fire pit. The cook

slapped whole fish and mounds of dough against the sides of the
pit, bringing everything to a blackened crisp. Our fish came on
chipped plates with the meat dropping off the bone by the handful,
accompanied by slabs of Yemeni bread two feet long and emitting
clouds of fragrant, yeasty steam. For dessert, the cook slathered
honey and chocolate on a slab of fresh bread and then rolled it tight
and chopped it into pieces. I think that seven-dollar meal was the
best we had in Africa, or maybe anywhere.

◇◇◇◇◇◇

Kampala. Muscat. Tripoli. Asmara. Our relationship was deepen-
ing at each dateline. These were the same exotic locales I used to
stare at longingly on airport screens; now I was waking up in them,
with Courtenay. People will go on and on about the risks of working with your spouse, with even more vehemence than they give
the don't-have-your-roommate-be-your-best-friend spiel. They're
not wrong—but it's like anything else. No risk, no reward. I've
been given the silent treatment in Burundi, Congo, Libya, Eritrea,
Uganda, and the Seychelles, at least fifty countries by now. I've
been called a "pussy" in front of several hundred armed men. You
wouldn't be an idiot to think "Dumb-Dumb" was one of my given
names.

But in the early days, and even during the most protracted wars
of attritional silence, the comfort of always having Courtenay
nearby and the pleasure of exploring together that open road across
Africa was something I would never trade away. Courtenay enjoyed this life, perhaps because it was a professional interlude. For
me, it was the closest I've ever come to living my dreams.

At a truck stop near the border of Zimbabwe and South Africa,
we met a white Zimbabwean farmer who walked with a limp.
He was loading his pickup truck with several hundred pounds of
groceries—corn flakes, cheese, white bread, apples, frozen sau-
sages, yogurt, toilet paper, boxed juice, dishwashing soap, ground

beef, provisions you couldn't buy in Zimbabwe. We asked him about the economic crisis—we were doing a story about Zimbabwe's collapse after a bungled election—and the white farmer told us that the trouble began years ago, when Rhodesia, which had been led by whites, gave way to black-run Zimbabwe.

"Now, I don't want to sound like a racialist," he said, quite earnestly. "But these people can survive on very little. They're not like us whites. They don't need a hamburger or an apple. They'll be fine for a month with a slab of rancid donkey meat."

That slab of rancid donkey meat made a deep impression on Courtenay. We were still arguing about it—she said it was indeed racist, or racialist, showed a deep disdain for blacks, and I said no, the farmer was just admitting blacks were harder, that they wanted it more—when we arrived at the border fence an hour later. I asked Courtenay—rather sweetly, I'd say—to get some shots of refugees shimmying under the wire that marked the international line.

Instead, Courtenay set up her tripod in the middle of the road and started shooting the moon.

"Just shoot the fence," I said.

"Uh-huh."

"Don't waste time on that."

"Just give me a sec, will you? Do you know how annoying you can be? You have an opinion about everything. Arguing with you is like arguing with a crazy person. Or a Republican. Go make a call or something."

New York loved the moon. They ended the video with it, making me wonder: I've been doing this kind of work my whole professional life, and Courtenay's been at it only a few months. Maybe I'm not so special after all.

◇◇◇◇◇◇◇

The Courtenay-and-Jeffrey show arrived at the Bukavu border point by foot, which is the best way to cross into a country. That way you get the full impact of a new place—its smells, its music, its weather, its spirit, tough to do in an antiseptic international airport. We had just come from Rwanda, which is neat, clean, and sullen. At the Bukavu border point loud *lingala* music pumped from blown speakers; drunken police shouted at women carrying every fruit imaginable on their heads, and the women shouted back; taxi touts, money changers, and vendors of cell phone scratch cards and red-skinned peanuts bawled out the prices of their wares.

A small man in a white coat emerged from this crowd. He walked right up to us and seized Courtenay's arm.

"Yellow fever?" he asked.

"No, she doesn't have yellow fever," I said.

"No yellow fever, no entry," he replied, tightening his grip on her arm. I grabbed her other arm. Courtenay stood between us, not sure what to do. It took me a second to decipher what he was talking about.

"Oh, yellow fever *cards*," I said, whipping them out.

He frowned—I'm sure there was some *kitu kidogo* opportunity in this—but he also let go. I noticed then that his white coat had "Doc" written in Magic Marker on the pocket. Apparently he was the port health officer. We breezed past him into the biggest, poorest, most screwed-up, and possibly most interesting country in sub-Saharan Africa: the Democratic Republic of Congo.

Congo is terrifying, but it has an uncanny ability to get into your pores and stay in your bloodstream. It's one of the most physically blessed places on earth, which I began to appreciate the moment we walked up to the gates of the Orchid Hotel, perched on a hill draped in pink hibiscus blossoms and other tropical plants that couldn't have looked much greener or happier. Lake Kivu stretched out in front of us, and beyond that, sculpted mountains rippled away for miles and miles. Never before or since have I witnessed foreground and background in such fierce competition for sheer beauty.

The Orchid was run by an elderly Belgian man, Marc, who struggled to adhere to the highest European standards. His waiters dressed in bow ties and crimson shirts and moved in whispers, depositing at each table a small blackboard with the specials of the day printed in neat chalk—Marc's filets were the most tender for several days' drive. He served frog legs and snails, in sauce de la crème. This was not the Seven Brothers.

"This is like an illusion," Courtenay said as we sat on the Orchid's deck, sipping frosty Chimay ale imported from a monastery in Belgium, the former colonial master, four thousand miles away. The black lake stretched before us, calm as a swimming pool, big as a sea.

When deep night fell, the fishermen paddled out and we watched the horizon slowly fill with little orange lights, kerosene lamps swinging from the bows of their boats. It soon looked like a whole city out there, or like a constellation of stars that had fallen lightly on the surface of the water. It was a pretty lie the fishermen were telling the fish. The fish liked to feed on nights with a full moon; the light of lanterns drew them from the depths.

As we headed back to our room, the air now cool, like in the mountains, we grew quiet. We had a long day in front of us. We weren't here for the views. We were slipping into Marc's sheets, of an indulgent thread count, super soft under our fingertips, for the same reason that all too often put us on a plane or in a bus or in the back of a dugout canoe. We were here for the death.

◇◇◇◇◇◇◇

The next morning we drove to the hospital, windows down. Brightly painted shops slid past, guys hanging out in front, leaning on each other, happily eliminating personal space. Bukavu, like so many towns we rushed through, was crammed with life. People in colorful clothing thronged the streets, and the first few beats of music we heard from a radio made me want to dance. As we passed the market, I could smell roasting corn. I wanted to take Courtenay's hand, jump out of the car and hurl my notebook and her camera down the side of a mountain. All that I'd experienced during my first trips to East Africa was still out there, practically waving to me, but we didn't stop, we almost never stopped. I had yet to figure out a way to make a place's friendly, life-affirming vibe newsworthy.

I'm not saying this was the only way to cover the region. I could have written more about culture, the economy, sports, technology. Maybe I should have. But I instinctively skewed toward human rights abuses and conflict. It wasn't as simple as my having adrenaline junkie qualities or once-a-cop-reporter, always-a-cop-reporter, or that I was trying to bring a Hemingwayesque glory to death. I felt irresponsible sinking time into a lighter story when I knew that one short plane trip away, people were being slaughtered. This was the *New York Times*, after all, the paper of record read by diplomats, intelligence services, and decision makers around the world. A story in our pages really does have the power to put pressure on governments to adjust their policies or the United Nations to send in more peacekeepers (though that's hardly a magic bullet) or a nonprofit to divert more of its resources to a specific area or need. Many foreign correspondents for other big media houses had left Africa; our competitors had cut back on their staff. And while Kenya had a vibrant media scene, most countries in this region, including Congo, didn't. The local journalists often lacked the resources—and the freedom—to cover conflicts or atrocities. The result was that if I didn't write the story, maybe nobody would. I tried not to be sanctimonious about it, but I couldn't forget what Martin Luther King Jr. once said: "The ultimate tragedy is not the oppression and cruelty by the bad people but the silence over that by the good people." I don't know if I qualified as one of the good people, but I wasn't happy with the idea of staying silent.

Compared with Brooksville, where the news was literally pushed through the door, so much of this job turned on deciding what the news was, which struck at the core of how to interpret the journalist's mission. Are we here to bear witness? Or are we here to drive change? I wish I knew the right balance. Sometimes I could see how depressing my stories were. I'm sure they depressed readers; I know for a fact they depressed me. And I didn't want to misrepresent a part of the world that I cared for deeply. But you know how it usually goes with news. News is *not* the millions of sensible moms taking care of their kids. News is the one broken mom who drowns her kids.

It took us a half hour to get to Panzi Hospital, the biggest in the area, where the survivors of the bush wars came, if they could make it that far. At independence, Congo was said to have more hospital beds than just about anywhere else in sub-Saharan Africa. That was a long time ago. Panzi sat at the end of a dirt road, its outdoor hallways covered in sheet metal, the ceiling fans hanging listlessly, like propellers of crashed aircraft. The hospital's director, Denis Mukwege, a large man with a squarish face and yellow, unblinking eyes, was a gynecologist trained in France. He didn't have to be here.

"When the victims come, you can tell by the wounds where it happened," he started to tell us. "In Bunyakiri, they burn the women's bottoms. In Fizi-Baraka, they are shot in the genitals. In Shabunda, it's bayonets."

I scribbled everything down fast, pausing only to ask about the words I didn't understand—Mwalimu Nanji, my old Swahili guru, hadn't felt the need to teach us *chuki* (hate) or *visu vya banduki* (bayonets).

"Some of these girls whose insides have been destroyed are so young that they don't understand what happened to them," Dr. Mukwege went on. "They have this odor, there is so little tissue to work with."

He rubbed his face.

"Why would you ever rape a three-year-old?"

Post-traumatic stress can make people do bad things, maybe drink too much or blow away their wives. But Dr. Mukwege, who performed ten fistula surgeries a day, transmitted this faint but perceptible inner glow, a sense of calm, of having arrived exactly where he wanted to be. Very rich people, in the comfort of their own homes, when welcoming in a guest, sometimes give off this same air, of deep satisfaction with themselves and their station in life. But usually, soon enough, something aggravates them—maybe a defect in one of their things, or people around them simply not moving fast enough. Dr. Mukwege was imperturbable. There was always something immensely serene in how his eyes rested on people, and this serenity went deeper than the spaced-out smile of a sadhu or the drone of a monk slapping a prayer wheel. It seemed to flow from the knowledge he was doing just about all that was humanly possible to help others.

In recent times, more women have been raped in Congo—nearly two million—than anywhere else in the world. Denis Mukwege has helped them more than any other doctor.

"Come," he said. "Time to meet some of the girls."

When Belgium's King Leopold II hatched a plan in the 1880s to gobble up Congo, he hired the most morally bankrupt explorer of the time. Henry Morton Stanley "shot negroes like monkeys," in the words of Richard Burton, no daisy himself. Stanley was a journalist by trade, psychopath by practice; he was also a proud American. Tossing a few strings of glass beads to cowering chiefs, he swindled the Congolese into signing away the rights to their own country. Leopold then sent in "the Administration"—pith-helmeted officers ordered to collect mountains of ivory, which Europe needed for billiard balls, piano keys, snuffboxes, and false teeth. Leopold's team was also interested in rubber, a commodity that was booming back then, thanks to the recent invention of the inflatable tire. If a village didn't meet its rubber quota, the Belgians might burn it down or even chop off a few hands to make sure everyone was paying attention. As Conrad wrote, Leopold's operation was "the vilest scramble for loot that ever disfigured the history of human conscience." The next decades weren't much better, and when the Belgians finally let go in 1960, Congo had been so abused it immediately began to crack apart.

Since then there's been a never-ending succession of interlocking murky conflicts over land, ethnicity, politics, and most especially minerals. The 1990s were the worst, when half a dozen other African countries invaded to plunder Congo's gold, diamonds, copper, cobalt and tin ore. The International Rescue Committee, a private aid group, released a study in 2007 asserting that 5.4 million people had died in a decade, making Congo's war—which doesn't even have a name—the deadliest conflict since World War II. Though I've occasionally used that factoid to turn heads, I don't know if it's actually true; it's based on mortality surveys and estimates of "excess deaths." On good days, I don't let myself use it, even though I concede its utilitarian value of getting people to care about Congo.

We had been told that armed groups had recently taken over several lucrative mines in eastern Congo and were using the profits to buy guns and terrorize people, especially women. I never got a straight answer for why these armed groups were so flamboyantly brutal to women. One Canadian professor I met on the Orchid's veranda wondered if all the war had simply torn apart social norms, devouring what little decency was left.

We followed Mukwege to one of the bare but neatly swept examination rooms, where he introduced us to a young woman who had the confusion of a child in her eyes. Mukwege said "Pardon" and disappeared, leaving Courtenay and me alone in a small room with a quiet and visibly damaged soul.

Courtenay didn't sit down. She opened the curtains, stepped back into the middle of the room, glanced out the window, and sized up the light. She had learned all this so fast, and I felt pride and also a bit unsettled seeing her shift so effortlessly into capture mode. It was like watching myself in the mirror. The young woman's eyes delicately followed what Courtenay was doing. Her name was Zawadi.

"I went out with my friends to look for some wood," Zawadi began.

Men with guns and dreads suddenly appeared—the Rastas, a new rebel group who terrorized the hills wearing shiny sweat suits and swamp boots. They lashed the women to trees with rope, untying them only to rape them. That's when they discovered that one of Zawadi's friends was pregnant. They told her to stand.

Zawadi brushed a strand of hair from her eyes and paused. Courtenay adjusted the camera slightly, one hand on the zoom button, the other on the tripod handle, to get in tighter on Zawadi's face.

The Rastas cut open the woman's belly with a field knife, ripped out the fetus, and threw it to the ground.

"'Eat it,' they told us. 'Grind it up and eat it.' They called it stew."

The next day, Courtenay and I walked down to a little beach behind the hotel. Lake Kivu was sparkling. We plunged in and the water felt so good. It had none of that fishy lake taste that I had grown up with in Chicago. Fed by streams running down the green mountains and heated by a powerful sun, that lake is fifty miles long and more than a thousand feet deep.

While we were paddling out, Courtenay said she was beginning to feel curious about herself.

"It's so weird," she said, treading water next to me. "My greatest fear is to be raped by an armed stranger, and here were some of the worst stories I've ever heard, and I was worried about the lighting."

She had always been so empathic; I remember how on our first trip to Tanzania the poverty had demoralized her. But now she was a journalist, looking out for her shot, her needs, quickly building efficient walls around her heart. Our outlooks were fusing; our separate, most intimate thoughts as close as they'd ever been.

"I don't want to complain about something stupid," I said as we headed back to shore, slowly paddling. "But the desk wouldn't let me use the word *scenario*."

"Why not?"

"Apparently there's some *Times* fatwa against it. Supposedly *scenario* should only be used as a Greek dramatic term."

"Does someone actually sit around thinking about these things?"

"Probably. And worse, they cut out *fetus stew*."

"Why'd they do that?"

"Take a wild guess."

"Too *ooga-booga*?"

⬦⬦⬦⬦⬦⬦

The pre—*ooga-booga* era was getting hazier. I—we—could go anywhere I could find a story, and sometimes I was so excited about the coming day that I couldn't sleep. To get everything ready for our first trip to Darfur, I set off for Khartoum a couple days before Courtenay, which I sometimes did to save the video desk money. I'd find a driver, start working with the fixer, apply for the internal travel permits, get everything set for us to push off into the hinterland as soon as she got there. I was eager to get a piece of Darfur, to see how it had succeeded in capturing the imagination like no other African war, even though Congo's, Somalia's, Burundi's, and Rwanda's were all far deadlier.

A big reason was the unrivaled firepower of celebrity. George Clooney, Mia Farrow, Don Cheadle, Angelina Jolie, Ryan Gosling, and a growing cadre of American politicians, including the junior senator from Illinois, Barack Obama, journeyed to either Darfur itself or the refugee camps across the border in Chad and presented this conflict as a straightforward case of an oppressive Arab government crushing innocent Africans, with a hint of the crusades. Across American college campuses, a rallying cry rang out: Save Darfur!

Darfur had cracked open at a time in human history when everybody had a cell phone and many had a sat phone. This made it relatively easy to relay news of battles and atrocities quickly, which wasn't true when Congo, Somalia, and Rwanda blew up in the 1990s. And Darfur was very visual. Men in turbans, women in veils, horses and camels, crumbly dunes, huge skies: it lent itself to TV. But unfortunately for Sudan, Darfur was hardly the only fire. Sudan has been at war with itself since independence in the 1950s. By 2007 there were rebels in the east; rebels in the Nuba

Mountains; countless different rebel outfits in the south; violence flaring in the Abyei region between farmers and nomads; and a new, little-known liberation movement that had just started to bud in the leafy reaches of the upper Nile in Nubia, according to my rival Eddie Sanders, of the *LA Times*, who had scooped me again. Come to think of it, the last time I'd seen Sanders, at the mall near our house in Nairobi, he had been exceedingly friendly, which should have been a tip-off.

Maybe I had wasted too much time in the office trying to organize all the overlapping and internecine conflicts, making a stack of neat, color-coded file folders for each rebel group and each war: Darfur, Nuba, North Sudan–South Sudan, the Beja, the Murle, the Miseriya, the Agok Dinka, the SLA, LRA, JEM, SPLA, SSDF. It took me years to realize how futile this was. Rebels (save one group I knew) didn't have neat goals or follow clear geographical lines. Take the LRA, the Lord's Resistance Army, a flamboyantly cruel rebel outfit that clubbed old women to death, made children kill their parents, and rammed padlocks through people's faces. They were Ugandan by origin but supported by Sudan based in Congo and making incursions into the Central African Republic. What folder did they belong in?

When I stepped off the plane in Khartoum, with some of those same file folders tucked into the back pocket of my laptop case, the sky was an ominous shade of pink. I felt the first puffs of wind. As I got out of the taxi on Abu Sin Street, I saw the fruit vendors looking up, muttering.

I checked into the hotel, the Dandas, new and therefore a bit uninspiring. I pushed together the two double beds to make a king, knowing Courtenay was on her way. The phones didn't work, so I went out to the balcony and set up my satellite transmitter, but the wind was picking up now, and so much dust was swirling in the air, that my BGAN—short for Broadband Global Area Network— transmitter wasn't getting a strong signal. Like so much of my expensive gear—my Italian hiking boots whose rubber soles split in the

Tanzanian sun or my IBM laptop that died on me in Juba because of the heat—my $3,000 BGAN was apparently not made with Africa in mind. I switched back to my sat phone and finally got through.

"Just got to the hotel, it's not bad, not great, but not bad, you'll like it. What's going on with you?"

"Nothing."

"What's wrong?"

"Did you check your e-mail?

"No. It's really windy and dusty here, BGAN's not working. Why?"

"Check your e-mail," she said flatly.

"Okay."

"Check your e-mail," she said again.

◇◇◇◇◇◇◇

The Zulus used to say that every so often there needed to be a big battle, a cleansing. Afterward the soldiers would cut open the corpses of their fallen enemies to purify their weapons. They called it "the washing of the spears." I guess I always knew there would be a washing of the spears.

When I opened my e-mail, I felt a tightness in the left center of my chest. My heart rate accelerated. My lips went dry. Courtenay had read the e-mails. She had found them by accident. She hadn't been snooping, she had just been looking for some letterhead on my old computer, the one from Iraq, and stumbled into a message from Elizabeth.

"Sweetie, please," I begged. "Come here, let's talk about this in person."

"The last thing I want to do is a stupid video with you, you cocksucker!" she shouted through my sat phone. "How could you do this to me?"

◇◇◇◇◇◇◇

I took a taxi to the airport. I didn't even want to look the driver in the eyes. When I saw Courtenay emerge from the terminal, flannel shirt, blue backpack, hair in a ponytail, I stepped toward her. I felt this urge to pull her close. I needed to tell her we could get through this.

"Don't fucking touch me," she said.

We didn't speak much on the drive in; we sat in the backseat, heads turned away from each other, staring out the windows. A haboob was about to hit. The streets were emptying. Waiters from the sidewalk cafés dragged in the last of the spinning sidewalk signs, the chairs, the wrought-iron outdoor tables, anything that wasn't bolted down. People scurried inside. I felt the wind lift off the street and shoot under the taxi, shaking it violently. It was like we were in a thin-walled capsule plunging deeper and deeper into sea. The pressure was increasing, the world we thought we knew darkening and becoming less familiar.

By the time we arrived at the hotel, the haboob had engulfed half of Khartoum, the other half about to disappear. The electricity sizzled out. We sat on the edge of the bed in the dark.

"All of them," she hissed. "Every single fucking one of them."

I didn't know where to begin.

"Ashley from LA?"

"Yes, Ashley."

"Samantha?"

"Yes, Samantha."

"That tennis girl from Oxford who stayed at your house?"

"Yes."

Dust slammed against the windows, the glass vibrating as the shrieking wind hit the hotel, forcing itself through every possible crack. I couldn't see the end of the street.

"Sweetie, we were apart, we were all fucked up—"

"Don't say *we*! *You* were fucked up." Her eyes narrowed. "Don't tell me you were fucking Elizabeth the whole time you were in Iraq. I will kill you if you were fucking Elizabeth the whole time you were in Iraq."

"Well," I said softly.

She howled. My mind was racing, eyes darting, I actually believed it was a question of simply finding the right words to explain things.

"We were in a long-distance relationship, you dumped me twice, you never wanted to live where I was, this all happened before we even got engaged. You know I would never cheat on my wife."

"I am the same person, you fucking idiot!"

She pounded her fist into the bed, sobbing. I edged toward her.

"I said don't touch me!"

I shrunk back.

"And now all those other fucking journalists, they know. You made me do this job, you brought me out here, and now you've made me the dupe!"

"Sweetie, I fucked up, this is about us, who cares what other people know?"

"*Who cares!* Is that really your answer!" She jumped up. "Do you want to try again?"

I felt queasy, helpless. It was like getting hit in the face and stumbling woozily to a mirror and suddenly seeing a gushing gash. It was too late. The damage had been done. I had wanted so badly to be a good person, but I was not a good person, I was not strong, I was not honest, I was not selfless. I was a stupid, weak, lying narcissist.

"You told me I had nothing to worry about! What self-respecting woman would stay in this relationship?"

My head was in my hands.

She curled up on the opposite side of the bed. The wind continued to roar like an ocean. I could taste the Sahara in my mouth. Sand was coming into the room. I hoped it would drown me. I had known the moment I crossed the lawn that summer, when I was twenty-two, that Courtenay Morris was going to be my wife. Nothing had ever been clearer.

I lay awake in bed as gusts continued to blast into our hotel, shaking the room. It was pitch-dark. All light outside had been extinguished. I could hear shutters banging, canvas awnings whipping back and forth, iron poles clanking to the ground as our marriage crumbled.

I snuck out toward morning to call Chicago.

"Dad," I started to bawl. "Courtenay wants to get duh, divorced."

"Wait, hold on, where are you?"

"Sudan."

"Where? You're breaking up."

"Khartoum. Sudan. There's a haboob going on."

"A what? Just hold on, let me conference in your mom."

Both my parents were professionals whose jobs included, to some degree, listening to people make excuses—my mom was a social worker, my dad now a judge. They listened to me cry. My dad asked me what I'd been thinking. All I could say was that I hadn't been thinking.

"She says a leopard can't change its spots."

"Well," my dad said, "tell her you're not a leopard."

For the rest of the week, an opaqueness ruled the sky. Even after the winds stopped, a blanket of dust hung over the dun-colored metropolis. I think several people died.

We carried on to Darfur. Anyone who saw us would have thought we were simply a quietly efficient married couple going about our jobs, writing things down, setting up shots, wasting no energy on superfluous conversation. Everything about Darfur was appropriately bleak. We saw veiled women working in the wadis, raising iron hoes high above their heads, sinking them into the sand. They were looking for water. It was a severe environment to attempt living in, and even the baby horses wore good-luck prayer scrolls around their necks. On the outskirts of Kas, a hard little town, we passed several hundred men wearing impossibly white turbans and robes and mirrored sunglasses, their camels lashed to trees with worn leather ropes, their PKM machine guns set up on tripods, trained on the road. It was a Janjaweed convention, as irresistibly visual as everything else. One man looked right at us, raised his hand, and waved hello.

We were covering a "seasonal massacre," as Courtenay put it, what happens in Wadi Bulbul every summer when the nomads cross the land of the farmers and the two sides come out to greet each other with belt-fed machine guns. Instead of trying to stop it, the Sudanese government just manipulates it for the government's own ends.

We went to the souk. I couldn't let anything stop the visit to the souk. The souk had always been an essential piece of the program, one of the few extracurricular activities we allowed ourselves, to remind us that we weren't just working, we were *traveling*. I was hoping things between us might finally be easing. There was nothing more I could say. I had confessed every misdeed, and I still loved her. She knew that. And we had worked hard to get to the very spot we were standing in right now. The souk was a crowded maze of stalls made out of sticks. I could smell incense, animal dung, sweat, and horses. We passed a blacksmith's booth that sold four-foot-long gleaming swords, and these were not decorative items— they could cut off someone's head with a single slice. Staring at those swords made me think back to all that I had heard about Sudan's president, Omar Hassan al-Bashir, the Janjaweed (which literally means "devil on horseback"), and the debate over whether Bashir orchestrated genocide. I don't think Bashir had to sit down the Janjaweed with a clipboard and say, "Okay, let's go through this one more time: Burn down the huts, kill the kids, rape the women . . ." The violence here was ambient, the destruction total.

As we walked farther into the market, Courtenay stared hard at me, like she wanted me to fuck off and die.

"You know," she said, "cheating really sucks."

"I won't do it ever again," I muttered. "You have nothing to worry about."

"That's what you said before! Don't ever say it again!"

TWELVE

◇◇◇◇◇◇

THE OGADEN DESERT, 2007

"Here?" I said to the driver. "You want us to get out *here*?"

He had stopped his taxi in the middle of a muddy field, the nearest lights miles behind us. It was night. Rain was falling. We still had at least thirty miles to go before we got in range of the rebels.

"Here," he said.

As if on cosmic cue, the sky cracked open. Musa looked at the driver, the driver nodded to Musa, and Musa bent down and grabbed the black plastic bag between his feet—his luggage. Musa had no way of knowing, none of us did—though we should have—but that at that moment he was enjoying the last hours of his liberty, thanks to us.

He opened his door and stepped out into a blast of rain.

"Let's go," he said.

We filed out, heads down, lightning marking the path in bursts. Musa was in the lead. Then Courtenay, who had just been given a new video camera and had helped me plot out this trip. Then me. Then Vanessa, a friend who lived in Uganda and came with us to shoot photographs. We hiked all night. Sometime around dawn, Musa allowed us to collapse under a thorn tree for a few hours of hard, greasy, dreamless sleep. Then we continued—for how long, I don't know; I stopped taking notes.

"Where the hell is this guy taking us?" Vanessa grumbled.

"I don't know, but he seems to know where he's going," said Courtenay.

After a few more steps, she shot me a look and said, loud enough for only me to hear, "I hope you know what you're doing."

The rain and clouds finally moved on. We arrived at the hilltop base late in the day. After Commander Peacock finished with his afternoon prayers, he walked us around and introduced us to the other fighters: Lion, Radio, Fearless, Soft Hair, Hero, Big Head, even one woman with chipped plum nail polish, a cheap plastic ring, a shy smile, and a fully loaded AK-47 whose nom de guerre was the Victim. The Victim and most of the other rebels didn't speak much English. As Peacock and the rest of us talked about the coming weeks, what we'd eat, where we'd go, what might happen, the other fighters stood quietly around, staring at us. What was unfolding was rare for both sides. All the rebels were of nomad stock, people who had been drifting across this land practically since Moses was fished out of the bulrushes, and we were the first team of Western journalists to visit. Whether it was asking where to use the bathroom or which hole to sleep in at night or showing them pictures on my laptop, every exchange felt like first contact. Both sides appreciated this and were more gracious for it.

Peacock never seemed annoyed or exasperated by his dual roles of rebel tactician and *mzungu* babysitter. He was always sharing things with us, in English broken but clear, bits of history, weather observations, rebel facts. He explained that his area of operations was a hundred thousand square miles—"Ten times bigger than Belgium!"—and that the rebels rarely spent more than one night in the same place. He showed us how to pluck little brown berries off the thornbushes, peel off the skin, and pop them into our mouths. "Ogaden chocolate," he said, smirking. It tasted nothing like chocolate.

As we walked, he constantly asked how we were doing: "Mista Jifri, how is your condition?" He schooled us in taking cover, should the Ethiopians attack, and how careful we had to be with rations. Being a rebel is like being in a national army, only with less food—often none. That afternoon I gestured to Manchoos, the cook, to refill my cup of camel milk tea (I was starving), and just as Manchoos bent down to lift the pot from the fire with his bare hands, Peacock appeared.

"Mista Jifri," he gently chided, like a patient camp counselor. "You know rule. One cup, nothing more, nothing less."

At that moment, looking at his yellow-toothed grin and that flicker of amusement in his eyes, I thought: Who the hell does Peacock remind me of? The gravelly voice, tired beyond its years, those amused eyes, the way he walked, slightly awkwardly, like his feet were too big. I spent the rest of the morning stumbling around in a hunger daze, racking my brain for Peacock's doppelgänger.

Peacock liked nothing more than to talk about the Front. Its full name was the Ogaden National Liberation Front, formed about twenty years ago, a descendant of Somali rebel groups that have been running around this desert for decades, unhappy that a region that ethnically was nearly 100 percent Somali had been tacked onto Ethiopia like an ill-fitting addition on an old house. Ethiopia is one of the most repressive nations in the world. The government, which is dominated by a small but powerful ethnic group from the north, has been systematically squashing dissent, closing down the last free newspapers, persecuting the last peaceful opposition political groups and marginalizing the peripheries like the Ogaden. Peacock and the other rebels felt the only way they could pressure their government was to attack it. "If we want development," Peacock said, "we need hurt them."

But Ogadeni civilians were the ones most hurt. While the Front occasionally scored a hit on a convoy or remote police post, the government's counterinsurgency measures were merciless and total. The entire population was paying a heavy price for the rebellion. Uniformed troops razed villages and slaughtered innocents. They threw a tight cordon around the desert, blocking commercial traffic and pushing millions of people to the edge of starvation. I got the sense, without one word in this direction ever being spoken, that the rebels themselves wondered how long they could hold on. They were desperate to bring some attention to their cause, which barely registered on the scales of Africa's wars, with much bigger conflicts continuing to burn in Darfur, Somalia, and Congo. That's why Peacock and Co. were eager to host us and why we were here.

When I asked the predictable question of what it felt like to kill people, Peacock seemed neither regretful nor proud nor even annoyed. "They shoot, we shoot, then you find bodies," he said quietly. "You never know which bullet." He seemed to be making a bigger point. Death, like most things for the Front, was a team sport.

Sometimes Peacock reached into the chest pocket of his fatigues and produced a child's exercise book lovingly draped in plastic. He carefully unwrapped it and read off the Front's precepts.

Rule No. 7 was my favorite: "The capital's in the bush and it keeps moving."

We walked ten to twenty miles at a stretch, shifting from camp to camp. By the fifth day, I was hobbling. The skin on the bottom of several toes had been torn off, making each of the first steps in the morning so painful I grew nauseous. Courtenay had essentially stopped eating—she was always too spent by evening to dive into the slimy strings of goat meat we received as a ration. We were always thirsty, and all we had to drink from were mud puddles and the rare stagnant stream. Of course we had forgotten purification tablets. So we just downed that water, as thick as blood, and hoped for the best. I once saw something small and dark swimming in the bottom of my bottle. The rebels traveled with a solar panel but it was very difficult using it to recharge our computers or camera batteries, nor did we really know how many days we would be out here. This meant we had to be vigilant each time we turned on one of our devices, adding to the stress.

When Vanessa got her period, I looked over to see her crying behind a thorn tree.

"Look, my pants, there's blood all over them."

Courtenay ran over to help. "Just sit on the ground and rub your butt in the dirt," she said.

It worked, covering up the bloodstains. But still, Vanessa was inconsolable. "Don't these guys ever drink?" she mumbled, sending Courtenay storming over to me. That's when she blew up about the water, though I knew it wasn't really about the water.

The next morning, two young fighters were staring at us, murmuring to each other.

At my first opportunity with Peacock alone, I asked him what they had been saying. He shook his head and kept walking. He had his AK slung over his shoulders behind his neck, hands over each end, like a man in a stock.

"Peacock . . ."

He was smiling so hard I could see his black gums.

"They said: 'Maybe Courtenay will love Jeffrey today.'"

The cheating revelations were still fresh. Courtenay may have still loved me, but she definitely didn't like me. Many days it seemed she felt simply stuck with me. She told me that she didn't like looking at old pictures of us anymore, that that was "cheating Jeffrey," which made me realize how my idea of "coming clean" had always been dumb. You can never come clean. There is no net cleaning. By removing your burden, you simply make someone else feel horrible. You always wash the spears in someone else's blood. I have few regrets in life, but here I wished I could redo everything. But I couldn't, which left me simply hoping that that clumsy, hurtful time would slip deeper into a softly entombed past, like the tracks we left behind in the desert that the evening winds gently erased.

◇◇◇◇◇◇◇

Ogadenis are some of the last true nomads. We saw entire families on the move—men slowly walking behind camels, little children bobbing on top, women clucking at goats, everyone and everything chasing the green grass that recedes southward with the rains and spells a continuation of existence.

We passed few towns or villages. I didn't see a single school, the legacy of decades of marginalization. Occasionally we glimpsed far ahead in the wavering distance a huddle of gumdrop-shaped shelters: a nomadic camp. As we tromped by, everyone would come out to look at us, and we'd see the whole camp lined up, one sunken cheekbone to the next. The nomads often dragged out a sack of rice or a scrawny goat whose throat would soon be slit, halal style, by an eager bayonet.

A woman sat on a log in front of us. Anab was her name. She wore a cover-up of bright colors; there were scars on her hands. As Courtenay clipped a mic to Anab's chest and then set up her camera, Anab looked at her the way many women in this region did, with this far-off, contemplative mix of trust and curiosity, intrigued by a white woman who moved so easily through the world, unveiled and among men, a glimpse of an emancipated life.

"They will kill me if they knew I was talking to you," Anab finally said.

"Who will kill you? What happened?" Courtenay asked.

Anab looked down at the pebbly sand where the tripod's legs rested.

"The Ethiopians came to our camp one night . . ."

They singled out several young girls, calling them rebel spies, which was just a pretext. The soldiers marched the girls back to their base. They fondled them roughly, then tore off their clothes. They took turns.

As Anab finished the story, her eyes went lifeless and blank.

A group of older men stood under a tree, waiting to speak to us. Each had a slightly different story that, taken by itself, might have seemed an exaggeration. But when there is enough harmony in the atrocities, you begin to believe them. The Ethiopian soldiers had slit the throats of their sons, burned down their villages, poured poison into their wells. They told us many of their friends had been publicly hanged and that the bodies of men they knew and loved were left up for days, desiccated and shriveled by the sun.

"The only people who are free are them," said one old man, pointing to the rebels. "They live or die happily."

The old man was among the thinnest, veins in his temples, face skeletal. As he finished, Peacock grabbed his wrist, which looked as if it could break as easily as a dried stick, and they walked off together to talk under the tree. When Peacock came back, he rubbed his face.

"He my dad."

In all of our conversations, Peacock had never mentioned his father. All he had told us about his background was that as a teenager the elders had sent him to attend a secret guerilla training camp in Eritrea, where Arabs, Darfurians, South Sudanese, and members of dozens of other African rebel groups hid out from their various governments. Peacock embarked on a degree in what can only be called Rebelogy. He took courses in sabotage, ambush, explosives, asset acquisition, and how to surf the Internet. Still, I don't know how he capped his anger, aware that while he was diligently applying his training, his family was being wiped out. He said his friends gave him the name Peacock because he seemed proud.

By the ninth day, our numbers had swelled. Our group was now close to eighty, and hardly inconspicuous. Most were young, thin, and quiet, equipped with an AK, a couple clips, and a plastic recycled vegetable oil bottle for water. As we marched along a riverbed, clouds of thin vapory powder rose from our shoes. Suddenly dozens more men emerged from the trees; they had been extremely well concealed. They rushed to us and exchanged long birdsong greetings, a flurry of excited Somali, lots of "Haa! Haa!"—*yes! yes!*—hugging each other with all their strength, eyes closed.

"Peacock," I asked. "How the hell did these guys know we were coming?"

Peacock flashed me a sly grin.

"We had appointment."

That night we got as close to rebel happy hour as we ever would. Manchoos boiled up a vast pot of rice, just enough for everyone. Peacock produced an old transistor radio and tuned in to Freedom Radio, the rebels' propaganda station. Another commander—the Professor, we called him, because he wore glasses—made a run into a nearby village, returning with a bulging black plastic bag and a naughty smile. Soon the entire rebel army was sitting in the sand, AK-47s and grenade launchers in their laps, sucking lollipops.

"Mista Jifri, how is your condition?" Peacock asked.

"Good, good."

"The men good too," he said, easing down next to me.

It felt oddly comforting to have so many armed men around. And it was a beautiful night, with a perfectly clear black moonless sky, so open and dark we could see stars all the way down to the horizon. We all were so contentedly fatigued, savoring being off our feet, enjoying the slight dip in temperature that dried the sweat on our faces. But Satir, one of the nobler-looking rebels, with a long aquiline nose and coppery skin, insisted on a dance. Everyone rose. The soldiers formed two lines facing each other and locked arms, slowly rocking back and forth to some deeply seated rhythm known to them alone. They picked up the pace, stomping the ground in their old cracked boots. The lyrics soon morphed into a deep, guttural, grunting sound, dozens of fighters lined up, arms linked, heads close together, *unn-uh, unn-uh!*—this loud, heavy, dramatic breathing done in perfect sync, communication by lung and heart. I was about to join in, but Courtenay, who was filming, said, "Don't. You're going to ruin the shot." She was probably right.

Part of me wanted to stay with the rebels for longer, my feet finally toughening up. But I knew we had our story, and when we were all gathered by a river, a long-awaited wide river that flowed swiftly from the spring rains and that we kneeled next to and drank from like it was Gatorade, I told Peacock that the three of us needed to go. Peacock didn't try to dissuade me.

I remember that parting well: we drove off in a shuddering dump truck, Peacock went back to the desert. I just hoped he wouldn't die in a few days.

◇◇◇◇◇◇◇

"Seet," the Ethiopian colonel said. It was an order, not an invitation. "Now, tell us, where are the terrorists?"

Courtenay, Vanessa, and I shot nervous glances at each other. We were locked in a room on an Ethiopian infantry base near Degehabur. Outside sat huge trucks, artillery guns, and tents with camouflage netting stretched over them. We had no time to get our stories straight. We hadn't said a word to each other in the truck over here.

"Sir," I began, "we are journalists. We have all the proper papers. You can call the foreign ministry in Addis and give them our names, and they will let you know who we are."

"American?" the colonel asked.

"Yes."

"Show me passports."

I eagerly fished mine out of my pocket. Courtenay and Vanessa did likewise. I handed all three to the colonel, who closed his fingers around them and thrust them in his pocket. It was the classic Kilimanjaro trick. Fifteen years had passed, and I still fell for it.

"You in detention," he said.

"What?"

"Dee-ten-shun," he cackled. "Pree-zon. Jay-oh. No go home."

"Wait," I said, feeling out the confrontational approach. "This is . . . is. . . . ridiculous. You can't . . . do this. We have a right to call the American embassy."

"You," the colonel stepped toward me. "Shut up."

He eyed me suspiciously, but for whatever reason he nourished a special hatred for Vanessa.

"I need to go to the bathroom," she said after what felt like hours of heavy silence.

"No." He glared.

Vanessa glared back. She had lived by herself in Uganda for years and seen it all, including watching a girl in a refugee camp throw up a three-foot-long worm—live. She wasn't used to taking any crap.

She stood.

"SEET!" the colonel yelled, rushing toward her and grabbing her shoulders.

"Get your fucking hands off me!" she shouted.

The colonel pushed her to the ground.

The soldiers stripped us of our phones, our computers, our cameras, our notebooks, our backpacks, our money, our pens, and even the scraps of paper in our pockets. They took everything, down to our toothbrushes. They split us up, taking me outside, across the base, to an open field of little white stones. I could hear a crisp but faint steady sound. Was that the same river where we had said good-bye to Peacock? The soldiers sat me on the ground, rifle barrels swinging in my face. By now, it was very dark.

"Tell us about the terrorists," the colonel said. "Talk."

"I'm a journalist, that's all there is to it. I'm not saying any more."

"We can do whatever we want with you," the colonel said. "Nobody knows you're here."

They left me sitting in the empty field for hours. My body grew cold. My feet numb. In the middle of the night, they marched me back to the office. Courtenay burst into tears.

"They took me out too. And when I got back and didn't see you, I thought, I thought . . ."

I hugged her tightly, burying my mouth in her hair. When you really fear for the integrity of your body and your life, really picture a rifle butt crushing the bridge of your nose or a high-velocity bullet blowing a grapefruit-size hole through your back, physical sensations take on new meaning. I wanted to drown myself in her deep, warm, brown hair.

◇◇◇◇◇◇◇

New York had no idea where we were. They didn't know if we had been kidnapped, killed, or got lost wandering in the desert. The irony was that before we set off, we were worried about the rebels. Not once did I worry about our faithful ally, the Ethiopians.

We were kept in a small room near the colonel's office. By day three, it began to smell of our unwashed bodies. There was one small window, and through it I stared at an endless column of trucks arriving. Each was packed with dozens of Ethiopian commandos wearing black ski masks. One after another, the trucks pulled up and the men swung their legs over the sides and poured out, seeping across that base like a thick, dark liquid.

I started to feel sick. There was no way I could deny it to myself anymore. We were stoking this war; we were altering its course. The commandos were starting from where we had been arrested and working backward. We had inadvertently tipped them off to where the rebel army was hiding. With a flash of panic, I suddenly remembered: The notebook! They took my notebook!

What was going to happen to Musa the messenger? Anab the rape victim? Peacock's dad? My eyes darted to Courtenay, sitting languidly on the floor. Why was I so careless with the things of value? I smacked my hand flat against the wall. I should have typed everything up, e-mailed the notes to myself via the BGAN, deleted the files while I was in the bush with the last of my battery power, and burned the notebook in the campfire. Instead I had left detailed instructions of how to hunt down the entire underground network of people who had just helped me.

The next day they packed us into a pickup truck. We were driven across the desert to another army base several hundred miles away. Plainclothes agents insisted on searching our computers. These men were professionals. They spoke perfect English, all the scarier because of it.

"Turn on your machine," one said. "If you try to erase anything, I'm going to really fuck you up."

I was sitting on the floor—they always had us sitting on the floor. I reluctantly pressed power. The agent smiled.

"Screen saver password?"

Early the next morning they put us in yet another truck, which stopped at a small commercial airport in the town of Dire Dawa, a place where Arthur Rimbaud once lived, running guns to the emperor.

"We're flying you to Addis," one of the agents said. "You might be charged."

"With what?"

"Aiding terrorists."

"At least can we call the embassy?"

"Shut up."

I walked into the airport in a daze. I ran my tongue along my fuzzy front teeth, I hadn't brushed in nearly a week. I looked around the drab terminal and was surprised to see across the room a white face. He must have been around forty-five or fifty, tallish, wearing zip-off pants, a mesh vest, and a big floppy hat, with a small camera around his neck. He looked like a guy from the Midwest all suited up for his first foray into the wilds of Africa: not exactly the most confidence-inducing outfit, but he was our last hope. I just needed to get word to him of what was happening. He could surely place a call, get through to someone who could get through to someone who could get through to Bill Keller, the American government— freedom. He couldn't have been more than thirty feet away, but we were surrounded by agents.

Vanessa tapped one on the shoulder: "It's that time of month," she said with a sugary smile. "I need bathroom." The agents waved her off, annoyed, toward the toilets on the other side of the room. I watched her carefully, gauging the distance, praying the floppy-hatted man wouldn't move. Right before she dipped into the ladies', she passed within two feet of him. Had she said something to him? I couldn't tell.

A few minutes later, the boarding announcement was made. Right before we stepped out the door, the man in the floppy hat surreptitiously angled his camera at us from across the room, and I saw his finger press down. It was a genius move. Now he had proof.

As we stepped onto the plane, I whispered to Vanessa, "What'd you say to that guy?"

She glanced left, then right, made sure no one could hear.

"I said as fast as I could: We're-three-NewYorkTimes-journalists-being-secretly-detained-call-the-US-embassy."

All the stewardesses were in on our detention. Ethiopian Airlines is government-owned, after all. They split us up, Courtenay sitting in a different row. When we landed in Addis, the capital, everyone else stood up in the aisle, mindlessly grabbing their bags from the overhead bins and shuffling out through the door to wherever they were going, free men and free women.

I rested my head against the Plexiglas window. I watched the man in the floppy hat disembark with the stream of other passengers. He was walking nice and fast, but not too fast. He was maybe a hundred yards away from the terminal, then seventy-five, then fifty . . .

Just as he was about to make it, two Ethiopian men in suits stopped him on the tarmac. His back immediately stiffened. The spit in my mouth dried up. Now they were going to arrest *him*?

He was marched away from the terminal, toward a small building with tinted glass doors.

The black glass doors seemed to magically open.

The man in the floppy hat disappeared.

◇◇◇◇◇◇◇

The prison was a secret site, an unmarked building down a crowded side street. I couldn't pinpoint where—Addis had changed dramatically since I had lived here, the streets now had been named, and glass-fronted shops had replaced the colonies of cardboard boxes where I had conducted the first interviews of my life. The gate slammed shut behind us. Heavily armed federal officers ordered us into a small room. They dumped our bags on the floor and fastidiously separated our electronics gear from our clothes, logging everything into a big book. We were booked. They even took my shoelaces. Courtenay and Vanessa were marched off with assault rifles at their backs. My last view of Courtenay was this placid expression on her face, as if she were sleepwalking.

My cell was dark, clammy, cold, and smelled like someone else's nervous funk. I kept thinking of that woman Anab who had been raped, the deadness that overtook her eyes. I paced the cell and punched the air, I even got down on the floor and did some push-ups—exercise can take your mind off things because it's one of two activities that doesn't involve any thought. But this time it didn't help, it was an illusion. I wanted to scream. Why had I been so stupid? The Ethiopians could do anything they wanted—try us, imprison us, keep Courtenay and me separated for years until we grew gray and old and lifeless. There was only one fact that mattered now. We were on their soil.

Night came. So did morning. A surly guard brought me a plastic plate of macaroni crawling with fleas. I ate the whole thing, pulling dead insects off my tongue.

When he came back around lunchtime, the guard stood at the door, empty-handed. He beckoned me out. I walked into the yard, blinking. I followed him through several courtyards, into another building, up a flight of stairs, and down a long hallway. He stepped through a doorway and motioned for me to follow. I was confused. We were in an office. Courtenay was sitting there, Vanessa was sitting there, a foreign ministry official I recognized from a previous story was sitting there, but still, there were armed guards posted at the door.

"Seet, Jeffrey, seet," the foreign ministry official said. I cautiously lowered myself into a chair next to Courtenay. I wanted to wrap my arms around her and ask, Are you okay? What happened to you? Did they do anything to you?—but all I could muster was "What is going on?" She looked okay, her face a bit mud-streaked, probably like mine—we hadn't seen a mirror for three weeks—but she didn't look scared. The foreign ministry official started to mutter something that resembled an apology, and the instant I sensed this was coming to an end, all my pent-up emotions, terror, relief, fury, regret, and despair, exploded. "You, you"—I couldn't even find the words— "don't you know we were just journalists trying to do our job!" My voice was cracking. I was shaking. Courtenay looked at me, worried. The official from the ministry slunk down in his chair. The guards at the door stepped closer. "Calm down, Jeffrey, calm down," the foreign ministry official said. "No!" I shouted back. "You calm down!"

"*Ten days* are words, but I experienced them as a prolonged dark age of despair." That's what the Egyptian political prisoner and poet Muhammad Afifi Matar wrote about his experience in a secret prison, and I felt the same way—though of course his age of despair was darker and a few days longer. The point is, a week in captivity is manageable if and only if you know it's going to be a week. But you don't. I spent every waking minute, hour after hour, day after day, terrified that I'd spend the rest of my life in an Ethiopian prison and never see Courtenay again.

They kept all of our electronic gear and notebooks, but they let us take back our moldering, salt-streaked clothes. At the prison's checkout desk, one of the guards pawing through our stuff held up a somewhat dense bag, Courtenay's signature gallon-size Ziploc packed with socks. He paused over it, feeling its weight. "Oh, that's nothing, just dirty clothes," Courtenay said offhandedly. "You can just throw it in with the other stuff." He did just that. Hidden inside that bouquet of smelly socks were the videotapes from the entire trip. That is when you know you have a winner. My wife outfoxed the Ethiopians, and we used those tapes to reconstruct everything. Courtenay's quick thinking saved the whole ordeal from being a total waste. When the story landed the following month, Courtenay's image of Satir and other members of the Front lined up with their guns, about to go on maneuver, ran four columns on the front page, above the fold. Her name was on the photo caption, mine on the story.

As soon as we stepped outside, I turned to Courtenay. "Are you okay?" There were tears in my eyes. Hers too. She nodded. The foreign ministry official was standing there, and so were the guards, so we didn't do more than squeeze each other's hands. Courtenay, Vanessa, and I then smushed into the backseat of the foreign ministry official's car and headed for the American embassy, a sprawling piece of property on a hillside forested with tall, straight eucalyptus trees. As we stepped out of his car, the foreign ministry official said, "Ato"—sir—"Jeffrey, please don't hold this against us. You're welcome back, anytime."

"Yeah, right," I said, and slammed the door as hard as I could.

The embassy had been instrumental in our release, and I'm sure it hadn't been easy—the American government tends to tiptoe around the Ethiopians, its friend in the volatile Horn, its Christian buddy in that sea of wild Muslims, as many see it. The United States has been lamely quiet about massacres, disappearances, and other human rights abuse inside Ethiopia, especially after Ethiopia allowed the CIA and Pentagon to fly drones from its territory.

The *Times* had contacted the State Department in Washington the day after we went missing, and Main State then contacted Addis, though that had been unnecessary. So had the valiant efforts of that concerned stranger, the man in the floppy hat. The Ethiopians had let him go after a couple of hours, minus his camera, I later learned, and he rushed to the embassy and informed them what was going on. But the embassy already knew. Everybody knew. Someone, perhaps several people, nomad spies, no doubt, had spotted us slipping off into the gravelly hills that first night. The Ethiopian military, the American military, and an unnamed "American government agency," I was told, had been tracking our movements, relaying the information back to Addis. The American government has always said that it provided training and intelligence to Ethiopian soldiers only to combat Islamists in the Horn, not to kill their own people, but the CIA's role in the Ogaden has never been made clear. "The minute you guys walked off into the desert," the American ambassador told me, "the whole Ogaden lit up." My dad had gotten that second call from Bill Keller.

The ambassador took us into his personal residence. He looked at us with parental concern, as if maybe we shouldn't be left alone or something else bad might happen. He insisted we spend the night, and his staff whipped up a meal of steak, salad, fresh bread, and cold beer, and after two weeks of goat seasoned with sand grains, washed down with a mud puddle, the word *amazing* comes up short. The ambassador told us that the Ethiopians were paranoid about the rebels and paranoid about journalists and that we had been very close to being tried in a military court, which would have meant years in prison. They thought we were spies collecting intelligence. "The prime minister's office," the ambassador said, "first denied that you guys were even being held." Eventually the ambassador succeeded in rescuing us from the clutches of our ally. Apparently the Ethiopians felt that by holding us incommunicado for a week and taking all of our equipment, they had made their point.

As we stuffed bread and beef into our faces, the ambassador and a young, clean-cut American wearing a Rolex who was introduced to us as a "political officer"—often the cover for a CIA agent—asked us questions. How many rebels had we seen? Where were they going? Who was the commander? Do we remember the name of the big river? Afterward—we didn't reveal much—we retreated to a back bedroom where Courtenay and I washed up. She emerged from the shower, skinny, sunburned, arms streaked with red scratches from the miles of thornbushes we had walked through. For the first moment in weeks, it was just she and I.

The two of us stood in that well-appointed guest room, by a tall window covered in long, white drapes, free as the kids we used to be. It felt like that for a second. But as we stood there, and I swept her up in all her soap-smelling nakedness, it felt different. We weren't kids anymore, and this wasn't Ithaca. We had fought and lived apart and survived. We had moved continents and survived. We had been kidnapped by an officially recognized government and survived.

As I stood hugging her naked, the skin of her back so smooth under my hands, I was just hoping we could survive the damage I had done. We were different now, and there was nothing I could do to take it back. I buried my face in her neck, thinking: This is all I need, my freedom and you. Take everything else from me. It doesn't matter.

THIRTEEN

◇◇◇◇◇◇◇

NAIROBI, 2007

"Hello, ladies and gentlemen. Your first officer speaking. We are now entering Kenyan airspace. There's a really nice view of Kilimanjaro out the left side of the aircraft. It's about twenty-five degrees Celsius in Nairobi, wind blowing in from the east. A few scattered clouds . . ."

Whenever we returned from a country like Ethiopia, I felt a silly flood of happiness simply landing at Jomo Kenyatta International Airport. I felt relatively safe here, I felt rooted, I could communicate, I was beginning to know my way around. As an old-hand expat in Nairobi had told us in the early days, "After you go to some of the places you're going to go, you'll get back to Nairobi and think it's Paris." We walked off the tarmac in a neat line led by a Kenya Airways attendant. The air always felt fabulous. At 5,500 feet above sea level and one degree south of the equator, Nairobi has the dreamiest climate in the world. It's the only place I've ever lived where even the nicest homes don't have heating or air conditioning—you don't need it. Nine days out of ten, the air outside is room temperature. On the drive back from the airport, I'd roll down the windows to feel it on my face and my bare arms. When I got home, there was always at least one window open somewhere, a trickle of breeze stirring the curtains, a breath of the outside, inside.

I hadn't been paying much attention to the news in Kenya. As a foreign correspondent, that was the dearest compliment I could pay it. Our first year in East Africa passed with trips to and from Somalia, Ethiopia, Darfur, Burundi, southern Sudan, northern Uganda, eastern Democratic Republic of Congo, all the hot spots. In Nairobi, there wasn't much going on, except for some guys on TV talking about the next election and rumors that KFC was coming.

Mid-December is what I call the shiny season, when Kenya is most heartbreakingly beautiful. The rains have just finished, and everything is green and lush. The light is bright and clear. The scent of jasmine is never far away and the air tastes so pleasant you want to drink it. I was standing in the *Times* bureau, admiring how the sunshine beamed off the polished parquet floors, when Courtenay called.

"There's two lines," she said.

I didn't know what to say back.

"The second's faint, but it's definitely there."

I clutched the phone.

"Okay, okay. I'll be home as soon as I can. Just finishing up three hundred words on the Shabaab taking another town. Give me twenty minutes."

In the ideal version of my life, I tell myself that the night of conception was during one of those sultry power outages we kept having in November. The electricity would suddenly cut out, but we wouldn't bother to light a candle and the two of us would move toward each other in the dark, the only sound outside the curtains of rain washing through the banana trees. That kind of rain closed off the rest of the world.

I banged out my Shabaab dispatch, locked up the bureau, jogged out to the truck, and sped away. When I got home, Courtenay came out and we sat on the porch, by the outdoor fireplace, and propped up our feet on the coffee table, legs straight, so Rudy, an old Lab we'd adopted who was so fat we called him the Black Tube of Fur, could waddle under the little bridge we formed and rub his back on the bottom of our legs. We used to joke that the Black Tube of Fur—who was about seventy-five in human years—was our son, but now we would have a real child.

"I guess we should start thinking of names."

"Already?"

"Yeah, why not."

"What about Rocky?"

She didn't even deign to answer.

Somewhere in the swirl of happiness, relief, and terror about impending fatherhood, I allowed myself a moment to stand back and see this for what it was: We were going to start a family in East Africa. Kenya had made my friend Dan who he was, and I'd always envied him for growing up here, for exploring this place with the singular curiosity of youth. But the longer I lived here, the more I began to accept that I might never truly belong. I loved it more than I even anticipated, but I was always slightly off balance, self-conscious, constantly making comparisons between here and home. For Baby Gettleman, it would be wonderfully different. He or she wouldn't be burdened by that. Here would be home.

A few days after the pregnancy test, the 2.16 of us headed down the escarpment of the Rift Valley to Suswa, a small town in the shadow of a volcano. We still had time to cover a few more stories together. Suswa was the site of one of the last major rallies before Kenya's presidential election, and as we exited the car, we were swallowed by a sea of red. This was the heart of Maasailand, and thousands of Maasai were gathered in a field, most of them wearing a *shuka*, a bolt of red cloth draped over the shoulder like a toga, a lot of the men giddy from a home brew called "Ups," made from roots, herbs, and honey. I had no need for the stuff; I was feeling pretty Ups already.

"Wanakuja! Wanakuja!" someone yelled out. *They're coming, they're coming!* Three helicopters began to drop slowly, like spiders on a string, politicians inside, clouds of dust boiling up from the earth. The Maasai squinched their hooded Nilotic eyes shut and yelled even louder. Five thousand *rungus*—traditional gnarled wood clubs—shot up. From their *shukas*, some men even produced Nokias and started taking photos.

Another old hand, an elegant woman named Dodo—old hands love to inflict their wisdom on the young and innocent—had told us upon our arrival, "It's a little late in the day for Africa." But it wasn't a little late in the day for Africa. We had arrived at the perfect time. We were witnessing the fusion of the old and the new.

The scene reminded me of the time when Courtenay and I visited Brazzaville, capital of the Republic of Congo, the lesser known and usually less murderous neighbor of the Democratic Republic of Congo. We watched two women walk down one of Brazzaville's main avenues with briefcases balanced perfectly on their heads. At the entrance to a glass office building they stopped, pulled the briefcases off their heads, and walked right in. Tradition and modernity coexist in Africa, just like anywhere else. It might look like a contradiction, a conflict, a clash, but it's not. That's what was so interesting about Kenya. It was more modern and more traditional than so many other African countries. What other place had helicopters and *rungus*, sushi and *shukas*, just as we *mzungus* liked it?

Kenya's politics held the same tensions, the coexistence of the old brand of tribalism with the relatively new demands of democracy. This election was going to be the first competitive race in Kenyan history between two heavyweights from rival ethnic groups— Mwai Kibaki, a Kikuyu and the incumbent president, who had been in politics since independence, versus Raila Odinga, a rich Luo and leader of the political opposition, who positioned himself as a champion of the poor, driving a candy-apple-red Hummer through the shantytowns. Odinga's opposition party, which had hired American-educated consultants, was leading the polls, paving the way for a peaceful transfer of power, extremely rare on the continent. But this was Kenya, after all.

◇◇◇◇◇◇◇

December 27, 2007. Dawn. Mostly clear skies. Courtenay was six weeks pregnant and not feeling so hot, so I set off to the polls by myself. I staked out the entrance of a school, press pass dangling around my neck, bugging voters with all the obvious election-day-in-Africa questions—Who are you going to scratch your X next to? What does today mean to you? Do you think there's going to be trouble? It's hard to rebel against stereotypes when you have two hours and four hundred words to play with.

The lines were nearly a mile long—young women jiggling babies to keep them from crying, older women with field scarves tied around their heads, suited professionals, septuagenarians, young muscular men with tilted ball caps looking almost too cool and self-possessed to wait in line for anything. Everyone faced forward. The lines advanced slowly. There were no snacks, no water, little shade, and a rising sun. I wasn't feeling especially neutral, witnessing this. I got a lump in my throat just scribbling notes. This wasn't America, where it usually takes no more than fifteen minutes to vote, and many of us don't even bother.

Around dusk my phone rang.

"Where are you?"

"Kibera," I said—Nairobi's biggest slum. I could hear anxiety in her voice. "Something wrong?"

"I'm . . ."

"What? Can't hear you. It's crowded as hell in here."

"I'm blee—"

"Say again, sweetie, say louder."

"Did you hear? Bleeding."

At that very moment I was watching two young men trying to squeeze through a window in the school, braving the lashes of police officers, that eager to vote.

"When can you get home?"

We sat quietly on the couch, Courtenay trying to sip a bowl of soup, light-headed from the blood loss. She grimaced as each wave of pressure shuddered across her midsection. I stroked her hair, brushing it back from her forehead. She was losing the baby.

Neither of us voiced the question we were both thinking as we stared at the election numbers on the screen. Had we waited too long? Was this the cost of my taking thirty-five years to figure out which way was up? "There is always a cost," a Save the Children accountant in Ethiopia used to say. I thought he was just talking dollars and cents, but now I got it. I had begun to sense it when, a few weeks earlier, we had been sitting in the doctor's office, giddy with our new station in life, and the doctor casually let slip the term "geriatric pregnancy." That wiped the smiles right off our faces.

When you really want to have a child, you allow yourself moments of intense, self-indulgent despair contemplating a future without one. If you're struggling to reproduce *and* living in Africa, that despair is especially acute. There are babies everywhere, slurping Fanta in the back of buses, strapped to the backs of their mothers hoeing fields, waving to you from the side of the road, babies carrying babies. Africa is the most fertile continent. Even with increased access to contraception, Kenyan women still average four children, Ethiopian women five, Somalis six, Nigeriens seven. Courtenay and I were desperate to make just one.

I fried up some grilled cheese and sawed off the crusts. She didn't touch it.

"I need that antibody shot," she mumbled. Courtenay's the rare Rh-negative. The mixing of blood could be very harmful. But nobody was picking up the phone at her doctor's office. The entire nation was frozen. Offices were closed, stores were closed, schools were closed, everyone was gathered at home, glued to their TV or radio set, the highways as clear as runways in the bush. Elections are anxious in most of Africa, even in Kenya. They are not just a race. They are a test. The key question is never who wins. It's whether the loser accepts.

◇◇◇◇◇◇

"This is weird," Courtenay said, when I came downstairs the next morning and found her curled up in front of the TV. "Last night Raila was up by a million votes. Now it's a dead heat."

"Is it okay if I go?"

"You should. And let me know what's happening."

I rushed downtown to election headquarters, located in one of Nairobi's high-rises. The tallying center gave off a bad sweat. Hundreds of people were squeezed into a low-ceilinged room, the size of maybe four classrooms. Election observers shook bundles of paper, opposition leaders pleaded with election commissioners to stop counting the votes and investigate the growing allegations of fraud, the commissioners sat impassively on a podium, the chairman cleaning his glasses. Riot police began to assemble outside, dressed like mutant Ninja turtles in green padded vests and black helmets. I could hear their plastic shields knocking into each other as they formed into lines.

"The press have the figures, we have the figures!" shouted William Ruto, a young opposition politician. "They're just changing ones to fours, sixes to eights!"

The opposition couldn't believe what the government was trying to do. It was massive rigging, in the open, slow-motion theft. The president's men couldn't stuff ballot boxes—you can't do that in Kenya—so they were simply topping up the vote tallying sheets as those sheets were transported from rural polling places to Nairobi. Some areas were now being recorded with turnouts of 115 percent. An EU official announced that its own observer had witnessed poll workers in one constituency announce on election night that Kibaki had won 50,145 votes. The total from that same constituency now being entered in the national tally was 75,261. You do that enough, and you can close any gap.

Just before nightfall, the election commissioners announced that they were ready to declare a winner, and it wasn't Odinga. Ruto and other opposition leaders were still holed up in the tallying room, shouting, "Hapana, hapana!" *No, no!* A whistle blew. The Ninja turtles poured in. Batons swung in wide arcs, men in suits scrambled toward the exits, chairs went flying, people screamed. This was a riot—indoors. I leaped back and flattened myself against a wall as the election chairman made a hurried exit, a crowd chasing him, yelling: "We want justice! Kenya has spoken!"

Odinga declared the election a fraud, which it was, and Kibaki rushed his swearing-in. An hour after the last "votes" were "counted," he stood stiffly in the backyard of the State House, his right hand on a Bible, his cold, dry lips muttering the oath of office. Within minutes, thousands of young men poured out of shantytowns across Kenya, waving sticks, smashing shacks, burning property, screaming, "No Raila, no peace!"

The next day was New Year's Eve. At 9:00 p.m., when I should have been two hundred miles up-country, I was straightening the bow tie on my tux. Courtenay was next to me, in a long, flowing evening gown. The election had been a miscarriage of justice, but we were fighting off the depression of our own loss, and figured the New Year's Ball at the Muthaiga Club would be a welcome distraction. The Muthaiga Club was the old settlers' joint, a place where the first Lord Delamere used to chip golf balls on the roof and where, in the film version of *Out of Africa*, Meryl Streep makes a dramatic appearance in the men-only bar. Not far away from the bar (still men only) was the club's resident lion, shot dead in 1905, his mangy head imprisoned in a large glass box.

The ball was fine: fillet for dinner, brandy snaps for dessert, Village People for music. At the stroke of midnight, red-faced Brits and white Kenyans took to the floor to exchange sloppy kisses and sing their song.

I had to lock myself into a bathroom stall to use my cell phone because this club, like all country clubs, has its own thousand fatwas—no open-toed shoes, no laptops, no exchanging business cards—but the most vigorously enforced was no cell phones. I sat on the toilet. I could smell the ammonium from the urinal cakes and that slightly nutmeggy scent of Imperial Leather soap. I dialed the police spokesman. From my stall, I could hear drunken singing.

"Should old acquaintance be forgot and never brought to mind . . ."

The police spokesman was talking faster than I could write: Coast ten dead, Nyanza twenty-two dead, Western thirty-five dead, Rift fifty dead.

The door swung open, the singing suddenly louder.

"For auld lang syne, my dear, for auld lang syne . . ."

Someone stumbled into the bathroom—I heard the blurt of a zipper, then a blast of piss. "My goodness, am I squiffy!"

Women were being raped. Factories were being attacked. Thousands of people were fleeing, IDPs. The police spokesman could hardly utter the term. "In the history of Kenya," he said—I could hear his voice skip—"we've never had IDPs." He was referring to internally displaced people, which I had seen in Congo, Sudan, Burundi, Uganda, Rwanda, Somalia, just about everywhere else. Some Kikuyus were even fleeing across the international border into Uganda. Uganda? It was the advent of a new creature in Africa: the Kenyan refugee.

"We'll take a cup o' kindness yet for auld lang syne . . ."

◇◇◇◇◇◇◇

On the first day of 2008, Courtenay and I stood on a hilltop overlooking the Kibera slum. Several *mzungu* ambassadors were gathered nearby. From the safety of our perch, we peered down into the flaming shanties, where mountains of tires burned and police in riot gear battled stone-throwing mobs. We coolly discussed how long this might last and how many people might be killed. We might as well have brought picnic baskets and parasols, like the fine ladies of Washington watching the debacle of Bull Run. Courtenay still looked paler than normal but said she felt better.

"The church, Jeff, the church in Eldoret. It sounds like something out of Rwanda. Can you get to the church?"

"Yeah," I told New York. "I can get to the church."

Everybody wanted to get to the church. All the roads into Eldoret, a somewhat soulless town in the middle of the Rift Valley, were barricaded, so the only hope of getting there was by air. I couldn't believe our stroke of fortune: we had scored a small helicopter leaving out of Wilson Airport, the old colonial one, often used by *mzungus* to get to up-country polo matches. The pilot was a guy named Chief, a big, good-looking Kenyan possessed of all the confidence and command presence you'd expect in a guy named Chief. True to role, he wore aviators. I was happily buckling up when Chief turned around from the controls to eyeball the five of us through his mirrored shades.

"Someone's got to—" he yelled over the rotor noise.

"What'd ya say, Chief?" I yelled back.

He held up four fingers.

"Four pax. Four."

"What are you talking about?" I couldn't believe it. "We made a deal."

"Hapana. Too heavy. I can only take four."

There was Robin, on the left side of the aircraft, a small, wiry Australian journalist for the *LA Times* who agreed to pay half, crucial for me not getting fired for profligacy. Next to her sat Anastasia, American, large round face, pushy but talented—she was our freelance shooter, and if I kicked her off, the next time I was in New York the head of our photo department would take out a serrated knife and castrate me. Then there was Tony, a kind, slightly balding, well-liked Kenyan photographer whose agency didn't have much money to contribute, but I felt it would be risky to land in a war zone without a Kenyan. And then there was Courtenay.

"Sweetie . . . ," I mumbled.

Courtenay was wearing an embroidered shirt she had bought in Khartoum and a sun hat with the strap cinched under her chin.

She was sitting next to me, her black zipper pouch stuffed with extra tapes.

Hurt flashed across her eyes.

"Okay," she said softly. "Okay."

She climbed out of the helicopter and stepped into the sunshine. To this day I can still see her trudging back toward the terminal, camera over her shoulder, pants swishing. Tears stung my eyes as Chief adjusted the cyclic. I'd separated them again, Africa and Courtenay. As the skids lifted off the ground and I could feel my stomach rise into my throat, I was filled with self-hate and a familiar sense of shame, the shame of betrayal. Video was the third piece, and if it hadn't been Courtenay holding the camera, I would have asked the video person to leave. But it was Courtenay. I wanted to kick out the windows. What was wrong with me? I knew what was right: to draw a black circle around us and make everything else outside that circle immaterial.

The countryside was striped with burns. Some farmhouses were smashed and smoking, others untouched; there was a pattern down there, I just couldn't figure it out. The Assemblies of God church was still standing, barely, its mud walls blackened, roof gone. As soon as we landed, Chief nodded to me to get out and do my thing. My heart wasn't in it, but I was paying for the chopper by the hour, so I had to work fast. The first person I saw, I pounced on, a disheveled little man sitting blank-eyed on the ground, twirling a blade of grass between his fingers.

"Habari yako, ndugu yangu?" *How are you, my brother?*

"Mzuri," he mumbled reflexively, *Fine*, the invariable Swahili response. His name was Daniel, a Kikuyu bricklayer. He had been hiding in the church with a few dozen other Kikuyus, hoping for safety in numbers. Then eight hundred Kalenjin showed up.

Daniel and some of the other men ran away, thinking the Kalenjins were after them. The mob didn't give chase. They surrounded the church, now filled mostly with women and children, and stuffed mattresses and bicycles in front of the doors, barricading the exits. The mob let out some war whoops—"Hae ho, hae ho"—as an aspiring politician who had just lost a race for parliament shook out a jug of gas. A match was struck. The women and children clawed at the mud-and-stick windows, trying to get out. A few made it, including one mother whose hair was burned off, but the baby on her back tumbled into the flames. The church went from refuge to oven, then mass grave. I put every sentence Daniel spoke into my notebook, but I couldn't believe it all. Massacring women and kids? This wasn't Rwanda, this was Kenya. I stammered out loud, "Why didn't you run to the district office? Where were the police?"

Daniel laughed bitterly.

"Police?"

◇◇◇◇◇◇◇

Kenya was disintegrating. Everything was breaking down. Mobs barricaded the highways, ripped up railway tracks, ransacked shoe shops, burned schools to the ground. There were no police, no fire engines, no emergency services. In many areas, the cell phone network collapsed and water and power were shut off. Ethnic grievances that went back decades, over land, power, wealth, and opportunity, were exploding. The government was nowhere to be found. Bodies were stacking up outside the morgues, rotting in the sunshine.

During riots in Nairobi, Courtenay and I, along with several journalists who had jetted in from Europe, got stuck behind a line of protesters at the Serena Hotel. The Serena was an expensive hotel, though a bit dated, with all its dark wood and doormen in tails. There were about eight of us at a table in the bar, drinking beers and soda, waiting for the streets to clear. We started talking about previous mayhem stories, and a freelancer from London abruptly turned to me. "Jeff, you got kidnapped in Iraq, right?" All eyes swung my way. I didn't feel like getting into this, especially in front of Courtenay. But I didn't want to disappoint, either. A key factor of being successful is believing your own bullshit, so I squared up with the table and started at the beginning. The road. Those date groves. That curve.

Right when I reached the Mr. Greck part, with all the assault rifles in my face, Courtenay piped up, a tad more animatedly than normal.

"I got a voice mail from Bill Keller, telling me to call him," she said.

I stopped talking.

"I was in court that day," she went on, her voice a little steadier. "I used to always keep my phone off in court, but that day for some reason I had left it on, and I heard it ring.

"In one of the breaks, I went out to the vestibule and listened. And when I heard Bill Keller's voice, I thought he had died."

The table went uncharacteristically silent. I knew what she was doing, but if you didn't know Courtenay, there would have been no way you would have ever sensed it: you would have simply thought this was seamless coupledom, a duet of a cliff-hanger, two people in love telling in stereo the story of how they overcame the worst moment of their fused lives. But I knew otherwise.

"How did he know to call me? How'd he get my cell phone number?" Courtenay asked. It was a good question. "It was really weird. So I called Bill, I called Diane, his secretary—I couldn't reach either of them."

Everyone was listening. The pain and anxiety of being in the dark about what had happened to me was much more interesting than the primary tale itself, whose conclusion was obvious.

"So I instinctively called my mother—my mother's first fiancé was one of the first men killed in Vietnam, a West Point grad, they had been engaged almost a year when she got the telegram, and somehow I knew my mom would know how to deal with this. And when she picked up the phone I said, 'Mom?' and she said, 'It's over.'"

Courtenay teared up. It was an incredibly powerful story, its delivery practiced and refined over the years, just like mine. I quickly
finished up my side of things, and the conversation swung to some
other hellhole. Sometimes when Iraq came up, Courtenay would
look down, embarrassed, feeling as if everyone around the table
knew what had transpired between Elizabeth and me. Other times
she tried to reclaim what had happened that day, that spring, that
war, inserting herself in the story because there had been another
woman in that story. Listening to her struggle to pull this off gave
me a whole new view of myself. Maybe I had been created to make
her life hell.

For the next two months, I wrote a story on Kenya every day.
Courtenay made a record number of videos. Never again did I opt
for a chopper ride or any other mode of transport that would divide
us. We were so busy we didn't think much back to the miscarriage.
Neither of us had ever worked so hard, and not since then have we
worked so hard together.

Everyone spoke to us on the record, spelled out first and last
names, even posed for snaps with their looted goods, flaming
torches, and long wooden death clubs. They were supremely confident they would not be punished, and they never were. Not the
four guys, all identified by eyewitnesses, who led the burning of
the church. Not the cop caught on television shooting two un-
armed protesters and then kicking their bodies to make sure they
were dead. Not the rioters in the Rift Valley who hacked people
up, though my editors didn't like that term; they changed it to
killed.

Kenya's implosion was a delicate story to report because it
played perfectly into Western stereotypes, and some of my stories
came off sounding as though the bow-wielding "tribesman"—we
could call him Mr. Ooga Booga—had always been hiding inside
the man in the suit. I wanted to be vivid but not lurid. I was constantly struggling with how to present this. What if people had
used poisoned arrows to kill each other? Was I not supposed to

report that? In other stories, in other places, I always tried to be as specific as possible about how the violence was meted out—by pistols or bombs or missiles or belt-fed machine guns.

Another question was how much of this bloodshed was political and how much was ethnic. It definitely looked ethnic. The country was segregating itself right in front of us. Kikuyus were fleeing to Kikuyu areas, Luos fleeing to Luo areas, Kalenjins fleeing to Kalenjin areas. On a highway near Naivasha, I watched country buses slide past each other, going in opposite directions, the roofs piled high and messily with chairs, couches, blackened cooking pots and bundles of clothes, the faces of children of different ethnic groups pressed to the glass, staring at each other as they passed. This didn't seem to be about money. This didn't seem to be about class. We happened to be in Kisumu, in the Luo heartland, right when a string of buses carrying displaced Luo families pulled into town. Every head on the street turned and cheers erupted. Fists shot into the air. It gave me chills. The people on Kisumu's streets didn't necessarily know these newcomers, didn't know where they came from, probably didn't have a place for them to stay. But all that mattered was one thing: They are us.

I interviewed university students on patrol in the rolling, corn-stocked, ethnically split hills of the western Rift, carrying homemade guns built from wood, nails, plumbing pipes, and umbrella springs. These young men said they had plenty of friends of different tribes back in "uni," but up here, it was different. "Why is it different?" I asked. "Because this is about family," one said. For years, politicians on all sides had stoked their bases by casting aspersions on other ethnic groups, talking about dangers to "the community." There was tinder lying everywhere in Kenya. The stolen election became the fuse, and the result was front-page news around the world.

"Scoop!! i was just thinking about how you always seem to find the chaos no matter where you go. crazy shit happening," an e-mail from Benny read. "i just took over Africa in a game of risk.

it was pretty easy i don't know what the problem is. things here are going well. i started a new drug that was actually shown to be effective in clinical trials. that's a first for the als world. on the movie front, we got into four or five festivals this month. i really can't keep track. Greece, Australia, Wisconsin, Illinois, Denver. you know my shit is good. damn, that's one baddass paralyzed mute motherfucker."

That badass paralyzed mute motherfucker wasn't succumbing to his disease. His doctors had basically told him to go home and wait to die, but whatever was in Benny's DNA, it wouldn't allow him to do that. He was determined to finish his movie about traveling the world, searching for a cure for ALS. Roko was right by his side, handling the camera work. The two of them met survivors in Greece; they interviewed traditional medicine experts in China; they climbed Masada in Israel, Benny dragging himself all the way to the top. When he tripped and cracked his head on a marble step in Hong Kong, Roko jumped in the ambulance with him and tried to cheer him up, saying he was "indestructible." *Indestructible, indestructible*, Benny repeated, gradually coming out of his shock. Then he started cracking up. That became the name of his film: *Indestructible*.

The death toll kept climbing.

Father Michael Kamau.

Constable Peter Ginthinji.

Elias Wafula.

Two hundred, three hundred, four hundred—and those were only the documented cases, the corpses affixed with a strip of white medical tape on the forehead, printed in all caps above the open eyes "PEV": post-election violence. The first PEV victim we saw up close was lying faceup in the Mathare slum, just a few miles from our house. He was a young man, his shoes already stolen by the time we got there, but at the same time, someone had put a white plastic bag over his head, an attempt at preserving dignity.

Courtenay looked intensely at the corpse for bullet or arrow holes. She was developing the same scientific fascination with death that I used to have.

In the Nandi Hills, we followed a beautiful but empty road. The emptiness should have been a sign. We took a curve. A mob suddenly appeared in the middle of the highway, a blur of colors and motion in a space that should have been clear.

Jeremiah, the driver, began to slow.

Checkpoints are the badge of anarchy. Richard, the *New York Times* driver, a Luo, could take us only about twenty miles from our house before we hit a hard-core Kikuyu area where mobs had set up checkpoints. Before we were even close, we had to switch cars for a Kikuyu driver. But that guy could go only another hundred miles west, up to Molo. After that, it was Kalenjin country. When we neared Kisumu, we hired Jeremiah, a Luo, because Kisumu was Luo country. It took a lot of logistics and a lot of Kenyan shilingi.

The men closed the distance to us, swallowed us, flowed in front of the car, around it, behind us. Once those wheels stop, it's too late, it takes no more than ten grown men to prevent a stationary car from getting away—ever see that video of the Northern Ireland army corporals getting lynched by a mob? More and more men ran into the road, the sun glinting off their machetes.

They started yanking at the door handles. Many wore weird, scraggly hairdos. Then I realized, wait, those aren't hairdos, they're colobus monkey wigs. Kenyans are usually considered reserved, neat, proper, the "Englishmen of Africa." Don't they love tweeds, tea, misty highlands, and golf? But Kenya was unraveling far faster than anyone would have ever predicted, and when law and order break down, people feel a sort of freedom to do whatever they want. Why had these young men chosen colobus monkey wigs, of all things? Maybe to signify that today was different from yesterday, or to link today to an idealized image of a nobler past, long ago, when chiefs and warriors wore such things. The men started pounding on the windows. I was rigid with fear. I had put us on the wrong road, again.

"Unaenda wapi!" *Where are you going!* one yelled out. He was wearing military fatigues and a jaunty skipper's hat.

"Huyu!" Another pointed a machete at Jeremiah's head. "Ana kabila gani!" *This man! What tribe!*

If Jeremiah had been a Kikuyu, he would have been dead.

Some of the guys chomped stalks of pulpy sugarcane. Others were stumbling drunk. One thrust his head through Jeremiah's open window, bloodshot eyes darting around at all of our stuff.

"Don't be scared, don't be scared," I whispered to Courtenay. She was pressed right next to me. It was pleasantly cool outside, but sweat dripped out of my armpits.

Courtenay smiled at the men, which seemed to surprise them. The drunk ringleader, the one with the jaunty skipper cap, abruptly stepped back.

"Go, go, just go." He waved us through, suddenly seeming ashamed. "Go!"

The mob safely behind us, I looked over at Courtenay.

"Holy shit, honey, you weren't totally freaked out?"

"Nah," she said. "They're just kids. They're like my old clients."

◇◇◇◇◇◇◇

David Githuri Kariuki.

Lucas Sang.

Cynthia and Wycliffe Awino, nine and seven years old.

Five hundred, six hundred, seven hundred.

Near Eldoret we found one last Kikuyu farmer. He was by himself, sitting alongside the road with two gunnysacks of corn. We asked where he lived, and he took us to a beautiful homestead with a tall avocado tree leaning over the house. His house had been burned, and so had the avocado tree, whose leaves were black. His name was Francis Kariuki Kamau, and as we stood in his small living room, where the paint had been scorched off the walls, he fought back tears.

"I knew these people," he said.

"Which people?" I asked.

"The people who did this. The night they came, I told my wife, don't be scared, I'll go talk to them. So I went outside."

("Sweetie," I whispered as the farmer paused to look out the window, "let's get this guy." Courtenay turned on her camera. I dropped back, by the door.)

"They were our neighbors, just over there," he said, motioning his hand vaguely toward the hills. "So I asked them, 'What's the problem? Why are you killing us? We've been friends for years.'"

Between his words, it was very quiet. All the neighboring farms had been destroyed. Many people had been killed. All we could hear outside was the barking of hungry, ownerless dogs.

"But all they said was, 'Leo ni leo.'" *Today is today.*

"I've lived here twenty years," he said. "Twenty years. Is this not my home?"

It was one of those questions that hung in the air.

Francis shook his head. "Leo ni leo?" It would never make any sense.

Leo ni leo. Today is today. If I could figure out why the mob in Eldoret had uttered that, of all things, then I could figure out a lot about sub-Saharan Africa. What explains how that switch was flipped so easily? It was flipped in Rwanda, flipped in Burundi, flipped in many nations in Africa. How could a tribe be benign one day and fatal the next?

Before we left, Francis dug into the front right pocket of his torn trousers. He produced a tiny key and slowly closed the front door, which was covered in soot. He locked the small padlock. It seemed important to him to keep up the fiction that he had something left to steal.

As we drove away, Courtenay began to cry.

"Where's that guy going to go? He has nothing."

Our fixer sat in the front seat and just laughed—at the hopeless-ness of it all.

"Is it land?" he said.

Our fixer was a jolly, heavyset Maasai named Reginald.

"Is it tribe? Is it politics?

Reginald looked out the windows.

"It's kind of everything."

◇◇◇◇◇◇◇◇

It was kind of everything, but everything seemed to stem from one thing: Kenya had failed to build a nation. It had done better than many of its African cohorts at building a state—there was a func-tioning bureaucracy, a clean capital, a national airline, an army, navy, and air force, relatively strong controls on firearms (what kept the election death toll from reaching the tens of thousands), but Kenya still struggled with a sense of nation, a sense of Kenyan-ness. Of course, there was enough national pride that many Ken-yans were outraged at the election being stolen. But Kenya was a society deeply divided. Those same traditions that we *mzungus* found so quaint, like five different languages being spoken on the streets, were evidence that Kenya had never fully cohered.

This is the existential challenge for nations created on a carving board. In much of the rest of the world, countries have borders that follow mountain ranges, rivers, and other geographic boundaries. Look at Europe. It's a confederation of blobs. Not Africa. There are more suspiciously straight lines and harsh right angles running across this map than any other through desert, bush, lake, and tribe. The borders between Sudan and Egypt, or Botswana and Namibia, or Libya and Chad, or Kenya and Somalia, and circumscribing the Ogaden Desert, for that matter, still bear the straight-edged ruler marks. Many of these were hastily drawn in the 1880s and 1890s by *mzungus*. The only African countries that succeeded in overcoming this and building anything close to a national identity were those that took forceful steps to neutralize ethnicity or tribe (I use the terms interchangeably).

Julius Nyerere, Tanzania's revered first president who took the reins in the 1960s, mandated that everyone speak one language, Swahili, and kids go to high schools in different areas—like desegregation school busing. The result is that Tanzania today is one of the most peaceful nations on the continent. Even kooky Mobutu banned Western neckties and encouraged the taking of "Zairean" names, a legacy that has kept beleaguered Congo intact even after armies from seven different African nations ripped into it in the late 1990s like a pack of hyenas.

In Kenya, the divisiveness began with the *mzungus*. To fill the ranks of their growing colony and because there weren't so many pairs of white hands around, the Brits typecast the Kenyans: the Maasai were the *askaris*; the Kikuyus the farmhands; the Luos the teachers; the Kalenjins the cattlemen. Certain people did certain things. It was like the ethnic groups had been turned into guilds. In few African countries was ethnicity used so energetically to categorize people (the Belgians did something similar in Rwanda, and look what happened there).

But the Kenyans themselves dug those trenches deeper. Kenya's first president, Jomo Kenyatta, began the Kenyan political tradition of winner-takes-all, vacuuming up national resources not for the benefit of his young, needy nation but for his own family and his own tribe—in this case, the Kikuyu. The Kenyattas are now among Africa's richest families, though no one here is foolish enough to try to call them on that original sin. Kenya's next two presidents, Moi, a Kalenjin, and Kibaki, another Kikuyu, didn't change the basic calculus of discrimination. Access to land and power continued to be ethnicized. Certain jobs continued to be overwhelmingly filled by members of certain groups. The tribe's interest, not the national interest, was what mattered.

I call Kenya's political system an "ethnocracy." It is a democracy of sorts, or it's supposed to be, but even when it "works," just about everyone votes along ethnic lines. It's less bigotry than pragmatism. If the political tradition is that it's our turn to eat, then you as an individual have an interest in your guy making it to the trough. That may mean a better job for you or a road for your village. This also explains the spectacular corruption. A politician's record is irrelevant. If he's from your group, he's your man. As in politics, so too in war: during the election violence, though it looked like madness and felt like madness, there was a method to the killing. People ignored the law, but they followed certain rules. The death squads didn't just bust into a town and start slicing up the first people in sight. They set up roadblocks, pulled people off buses, checked IDs.

The staff in the *New York Times* bureau had worked together collegially for years, regardless of tribal affiliations. Hannah, the office assistant, was a Kikuyu, Richard a Luo, Hanson, the office manager, a Luhya. They spoke their own mother tongues sometimes when their cell phones rang—relatives calling from back home—but that was about the only sign of tribal affiliation. Now things were different. I walked into the bureau one afternoon and caught Hannah glaring at Hanson, saying in her typical mix of English and Swahili, "Hii ni hate speech!" *This is hate speech!* I had no idea what Hanson had just said. He was usually mild. But for the rest of the afternoon, a block of dead air sat between their desks, which were about six feet apart.

Lukas Matete.

Erick Ouma.

Mzee Zephania.

Eight hundred, nine hundred, one thousand.

The shelves of our supermarket were cleaned out, a run on water, bread, flour, Eveready batteries. Courtenay spent the mornings on the proverbial breadline, buying all the meat she could, freezing it, then joining me in the afternoons to shoot video. Driving into town, we passed police officer after police officer, positioned every few hundred yards on the main roads like a taut string drawn across Nairobi, their bodies vigilant and erect, each man, each face, carrying the apprehension of the entire nation. I felt none of the excitement I usually felt moving through a place on knifepoint. This wasn't news. This was our home.

Nairobi was eroding into a battlefield. Instead of smelling jasmine at night, I now stood on our porch and smelled burning tires. Many of the biggest thoroughfares were either deserted or a mess of tear-gas canisters, split wood, downed telephone poles, and fleeing people. Courtenay and I found ourselves trapped in a crowd on Ngong Road, frantically running away from police firing their weapons. All of a sudden we started choking.

"Holy shit," Courtenay gasped. "That shit hurts!"

Her eyes were streaming; clear snot poured out of my nose. We had just been teargassed and were simultaneously running, choking, crying, coughing, and then laughing at each other. If violence was becoming our new weather, this was our new forecast, and we'd better just accept it: Sunny, with a chance of tear gas.

Peter Buranda.

Esther Wangui.

Joyce Macharia, burned alive, two and a half years old.

Eleven hundred.

I'd stay up each night until nearly the break of dawn, haggling with New York over *hacked* versus *killed*, *tribe* versus *ethnic group*. The word *tribe* comes from the Latin *tribus*, which refers to the three original voting units of ancient Rome, and may have corresponded to the city's three biggest ethnic groups: the Latins, the Sabines, and the Etruscans. In that way, *tribe* has always been intertwined with ethnicity. Educated Kenyans use the term, so I felt it was patronizing to switch to the more politically correct alternatives my editors suggested: "community" or "ethnic group." I lost that one too. Frankly, there was no good term; each, in its own way, expressed value judgments or paternalism. Sometimes, after another exhausting night, I'd look out the windows of our upstairs bedrooms down at Richard and Alfred's small house behind our driveway, the staff quarters, and see the faint blue glow of TV light. Everyone in this country was mesmerized by the election violence. Nobody could stop it.

If Western-style institutions such as the police, the judiciary, the clergy, and local government all collapsed in Kenya, in the end it was Western-style capitalism that saved it. While the fighting was raging, a small group of executives and professionals began to form: lawyers, physicians, safari company owners, corporate bosses, and development consultants from all the major tribes, even a couple Kenyan cowboys. They met for breakfast in a windowless, wood-paneled conference room at the Serena Hotel, where they began their sessions by standing up, holding hands, and singing the national anthem. "Natukae kwa undugu . . ." *May we dwell in brotherhood . . .*

One man belted out the words with special passion. After the meeting, I walked over to him and introduced myself. George Mbugua was a fortysomething CFO of a growing water services company. He welcomed me and Courtenay into his home, where I saw two cars in the driveway, a set of golf clubs, and a painted drum in the living room that read "Jambo Africa"—"Do you like? I bought it on holiday, in Mombasa," Mbugua said. For some reason he had a hankering to hunt deer in Alaska, and he was proud to tell us, as he bounced an eighteen-month-old baby on his thigh, that he had just learned how to swim. Mbugua was the New Kenya.

"It's madness," Mbugua said about the tribal bloodletting, and he didn't use the term flippantly. To him it was incomprehensible— and evidence of an unsound mind—that people in the countryside and in the slums and even in the halls of parliament were willing to risk all the hard work and investment that had been steadily accruing and reduce it to char blowing in the wind.

Kenya's middle class was one of the biggest on the continent— around four million people making between $3,000 and $40,000 a year—and in an ethnically divided country, the middle class can be an awesome counterweight. They typically identify as much with their profession as with their tribe, and they have much more to lose than the guy kicking down shanties and screaming "No Raila, no peace!" The George Mbuguas of the world don't live by today-is-today. They're working for tomorrow.

For several weeks, while people in the countryside continued to slaughter each other with poisoned arrows and heavy *rungus*, the professionals at the Serena Hotel stuck to their morning meetings. They urged Kibaki's and Raila's men to lay down their arms for the sake of Kenya's economy. There was going to be no new election, that much was clear. But the hope was to form a power-sharing government—later named "the grand coalition government"—that would give Raila and other opposition figures enough power so they would tell their followers to stop killing, and the country could get back to business. When Kibaki still refused, Condoleezza Rice flew into town and wagged her finger at him, warning that the American government, which gave Kenya $1 billion a year, would not tolerate any more stubbornness. Kofi Annan pushed as well. So grateful were middle-class Kenyan wildlife rangers, they named a new rhino Baby Kofi.

Kibaki finally relented. Raila became prime minister. At a reconciliation ceremony, the two puffed themselves up, wearing beautifully tailored suits, acting as if they should be thanked, not incarcerated, for what they had unleashed. The killing finally stopped. The official figures were 3,561 injuries, 117,216 properties destroyed, and 1,133 dead. There is no authoritative list of all the names of the deceased.

A few days later, over lunch at the Nairobi Club, a scruffier version of the Muthaiga Club, Raila grinned at me: "Half a loaf is better than no loaf." As I watched him gobble down a buttered roll, he told me that there was an old joke that a Luo would be president of the United States before being president of Kenya. Barack Obama's father was a Luo, and Obama had just won Super Tuesday.

FOURTEEN

⬦⬦⬦⬦⬦⬦

NAIROBI, 2009

"Mista Jifri, how is your condition?"

At first, I thought I'd been dreaming. Many nights the roads came back to me, the places I'd been, the people I'd seen, Fallujah, Karma, the Shabaab, the Ethiopians, all mixing in that hazy REM reality tinged with the frightening power of prophecy. Sometimes I screamed for help in my dreams, a rifle barrel jabbed in my face, or just as scary, I dreamed that I had lapsed, that I had cheated again, that Courtenay would find out and I would have to face her and my life would be destroyed. I'd wake up in a sweaty heap next to her, immeasurably relieved.

But this wasn't a dream. I was half-asleep, Courtenay fully asleep next to me. I looked, bleary-eyed, at the phone in my hand: an 88216 number, which meant a sat phone, which meant someone far away. The moment I groggily said "Hello?" I heard that voice from the desert.

"Mista Jifri, how is your condition?"

"Peacock!" I sat up in bed. "Where the hell are you?"

"Secret place," he said.

"You okay?"

"Me, myself I have no problem. But so many terrible things have happened. I will narrate for you . . ."

He filled me in on the latest battles, casualties, and defections. Dozens of rebels, including many of the quiet young men who had helped carry our gear and look after us, had been bought off for a few hundred dollars and were now killing for the government.

"I must go," Peacock said after we chatted for several minutes. "The capital is moving."

How do you say good night to a rebel on the run, a young man who might be dead within minutes of whatever paltry words you settle on? I didn't have much time to think—"Okay, Peacock, be well"—and anyway I was too distracted, too tired, to say much more.

I was already a bit down on another front. Courtenay was having difficulty getting pregnant again after the miscarriage. We saw all kinds of specialists in Nairobi, New York, and Zurich who ran all kinds of tests. Nobody could tell us where the problem was. We were diligent never to miss that one-to-two-day window each month, no matter how exhausted. Some nights we were so depleted by Congo, Ethiopia, Darfur, and Somalia that all we could do was sit in our home office, staring at our computer screens, barely talking. "Okay, hon," Courtenay would finally say with a tired smile. She'd lightly touch me on the arm, which was a sign. "Time for another team-building exercise . . ."

The news showed little mercy. I could have written a story every day on Somalia alone. I was even grateful to cover the end of the Tom Cholmondeley murder case, because it kept me in Kenya for a few more days. The judge found Cholmondeley guilty of manslaughter and gave him eight months. The Kenyan public absorbed the verdict gracefully; he had gotten off easy because of his *mzungu*ness, but at least it wasn't a seventy-dollar fine. Because of the epic delays in Kenya's judicial system, Cholmondeley's total time in Kamiti Prison—an imposing colonial-era clink where hundreds of Mau Mau fighters had been hanged—was three and a half years. I saw him not long after he was released, his colossal blond head hanging over a steaming mound of chow mein in the food court of the Village Market mall near our house. He caught me staring and recognized me from the peanut gallery at his trial. He lifted his head, wiped his mouth, and smirked. I knew exactly what he was feeling. I had felt it multiple times. He was thrilled to be a free man.

But Somalia kept pulling me back. That country kept morphing, and now the trouble was coming from the coast—Somalia has the longest coastline on the African continent, 1,880 miles.

The tip had first come to me in another late-night call six months earlier, from a blocked number.

"Hello?"

"Mon frère!"

Shit. Louis. He always blocked his number.

"Got something you might be interested in."

"Sure, um, yeah . . ."

"Can you hear me clearly? You ready, my sleepy friend? Take this down. Plus eight seven oh . . ."

I could barely write but I knew I had something good when I heard +870. That and +88216 were the outlaw extensions, the calling codes for sat phones, the communication device of choice for Africa's rebels and diamond smugglers and the renegade general on top of a mountain on the Congo-Rwanda border with 1,500 baby-faced soldiers, several field guns, and an itch for more territory.

"That number will take you to the deck of the *Faina*," Louis had said. "Ask for the pirate spokesman."

This was it: the beginning of my two-year pirate phase. I'd heard about skinny Somalis taking a few ships here and there when I was in Mog in 2006. Back then, al-Shabaab had done a decent job fighting them, boarding hijacked ships and arresting pirates. But Somalia's new "government" couldn't control a few measly blocks in the center of its capital, let alone that long, squiggly coastline. By mid-2008 we were entering the greatest piracy craze since the heyday of the swashbuckling Barbary boys in the late 1700s. Landlubbers have always loved the idea of pirates, full of derring-do and embodying that sense of hyperfreedom that, at some level, we all crave—free of laws, free of society's expectations, free of borders, cruising around the open seas, reveling in the immensity of all that space. These twenty-first-century pirates were no different: tailor-made for Western consumption, which was somewhat ironic, since we had also produced them. If the United States hadn't bungled Somalia in 1993, then again in 2006, the phenomenon would have never developed into a billion-dollar global problem. The pirates were children of Somalia's chaos, pure and simple.

You had to hand it to them. The rich nations of the world had neglected Somalia, and Somalis had now found the perfect way, within their means and abilities, to make the world pay. Gangs of young men sped out into the open seas in battered skiffs, swarmed a ship, whirled up their grappling hooks, scampered up the ropes like a bunch of wet rats, and then forced the crew at gunpoint to sail back to Somalia. They hit anything that floated—Saudi tankers, Arab dhows, a Ukrainian vessel stuffed with tanks and other illicit arms, food ships, cargo ships, sailing yachts, once even an American guided-missile frigate (that one was a mistake). I clicked on Google Earth and saw dozens of hijacked ships bobbing off northeast Somalia, hundreds of hostages inside.

In no other country would a kidnapping ring so open be allowed to flourish. But this was Somalia. The pirates had the luxury of waiting for months in their pirate dens for the ransoms to be delivered by companies in Nairobi that specialized in shrink-wrapping million-dollar blocks of cash and dropping them by parachute. The pirates weren't exactly Robin Hood and Little John in Sherwood Forest. But the effect was similar. The multinational shipping and insurance companies paying for those blocks of shrink-wrapped cash were injecting resources into the world's neediest nation.

Louis's tip opened up the pirate underworld, and soon enough I was off to see a pirate captain in the flesh in a small town in inland Somalia, where he controlled his operation. Garowe was so overrun with pirates that there were even signs in the parking lots that said NO PIRATES ALLOWED—but that was a bunch of malarkey. Pirates ran that town. When I walked into a restaurant with Abshir Boyah, soldiers, police officers, a police chief, and all the red-bearded elders rose to their feet. To the world he was an internationally most-wanted man; here he was a king. As lean as a letter opener with a sharp haircut and a pearly smile, Boyah spent the next five minutes cordially shaking hands, working that room like Bill Clinton at a fund-raiser. Finally we sat down at a table covered with a greasy strip of vinyl and a squadron of flies. Boyah was one of the founding fathers of a pirate organization called the Corporation. He was considered a pioneer.

"Me eating with white men," he said through a mouthful of spaghetti. "This is like the cat eating with the mice!"

This all could have felt dangerous—it certainly did for the video department, which once again grounded Courtenay, but Boyah was grinning, and the president of this region, a guy we reached by phone and spoke to for about three minutes, had guaranteed my safety. (There are more "presidents" in Somalia than any other country in the world.) As we downed the oily camel meat and oily spaghetti, Boyah explained the business; I happily took notes. I loved the pirate story, at least at first. It was more fun than anything else I wrote about in Africa, and did less damage to me spiritually. In fact, the Somali pirates were the only newsmakers in my region who generated front-pager after front-pager without taking many lives. This wasn't a war. The pirates weren't bloodthirsty killers. If they got their money, nobody got hurt.

Many pirate kings displayed a certain criminal intelligence. They had to, to stay on top of operations that sprawled over thousands of miles of ocean and employed legions: translators, bookkeepers, mechanics, guards, gunsmiths, middle managers, boat builders, women who sold tea to the pirates, others who sold them goats. Boyah, who became a quite good source, told me he had "done" about twenty ships, that he never hurt hostages, that the Corporation had a printed handbook (he had no idea where his copy went), and that he wished he'd been wiser about investing his proceeds.

"But you know how it is," he said with a wave of his long fingers.

I had no idea how it was.

"Parties, weddings, jewelry, cars, khat."

"What was your first ship? Tell me about your first ship."

"Ah, you white men. You always want whole story. You know how this started? We were poor fishermen—" He held up his palms and rubbed thumb and forefinger together. "Foreign ships came in and started robbing our seas. Would we let them take all our fishes? No! We would *not* let them take all our fishes. We armed ourselves. We got brave. We are freedom fighters!"

They had freedom, yes, but they weren't freedom fighters, not at all—not like Peacock, who'd had a clear agenda to liberate a place and provide for its people. Those young men in the Ogaden were the last I'd come across worthy of the freedom-fighter name. Boyah's Corporation was just that.

"You know, it's hard to be the richest guy in town," Boyah complained. "It's not like three people split a million bucks," he added, referring to the extended clan system. "It's more like three hundred." He said that he also gave 15 percent to charity, especially to the elderly and infirm, adding, "I'd love to give them more."

It was a silly thing to hear from a gangster. But wasn't that the theme of living in sub-Saharan Africa, especially as a privileged *mzungu*? You could always give more. Can you pay for school fees? What about a loan to buy a plot of land? My kids want a TV. Can you help me? Being asked such things was a big part of living here, and I didn't categorically say no. But by June 2009 my attention was beginning to shift to all that I needed to do for us, to get everything ready. I had even bigger news. Something I had come to believe might never happen was about to.

◇◇◇◇◇◇

An hour after the power had cut out at the Aga Khan Hospital, at about five in the evening, Courtenay bravely pushed our son into the world. Tears burst out of my eyes. I was nearly thirty-eight years old, Courtenay was thirty-six, and like so many other couples who had waited too long, we began to dream of what it would be like to be parents with the sense that maybe we never would be. But now he was here, tiny, wet, eyes scrunched shut. Three kilos. Small but apparently healthy. The doctor shone a flashlight over his body, just to make sure. The next chapter of our lives began in that dimly lit birthing room—the rains had been weak for months. Kenya depends on hydropower, and a lack of rain means a lack of light.

We named him Apollo, and his early days weren't made any easier by the fact that my generation has gotten this backward, scrambling to establish our careers first, then starting a family. I envied my parents for chasing me and my sister around when they were in their twenties.

Not a day would pass without a call from New York or our international desk in Paris or some radio station, asking me about the latest pirate hijacking. I was getting into the truck one Saturday afternoon with a ten-month-old Apollo in my arms when the phone rang. Another ship? Won't these guys take a break? I couldn't reach my phone, so I sat Apollo up on the hood as I dug into my pocket. He looked so cute in his matching shorts set, those little chubby legs with no ankles. He started crying, as he usually did when I abruptly sat him down.

"Don't cry, honey, I'll be right here . . . Hello . . ."

Apollo soon wasn't crying anymore. He was screaming. I jettisoned the phone and scooped him up with one hand. With the other, I nervously felt the hood where he had just been sitting. The car had been baking for hours in direct sunshine. I could have fried bacon on the hood.

I held my bawling son in the air to survey the damage: the back of his exposed thighs had burned lobster-red.

Courtenay heard the howling and came running outside with a viperous look in her eye.

"What the FUCK were you thinking?" she said. "Give him to me. Go in the house. Get the dawa." (*Dawa* means medicine in Swahili; we were becoming like Hannah, Hanson, and so many others in Kenya, mixing the two languages.)

In Nairobi, everyone lived behind high walls. There were few parks or playgrounds, no trains to ride, no ducks out by the river to feed, so our compound became Apollo's area of operations. I marveled at how seamlessly he was a blend of us—Courtenay's wide mouth and slightly pouched eyes, which would nearly disappear when he smiled; my hair color, my chin, my profile. He toddled around the garden, chasing the ibises that swooped down to land on our lawn, always in twos, male and female; ibises are monogamous for life. Our plot was a quarter acre, modest by *mzungu* standards, but for a miniature human there was plenty to explore. Apollo helped Alfred, our gardener, rake up the orange flame tree blossoms and clip the thornbushes that formed our fence. Together they looked for chameleons and the monkeys that occasionally showed up to steal our mangoes. It was a whole new question of etiquette with a child: I tried to tell Richard or Alfred not to pick up after Apollo and to feel free to scold him when he whined or misbehaved. They rarely scolded him and constantly carried in his pails and dump trucks from the yard, which I hoped he didn't see.

Some of life's lessons I didn't want him to learn. Like the time when we were coming back from a weekend at the coast and security officials at the airport stopped us, telling us we weren't allowed to bring back any seashells—they had seen the shells in our luggage on the X-ray machine. "My shells?" Apollo panicked. "Daddy, they want to take my shells?"

I knew the game. I'd made dozens of trips to the Kenyan coast and brought back seashells on many of them. And it wasn't like we had raided a protected marine park; we had found these shells on a public beach. If there was a rule against keeping seashells, its enforcement was optional. That's what always impressed me about Kenya, its innate flexibility, especially when it came to the law.

I turned my back to Apollo, making sure he didn't see me extract the crisp 500-shilingi bill from my wallet. I walked over to speak to the woman running the X-ray. I waited for her to make the first move. She did: "Just give me a little something for soda." We shook hands enthusiastically, and I felt her fingers digging for the note in my palm. Apollo was thrilled to get his shells back, and since I've become pretty good at these bribery handshakes, I don't think he or anyone else noticed. I didn't want him to be cynical about how the world, or at least this world, worked, and see that daddy literally had a hand in it. I also tried to not to use the word *mzungu* around him, knowing the can of worms it would open. I liked it when he described people as "tan," "brown," or "peach."

As he grew, he asked with a twinkle in his light, khaki-colored eyes if he could eat lunch with Alfred. I knew exactly what he was up to. Childhood, even in East Africa, is nothing more than an epic quest for candy and TV. I'd look out the window and see him disappear into the staff quarters, the SQ, where Alfred and Richard lived. That building with its two small rooms, bare steel sink, and small electric burner was the height of my hypocrisy, standing there every day to remind me of how far I had not come. When I was with Dan, I used to make fun of what I called "the slave quarters." Now I got it. It was too futile to try to dismantle the entire system. But surely I could make the rooms nicer.

I'm not sure how much Apollo picked up on this, and I envied him for it. He was excited to spend as many lunches as possible in the SQ, watching cop shows and wrestling on Alfred's TV and learning to eat *ugali*, the maize meal staple that powers Kenya.

Alfred taught him how to tear off little pieces of *ugali* and dip it into sauce, patiently inducting him into another culture.

◇◇◇◇◇◇◇◇

We were now entering our sixth year in Kenya, and the standard tour was five. This meant one thing: New York could move us at any time. The South Africa job was about to come open, and it seemed a prudent move to try to grab it; that way I could guarantee staying in Africa for several more years. South Africa was the biggest story on the continent, with the strongest economy and a jagged crack running down the middle of it. Most Americans cared more about South Africa than any other African country; we instinctively recognized its tortured black-white issues. And if that didn't work out, I could wait a little longer and apply for the job in our office in West Africa, probably the richest part of Africa in terms of culture, fashion, and music and home to the Sahara's great old trading centers, like Timbuktu.

I knew it made sense, practically, to move on, but I also knew where my heart was. For me, eastern and central Africa still had it all—the striking harshness of the Horn, the comforts of Nairobi, Congo's immutable vibe, Swa Freaking Hili, which isn't spoken in other parts of Africa. I knew it would crush me to give this up, even if it meant learning more about other places. "Just stop obsessing about it," a fellow journalist advised me. He worked for a prestigious London paper and was on his way up—and out. "You shouldn't stay here that long anyway. As my boss always says, 'Africa's been the graveyard of many good careers.'" I was at a loss for how to respond. I felt my face heat up, as if this were a personal insult. I simply stared at him. I wanted to blurt out "Yo mama." But he was young and British. He wouldn't have gotten it.

That year, 2011, was even drier than the previous years. The spring rains had failed again. As I took Apollo for walks in his stroller around our neighborhood, I was struck by how droopy everything looked. Our street was lined with tall trees intertwined with heaps of flowering bougainvillea vines, quite possibly the most beautiful parasite in the world: but the trees glowed less green, the bougainvillea burst less purple. Some of our banana plants, among the hardiest in our garden, had died. We had to truck in water, which was a different color. I don't know where they got it from; Nairobi's reservoirs had run dry. Somewhere up-country, probably. After I carefully lifted Apollo out of the bath, I'd watch the red dirt grains swirl down the drain.

"This is gonna be bad," Louis told me one morning when I was out pushing Apollo's stroller and trolling for some news on my cell phone. "You should see the info."

"The UN doesn't usually share that with me. How bad?"

"Bad. The rainfall figures are dreadful, livestock prices are plummeting, global food costs are going up, and the goat-to-rice ratio is all out of whack. Even the camels are dropping dead. The aid groups are going to need some serious dinero for this one."

I kept walking. Apollo looked up at me from his stroller. There wasn't a cloud in the sky.

"This is going to be Somalia's worst year in a long time."

"Yeah?"

"Yeah. Take my word for it. By next week, they're going to start using the f-word."

◇◇◇◇◇◇◇

Asa Gettleman was born at the height of the famine. We had opted for the same hospital, and right as Courtenay was in the deepest, darkest abysses of labor, the power cut out, again. All the beeping machines stopped.

But this go-around, in a sign of the changing times, the generators kicked in. The Aga Khan Hospital had just been rehabbed and furnished with modern equipment. Asa, an old Hebrew name that means "healer," was born in the light. He was our chocolate-eyed beauty. His eyes were wide set and so dark you couldn't see his pupils. Courtenay's labor for him had been much harder. He was bigger than Apollo. His little grip was startlingly strong, and even from his earliest days, I could tell we had a warrior on our hands.

It was just as Louis predicted, and it was impossible not to see our own good fortune put in even starker relief. It had taken us two years to get pregnant again, and just when we had given up hope, we saw that blessed second line. When we brought Asa home the first night and laid him down in his fluffy white bassinet, fourteen children every hour were curling up in the sand, starving to death in Somalia's latest famine. Even though I had a new kid, I couldn't turn my back on this.

I became a ghostlike presence in our house, drifting in and out at odd hours, Apollo playing in his room with Thomas the Tank Engine, Courtenay sitting on the floor giving Asa his tummy time, me slipping quietly off with my computer, notebooks, PowerBars, and thousands of dollars in my pocket to ride the flying jalopies that serviced Somalia. I reappeared through the front door days later, filthy and exhausted. I was chasing death again, and it was becoming more concentrated at each stop. At the Dadaab refugee camp near the Kenya-Somalia border, thousands of people materialized every dawn out of the thin desert air. They sat at the camp's gates, masses of them, little kids so dazed they couldn't cry and proud nomadic men reduced to begging for a pack of glucose biscuits. Mothers with babies wrapped in bundles on their backs sometimes did not know, until they reached the camp and untied their bundles, that their babies had died along the way. There was a graveyard directly across the road, for such things.

"Sweetie, I don't think I can do this anymore," I told Courtenay over the phone when I was in Mog, the epicenter of the famine. I felt a certain relief uttering that out loud. Maybe this would be it. I wiped my eyes. I was standing in a pediatric feeding center, feeling like a vulture. The whiff of diesel hung in the air—that's all they had to clean the floors. The nurses wore filthy smocks and would barely look at me; they didn't have enough IVs or oral rehydration salts. They didn't stand a chance. The famine had crash-landed in one of the poorest, most ill prepared places in the world. All around me, dozens of little kids were quietly fading away, their glassy, unblinking eyes locked on the ceiling, every rib showing beneath skin as translucent as rice paper.

"They're so skinny," I said. "They're not going to live. I know they're not going to live."

"I can't even imagine what you're seeing," Courtenay said.

"All I'm doing is thinking about you guys. All I want to do is just come home."

"You can't," she said. "You've said it yourself. The Somalis are the rejects of this region, their government is horrible, they're treated like dogs in Kenya, no one cares about them. What you're doing is too important. Don't think about the kids. That's too painful."

The news of suffering takes a new shape when you're a parent. Fatherhood peels back a layer of skin, exposing a network of nerves I hadn't known existed. Could I imagine anything worse than watching Apollo or Asa dying *slowly* in front of me, their skin flaking off like chipped paint? I worried when they got a fever.

"Dak-tur, dak-tur," an old man yelled out, leaning over a small girl. He waved to me frantically. "Firee, firee!" *Look, look!*

The old man thought I was a doctor. My first-aid skills had not advanced much in the past few years. Still, I wanted to help.

"Can you take this out?" He motioned toward the IV. The girl didn't need it anymore.

While I was talking to Courtenay on the phone, another child died. She looked about Apollo's age, though it was hard to know for sure because her face was wizened. The old man, her father, quickly covered her up. He wrapped her in a coarse blanket and walked stiffly out the room, the bundle in his arms. I followed a few steps behind.

We moved out into the bullet-pocked streets. People were selling pyramids of oranges from wooden carts. Powdered milk and sacks of grain sat on the shelves of the little stores we passed, the very food that little girl had needed to eat. It didn't seem to make any sense, but famines are caused by shocks to the food distribution system, not necessarily by poverty per se. There was still plenty of food in Somalia; it was just relatively expensive because of the drought and the rise in global food prices. I could tell from the old man's raggedy clothes and the way he moved uneasily through traffic that he hailed from the deep, dead land in the middle of the country, and that he had no money. We kept walking. I followed him for blocks. He knew I was there, his look told me it was okay.

At the edge of the city, where the streets faded into sand and bands of gunmen lurked, I stopped. He kept going. As I watched him disappear toward the ocean, a diminishing, hunched-over figure in the unrelenting light, I realized that however crazy this world gets, however accustomed to misery someone may be, we are all the same. No one ever totally gives up hope, no one is made in such a way that he is grief-proof. Not even in Somalia. Everyone seeks, till the very end, to preserve whatever dignity he can. The old man went off to bury his little girl properly. I didn't ham up that story. It was a watershed for me. I played it straight, no more-is-more. Sometimes, enough is enough.

More than 2,000 years ago Herodotus wrote, "In peaceful times, children inter their parents. In war times, parents inter their children." More people perished in Somalia's famine of 2011 than during the famine that Dan covered in 1992. The number exceeded 250,000, and most were children. Famines are not natural disasters. Famines are man-made. Droughts happen from time to time. But in this century, for any drought to metastasize into a famine, it takes a monumental breakdown in the economy, in relief efforts, in communication, and in the customs and traditions that usually keep places like Somalia from totally unraveling.

Al-Shabaab diverted rivers during the driest days and locked the half-living in camps that had no food. Why would you do that? I tried to call Abu Mansoor, my old Fanta friend, to find out. Al-Shabaab didn't like the West, but this was so much more ruthless than simply banning UNICEF or Save the Children from their territory. But I couldn't reach Abu Mansoor. I had a number for his younger brother, a smiley kid who once shot crocodiles in front of us, back when the Shabaab helped distribute emergency food during flood times along Somalia's swollen rivers. But the smiley brother was being hunted and had gone underground as well. And the news was moving fast, pushed forward at a relentless speed by that unpleasant truth of how war creates excellent conditions for a certain form of capitalism. Thugs in southern Somalia were now charging weary famine victims a "shade tax" to rest along the road under "their" trees. Other warlords, in zones the government allegedly controlled, "rented" refugees, paying famine victims a small pittance to camp on their land so the warlords could skim from the millions of dollars of relief supplies that flowed to such concentrations of misery. I wish I were exaggerating.

American policies didn't help either. There had been so much hope about Barack Obama: Kenya had declared a national holiday after he was elected, and there were ringing celebrations across the continent. A person of African heritage had risen to the highest position on the planet, the biggest of the Big Men.

But Obama's policies in this part of the world were simply con-tinuations of what came before—drones, mercenaries, sanctions, and SEAL Team 6. After one SEAL raid on a pirate camp where an American woman was being held hostage, word went around Somalia that the Americans had dropped a "face-eating bomb." They were just clean head shots, multiple ones.

Our stubbornly Manichean approach to counterterrorism blinded us to so many other delicate issues in this part of the world. "How is it," a Kenyan member of parliament of Somali descent asked me, "that with all those resources and all that knowledge, America keeps getting Somalia wrong, not just once, but every time?" At times like these, I found it hard to believe that it was we who had taken over the world. I didn't have any answers for the parliamentarian. Nobody did. During the Somalia famine, Obama's Treasury Department imposed rules that made it illegal for aid groups to pay taxes or access fees to the Shabaab. They were terrorists, and the United States, especially since the days of Bush, doesn't deal with terrorists.

But American aid experts knew the dangers of these rules: the Shabaab controlled half of Somalia, with millions of starving people trapped in its territory. And not all of the Shabaab, or even anywhere close to most, were terrorists; they were militants, "bad guys," in Bush's lingo, but men who posed zero threat to the United States. Still, those Treasury rules against the Shabaab had a dreadful impact. Fearful of getting in trouble, and not able to guarantee that some of their aid would not somehow end up in the hands of some Shabaab, many leading aid agencies opted to stay away from the hardest-hit areas in Somalia. This was collateral damage at its worst, essentially a replay of Vietnam's "destroying the village to save it."

During my first trip to the continent in 1990, I was proud to be an American. The way I saw it, we were the greatest, and I thoroughly enjoyed playing my role as the goofy cowboy, the loud talker, the sometimes ignorant but optimistic Yank. Slowly but surely, that once-unquestioned pride had gone from boastful to quietly assertive to dormant. I was beginning to see that America was as selfish as I had been in my worst days. The values that America stands for are superb; it's what we *do*, especially in those places few Americans care about, like the Valley of the Caves, or south-central Somalia, that makes a mockery of these values.

◇◇◇◇◇◇◇

There remained so much I didn't know, even on our own compound. With the beat spewing out endless emergencies, wars, hijackings, insurgencies, mass killings, and now having two kids, my ability to concentrate was beginning to deteriorate. I was constantly worried about the boys playing in the garden and getting bit by a black mamba—Alfred found a molted snake skin, a big one, right under our kitchen window, which freaked everyone out. Our utilities would frequently be turned off, for no obvious reason, and often we ran out of water from our reserve tanks and had to arrange for it to be trucked in again. The Internet didn't work. Asa's crying woke us in the middle of the night, and Courtenay and I took turns shuffling in and out of his room, half blind, trying to get him back down. Sometimes Apollo and Asa would be up at the same time. Apollo would drop silently out of his bed and creep into our room—in those footie pajamas, we couldn't hear him until he was right on top of us. Our kids were like the Viet Cong, or al-Shabaab, for that matter: They owned the night.

Each morning we'd wake up so dizzy with fatigue that things kept happening right in front of us that were impossible to decode on three hours' sleep. I stumbled downstairs one especially annoyingly bright morning to find Lucy in the pantry, digging through our nest of spare plastic bags.

"Shetani gani?" she was saying to herself—*What devil?*

Then I heard her mutter in English: "Where's my apron? Who took my apron?"

Lucy was our primary nanny, a squat, fifty-five-year-old Kikuyu woman who raised four kids of her own. I asked Courtenay what's the big deal, it's just an apron, why's Lucy so upset, and Courtenay said, "Well, it's just one of those things, it's like everyone has their own towel, their own apron, it's something we dole out and they're supposed to look after."

That missing black-and-white-checked apron soon became the talk of the compound. Lucy, Alfred, Richard, and Purity all looked high and low for it. Purity was our new backup nanny. She was a single mom with three young kids at home, and to take the job working for us, she paid a girl, Millie, from her neighborhood to watch her children. Millie also had kids, and hired a local girl back in her village to watch her own children. I like to think the whole chain of child care is a testament to Kenya's work ethic. Or maybe it's a testament to the hierarchy of poverty. I don't know many other countries where a nanny has a nanny who has a nanny.

Two days later, Purity sheepishly showed up with the checked apron, saying she had taken it home "by mistake."

"I knew something was up the minute Purity gave that back," Courtenay said. "How could she take Lucy's apron 'by mistake'?"

It was suspicious. But Purity was good with Asa, so we didn't push it. Purity walked around the house with Asa clinging to her neck, and when he woke in the middle of the night and cried, often he didn't cry for us. "Pur-a-dee, Pur-a-dee," was his SOS. He was beginning to look more and more like his brother, the same shape of head, but he had Courtenay's dark hair that in the right light gave off a rich luster. And if Asa was anything, he was fiercely loyal. He didn't seem to like Lucy at all, and Purity had little warmth for Apollo—once when Apollo misbehaved, she locked him in a bathroom and threatened to take him back to the doctor for more shots, a masterly way to inflict terror on a three-year-old. It made for a bizarre love quadrangle.

Soon enough we discovered Purity was stealing. Nothing big—a bag of sugar here, some laundry powder there, definitely a few rolls of toilet paper. We had a lot of all this stuff, and it didn't strike me as particularly egregious. Courtenay didn't see it that way.

"Stealing is stealing. I'm sorry, that's what it is. You can atone for it, someone else can forgive it, it can be overlooked, but you can't pretend it's something that it's not."

"I know, but come on," I said. "You don't really want to fire Purity, do you? She's great with Asa, and she has her own kids to support."

"You excuse so much crap in this country," Courtenay said. "You do, and you know it."

"Why do you think I do that?"

"Because you care about the people here and are apologetic, which is a form of racism in and of itself. Don't apply double standards. Don't have such low expectations of them. What would you do in the States? And worse—"

I suspected what was coming next.

"How can you trust her? After she's broken our trust, it's never going to be the same."

That was aimed directly at me, and I knew comments like that were part of the way it had to be from now on, that I had a debt to repay, and it was going to take time. But as long as I didn't get myself killed, we had time.

My dad says the path to a happy marriage is just saying yes. My parents have been married more than fifty years, so I don't automatically dismiss what my dad says, and in this case, I said yes. The worst part was seeing Purity say good-bye. Asa was curled up in front of the TV, hypnotized by Baby Einstein, and when she came up to him to give him a hug, he snapped out of his trance and squirmed away. She started crying. "Asa," she said. "Please. I'm never going to see you again."

It was only after she had gone that we learned the full extent of what Purity had been doing behind our back. She had been practicing *madawa*, a form of witchcraft, in our house.

According to Lucy and Alfred, Purity had cast a spell on Asa, making him love her and only her. Purity had stolen Lucy's apron because she needed to bring it to a witch doctor so he could put some *madawa* (medicines) on it, and the *madawa* acted as a repellent so Asa would never get close to Lucy, and therefore Purity's job would always be safe. Lucy and Alfred explained that this is why the apron was missing for exactly two days, just enough time to let the witch doctor do his work. I didn't believe in *madawa*, but that didn't matter: everyone else on the compound did.

After that, I started paying closer attention. When Mecha, one of our night watchmen, went to the bathroom one evening, I casually walked over to the table on our porch where he sat. I checked over my shoulder; the coast was clear. I picked up the gray-and-black composition book that the guards were always scribbling in, and that I had seen a couple thousand times but never been curious enough to open. As fast as I could, I whipped out my phone and started taking pictures of the pages—I'm sure the guards would have been happy to share their book, but it was more fun pretending I was a Cold War spy stealing secrets. In front of me lay an hour-by-hour chronicle of our lives, seen through the eyes of an *askari*.

1900: "Madame back in."
2115: "Clients return, all on board."
2300: "Nothing suspicious to report."
0000: "Good mid night post ok."

What did the guards think of us zooming in and out of the gate in a truck so fat they had to flatten themselves against the bushes so we could squeeze by? What did Lucy or Purity think of our drawers, stuffed with so many clothes that they were impossible to close? We had no serious material needs, and their lives were dictated by them. Once you start looking around your house through this lens, everything becomes suspect. One of the kids' favorite books was *If You Give a Dog a Donut.* I'd be very curious to know how many Africans have ever given a dog a doughnut.

Hanson was the Kenyan I worked most closely with. For the past thirty-five years, from a file cabinet of sun-spotted folders and a coffee mug crammed with well-thumbed business cards, Hanson Otundo had been running the *Times*'s East Africa bureau. He was a large man, with heavy, rounded shoulders, still strong even in his sixties, and every day that he lumbered through the door, he was helping me live my dream. He knew how to get our stove fixed when it stopped working, which seemed to be every other month; he handled the car insurance, he paid for airline tickets, he got our water turned back on; he was the intermediary between me and

the infuriating bureaucracy and low-level chaos that any developing country reliably produces. If anything ever happened to him,
I wouldn't know where to begin. Hanson had seen so many of us
young bucks come and go through that office door. But what did
he really think about us? How did he feel processing expense receipts for a sushi meal I'd had with Louis that nearly surpassed his
monthly salary?

I finally asked him.

"You can't feel jealousy for something you will never get," Hanson said. "What are we going to do? You are first world, we are
third."

I didn't know what to say. That was the awkward end to the first
and last conversation I had with him on the subject. The fact that
he didn't complain made me feel worse. Hanson had the same ac-
ceptance of our excesses that I had felt my first summer here when
I was surprised that poor people in Malawi didn't resent us for our
Nikes. I guess that's one of the greatest challenges of life, if not *the*
greatest: how to walk in a world so beautiful but so messed up.
Reporters spend their careers writing about the messed up. And
the messier it gets, for us, the greater the rewards. It was like what
I realized during the Willie the Crabber days: we need other people's pain to do our jobs well. I guess you could say the same about
doctors, but doctors take care of people.

At most newspapers, you're only as good as your last story. At
the *New York Times*, you're only as good as your next. One word
dictated the unforgiving metabolism of every person who worked
here: *produce*. But in my job, producing meant hopping on a plane,
and it was getting harder to do that. I used to love traveling but
the sight of my stuffed backpack waiting by the door now filled
me with despair. I wanted to catch every new word the kids said.
And it wasn't like I was going to a conference in Brussels. The
places I covered were inherently dangerous, and by virtue of my
occupation, I chose especially dangerous times to visit—rebels
closing in on Goma, a spate of assassinations in Mogadishu, deadly

riots ripping through Kinshasa. The instant I landed and spied the empty roads and the tension on the taxi drivers' faces, I felt like I was staring down the barrel of a loaded gun. I didn't want to even leave the airport.

Before I flew off one morning for Galkayo, a midsize town in central Somalia whose name means Where the White Man Ran Away, and where, incidentally, several white people had been kidnapped, I parted the folds of Asa's mosquito net. He was lying facedown in his crib, arms akimbo, legs spread—picture a homicide chalk drawing. He smelled like a warm pillow. I stroked his thick hair and whispered: "Don't forget me." It wasn't simply that I was sad to be gone for a couple days. I was genuinely worried about not coming back.

And I'm sure I wasn't alone. This was a dangerous time for many journalists. There was the chaos in the Arab world, NATO's bombing of Libya, and the Japanese nuclear catastrophe. Sub-Saharan Africa suffered several major wars and dozens of smaller insurgencies, a famine and hundreds of thousands of deaths. None of this captured as many headlines, but I felt good about the work I had done and was disappointed when I found out that the *Times*, which under Pulitzer rules gets three entries in each category, chose to nominate other foreign stories for the prize and couldn't squeeze mine in too. But the Pulitzer rules also say anyone can enter his own work. Of course it helps to be nominated by your paper because that makes it more official (and seem less self-aggrandizing), but individual journalists nominate themselves all the time. I called up an old graphic designer friend from Evanston to help me lay out my clips, and get the submission in order. Maybe this could be seen as yet another example of my willful failure to understand nuance, but I just didn't see anything wrong with standing up for my own work. I thought if I didn't enter, I might always wonder what if. So I took the path of least regret and sent in a fat envelope that was not so different from the fat envelopes of newspaper clips that I used to send from Brooksville, years before, unsolicited, to editors around the country. It never crossed my mind there would be any major fallout if I actually won.

When the news broke that I had won, the BlackBerry in my pocket vibrated for three days straight. Friends from Cornell, Oxford, Florida, California, Atlanta, Afghanistan, Iraq, Kenya, Somalia, Ethiopia, from different places I'd worked and different eras of my life, got back in touch after years of radio silence, sending kind messages. I know you're not supposed to derive satisfaction from others, but I felt so happy that other people were happy for me. At moments, it didn't even seem real, almost as if it were happening to someone else, and for those first few days I was like that Malawian kid with our soccer ball: *I* was on top of the mountain.

But then I started drawing heat, not from anyone inside the paper but from the snarkier corners of the Internet. "Does it *necessarily* make you an asshole to nominate yourself?" Gawker asked the world. Instantly, the attention shifted from the stories that won (eight from Somalia, two from Sudan) to the controversy of winning. Some friends asked me if I had embarrassed my bosses, and I don't think I had, The *New York Times* has built its brand on winning these prizes, but that question didn't go away. When I appeared at the fancy lunch at Columbia University a few weeks later to meet the other winners and collect the actual prize, I felt acutely conspicuous. Here I was, in this moment that many journalists dream about, which is supposed to be joyous and triumphant, a recognition that hard work can reach people, and I wanted to crawl under the table. I wish Courtenay had come with me but she had to stay back with the kids, and I just wanted the luncheon to end. That entire day, a queasy feeling swirled in my stomach. I couldn't wait to get back home.

When I showed my kids the prize, a crystal paperweight cut in a triangular shape, made at Tiffany's, Apollo said it looked like "a spaceship or an icicle." Asa said it looked like "a castle or nothing." I eventually put it back in its powder-blue Tiffany's box and softly closed the lid. I sent it from Nairobi to Evanston, where my parents put it in the living room, near a clay penguin my sister made when she was about eight.

◇◇◇◇◇◇◇◇

In journalism, when you're covering a beat, you follow certain stories. It gets to the point where you already have half the story in your head when you sit down to write because you've written ten just like them before. Sometimes, though, the stories come back; they follow you.

It was late at night, and I was resting in bed; Courtenay was reading *The Emotional Life of the Toddler.* I could hear Mecha the *askari* outside coughing in the darkness. My phone rang. The caller ID revealed Kenya's country code, although I didn't recognize the number.

"Mista Jifri, how is your condition?"

"Peacock?"

"Yes, I am Peacock."

I held the phone away from my face and squinted again at the number.

"Where the hell are you?"

"I am here, Mista Jifri, I am here."

In East Africa, Nairobi is the center of all things. All roads lead here—in fact only one road ran from the port of Mombasa, right past the patch of grass in central Nairobi where Roko and I were mugged many years ago, all the way to Goma, Congo. But still, it was a strange and unnerving sight to see Peacock in the doorway of my office. I barely recognized him. It had been four years. The drought and famine of 2011 had desiccated the Ogaden as well, causing thousands to flee. He was painfully thin and had shaved off his dreads. He was wearing a professorial sweater vest. His condition was not good. He now had a family, a wife and kids. The Front was all but dead. He was out of the game.

We hugged, and I said, "Please, please, sit down," as so many people had once said to me. I jumped up to get him a Sprite from the fridge, which he struggled to open with his long, bony fingers. He looked far more fragile than he had in the desert when he was being hunted down. "Nothing problem," he said in his gravelly voice, as he finally cracked the seal on the plastic bottle. I asked about the old gang.

"Musa, how is that guy?"

"Death-sentenced," Peacock said flatly.

"What about Manchoos?"

"Gone."

"Big Head?"

Peacock shook his head.

"Satir?"

Satir's face was on my wall, right behind where I was sitting. It was the one self-indulgence in my office, next to maps of the Ogaden and Mogadishu and a pirate chart in which the UN had actually used a little skull-and-crossbones motif to mark the latest attacks. After the Ogaden article ran I spent several hundred dollars dry-mounting the front page and framing it. It was Courtenay's picture beside my story. Peacock looked up at it. Satir was the one who had led that magical liberation dance late into the night.

"Shot through the heart," Peacock said quietly.

That framed story behind me was one of the highlights of my journalistic career. Human rights groups, aid organizations, and members of Congress seized upon it, calling for fact-finding missions and sanctions against the Ethiopian government. The story, in its entirety, was entered into the *Congressional Record*. Courtenay's video, probably her best, generated a half million views. We put what had been an obscure African conflict on the world map. But our work in the Ogaden didn't have the same effect as the story on Bahram. Because of the newspaper's reach, Bahram had been saved. Because I'd been sloppy enough to leave a notebook accessible to the Ethiopian military, Musa had been tracked down, the driver who took us to Degehabur had been imprisoned, several students had to flee the country, and Peacock's father had been arrested. He had been ill at the time, suffering chest pains, but the soldiers refused to take him to the hospital. He died in custody.

"Not one of his children attended the funeral," Peacock said.

We sat for a few moments, separated by a chunk of silence.

"Peacock," I finally asked. "Tell me the truth. Did our work do more harm or good?"

It was a question I had thought about plenty of times but never dared to ask. Journalists try not to think about it too much because if we did, it might be hard getting out of bed in the morning: Does my being here mess things up more than my not being here, despite whatever good intentions I may have? What really was my balance sheet? Would someone like Peacock have been better off if he had never met me?

Peacock rubbed his face for a moment, looked out the window.

"For people who personally suffered, it was problem," he said. "But your mission gave us wider audience. And you got experience with your own hand. It entered your emotion. It is part of your narration."

I looked out the window. I couldn't look him in the eyes.

"I have this tingling," Peacock went on. "Up and down my legs. It's why I had to leave. I am not well. Can you help me?"

I wasn't writing a story. Peacock wasn't carrying a gun anymore, and so he had no *news* value. Sitting across the table from him, there was very little distance between us, and I didn't allow any of it to remain professional.

I picked up the phone and called the Aga Khan Hospital. A receptionist answered.

"Hi, I'd like to make an appointment. My name is Jeffrey Gettleman, and I'd like to see Dr. Hooker."

"Very well," she said. "When would you like to come in?"

"It's not for me," I answered. "It's for a friend."

"Oh, okay. What's the friend's name?"

"Pea—" I whispered, covering the receiver. "Hey, Peacock, what's your real name?"

A few days later we walked together up to the fourth floor of the hospital, just down the hall from where Apollo and Asa were born. Dr. Hooker, a gentle neurologist, a member of the Indian professional class, took a long look at us as we filed into his office.

"So, how do you two know each other?" he asked.

"Long story, daktari." I smiled at Dr. Hooker. "Let's just say we met in the desert."

"I see," he said, beginning his exam, softly tapping Peacock's knees and feet with little rubber hammers. He looked into his eyes, felt very slowly up and down his vertebrae, measured all his vital signs. After a few minutes, he stepped back and told me to sit down.

"It may be irreversible," Dr. Hooker said. "Extensive nerve damage. Maybe paresthesia. It's difficult to discern the cause. A severe vitamin deficiency, perhaps? My guess is, it was his lifestyle."

I tried to explain this to Peacock, who sat on the examination table, chopstick legs hanging limply down from the white paper. He nodded stoically, then slid me a little grin. That's when it hit me. He's Benny. That's who he had always reminded me of—I had just failed to make the connection before. He had Benny's gravelly voice, Benny's slight hunch, Benny's irrepressible glint of amusement in his eyes, even now, while receiving a hopeless prognosis.

I wish I had done more to help Benny. At the very least, I could have called or written more often. As I was settling into my new life, the slope of Benny's descent steepened. The worst part was that he knew it.

"i am angry this month," one of his last e-mails said. "angry that i cannot walk without falling. angry that my arms don't move, angry that there's no effective treatment for als and a dozen drugs that will make my dick hard. im angry that i weigh 105. down from 177, i'm actually disturbed by that one. I'm angry that i cannot wake up before dawn make a cup of coffee and stand alone on my patio while the neighborhood wakes up. i really miss that one. i miss the past. i miss every woman i've ever slept with like my friends and family miss the way i used to be. the memories are stuck in my bones for the rest of my life, reminding me of what i have lost."

I don't know if I was consciously trying to atone for not being around more for Benny. But I felt no hesitancy in taking out a pile of Kenyan shilingi from the bank, buying Peacock a bag of expensive drugs, and helping him find a place to live. It wasn't great—one room in a large, institutional-looking apartment block off an unpaved road in Eastleigh, the neglected Somali neighborhood nearly buried under piles of sour-mash trash. The barred balconies dripped with drying clothes. Inside it was loud, reverberating with echoes. At the door to each apartment stood a small pile of shoes, but I noticed that there was only one kind of shoe from each pair. Peacock told me that's what everyone did, to make sure their shoes weren't stolen by neighbors. He quickly ushered me inside. I could tell he missed the Front.

I tried to check up on him as much as I could. He didn't have a job and spent a lot of time in his apartment, sitting in a plastic chair. He had been to our house, had seen the comforts and space we had, but like Hanson and so many others I've met out here, he didn't seem to resent us for it. He never asked for money, though he was still asking a lot of questions.

"Mista Jifri, you know man Samwell Harrington? He wrote book, something called *Crash of Civilizations*."

The title was one letter off but I knew what he was taking about.

"It good? Have you analyzed it?"

"Not yet, my friend," I said. "But I'll get it for you."

He introduced me to his wife, who had also been a fighter in the Ogaden; she was the one named the Victim, with the chipped plum nail polish, holding a loaded Kalashnikov. She and Peacock seemed especially close. Peacock gave me a picture they had taken in a Nairobi photo studio. Because he was so much taller than the Victim, the two are squatting on the floor, his arm protectively around her back, her hand placed lightly on his shoulder, a greater display of affection than I have ever seen in a Somali couple.

Like us, they had two boys, Abdisame, a tiny baby, and Mohamed, about Apollo's age. In addition to the money I gave them, the family lived off a few hundred dollars sent each month by taxi-driving relatives in the States. Here was an aging rebel fighter trying to raise his boys, and he didn't have enough money for "baby class," as they called it here, nursery school. Mohamed spent most of his day in their one-room apartment, watching TV.

"It not good for Mohamed to be so, so"—Peacock struggled to find the right word—"isolated. He need social contact."

Mohamed's only toy was that TV. He sat on the edge of the bed much too close to it, his eyes lit by the glowing screen. At the time, Apollo was into Legos, and when I'd come home from work and he'd run up to me with his latest creation, a spaceship or aircraft carrier he had built with almost an engineer's intuitive sense, I'd say, "Wow, Apollo, that's amazing," genuinely stunned someone that small could do that. Now, watching Mohamed zone out in front of a fuzzy TV, I realized that whatever talents or abilities our children have are almost irrelevant when compared to the material advantages or disadvantages they start off with.

I tried to explain a smidgen of this to Apollo, who also possessed approximately a hundred Matchbox cars. He agreed to part with exactly two: a station wagon with no roof and an orange race car missing a door. I presented them to Mohamed a few weeks later, and when we drove away, the little boy stood riveted on the balcony, one car in each pudgy fist, looking down at us, dust rising from the road. Later I bought him his own set that came in a nifty plastic wheel. And I gave Peacock money for baby class.

When I called the hospital that day, I hadn't felt like a Missionary, a Misfit, or a Mercenary. This was a new role for me. I had felt more like a public defender assigned to a case that I needed to handle with great care. That's really the best you can do in Africa, or anywhere else. A couple cases come your way, individual people, and you do your best to defend them. There's an old Talmudic saying that my pogrom-fleeing great-grandfather Morris, who arrived in America in 1914, would have known: To save one life is to redeem the whole world.

I'm not particularly religious. What I did for Peacock did not redeem the whole world. It was a very small act. But it felt right and necessary.

FIFTEEN

<><><><><><>

THE WORLD, NOW

It was becoming strange to return to the United States, stranger still to be standing shoulder to shoulder with my Da Vinci Brothers, all of us in suits and ties, some sprouting our first gray hairs, staring into Benny's grave.

Benjamin Saul Byer died on a bright July day. He was thirty-seven. He had never given up, pushing for an experimental surgery in which four electrodes were implanted in his diaphragm to artificially stimulate contractions and help him breathe. The surgery didn't take, and his breathing stopped.

Benny was buried in Arlington Heights, a suburb north of Evanston, and as we sat near the freshly dug hole, I heard the hum of traffic lifting off Rand Road. I'd seen so many people die, in different styles, but never as slowly as this, and not somebody I knew, not somebody who was such an inspiration in his own goofy, free way. So much of my life had been trying to control exactly where I was headed, and Benny had taught me a whole other approach. Without ever verbalizing it, he showed me that if you let life just come at you, yes, you may not be able to prevent some bad things from happening, but you also allow the best things to happen. Despite the ravages of ALS, Benny didn't die a miserable guy.

When the service was over, it didn't feel right to just stand up and walk away. I now understood why the funeral is always the hardest part of death. It is only then that you truly part. Having the body near you, even if it's inert, provides a trace of comfort. But when you walk away from that grave, and leave that person in the cold earth, alone, you walk away forever.

At an old high school friend's house, I caught up with some people I hadn't seen in years. After I told them what I was doing, I found myself in the middle of a small circle, the questions flying in. "Is it really dangerous? Is it really poor? What do you love about Africa so much?" After all these years, I still didn't have any snappy answers, and that last question stopped me cold. It's easy to explain why you *like* something. But love? That's tricky. That's a story, not a sentence. As I looked down at my shoes, I felt as if I had suddenly returned to the battered dining room in the old frat house with Milk towering over me, asking me what that first Africa trip had been like.

But then I felt something soft against my hand. I looked up. Courtenay was standing there, right next to me. She stepped in like a litigator.

"Have you ever been?" she asked someone.

"No."

"Well, if you had, you'd know."

My friends nodded thoughtfully, and Courtenay slid me a quick, knowing smile.

Driving back to my parents' house, I began to feel the full distance that we had put between us and our former selves. We hadn't moved to Kenya because we felt alienated from America or wanted to escape our roots. But that was the effect, whether we intended it or not. Even a place like Evanston, so congested with nostalgia, would never feel the same. I used to drive around, and it was as if I'd never left. Passing the houses we'd painted, I barely needed to squint to see us up there dangling from ladders in the strongest days of our youth. Those houses felt like our houses, like we had lived in them, not simply clung to the outside bricks for a couple weeks or snuck into the fridge to nick a few spare ribs. But I didn't see anyone up on the ladders anymore. Benny's death amplified this; in a weird way, Benny had been the heart of the Da Vincis. All I could do now was allow myself a few seconds of longing, to wonder what it would feel like if we could all come back from the past, alive and in one piece, and be together again.

We were becoming the lost *mzungus* in our own land. More accustomed to the roads of former British East Africa, Courtenay now drove a little too close on the right. I braced myself to hear the crunch of her whacking off the mirror of my dad's new Acura. When we swung past Haven Junior High, she couldn't believe it.

"Wait, that was your school?"

"Yeah, you've seen it before."

She had probably seen it a hundred times.

"No fence? No walls?" Courtenay shook her head. "Look at it, hon. Just out there for the taking."

That's some serious PTSD, I thought. But what did I expect? She'd been held at gunpoint, kidnapped in the desert, tear-gassed. She too had seen more than her fair share of freshly sliced meat. And now, thanks to me, a compound trimmed with razor wire and guarded by billy-club-wielding *askaris* was what she called home.

Apollo was the most maladjusted of us all. His grandparents in New York didn't know what the hell he was talking about when he started going on about *shimos* and *totos* and a wet *kitambaa* (that's holes, children, and washcloth; he knew only the Swahili words for certain things). During a stroll through Central Park, he suddenly tugged my sleeve, saying: "Daddy, daddy, quick, quick, what's that? It is real or is it a toy?"

"What?"

He jabbed his little finger at a large brown object about fifty feet away.

"That!"

My son had seen, in the wild, elephants, lions, rhinos, croco-diles, and lemurs leaping from the trees. At five years old, he could tell you the difference between a gazelle and an eland, a wildebeest and a waterbuck. But there was one species he had never encountered that blew his little mind: an Upper West Side Labradoodle.

The two of us admired it for a minute, its poufy fur and dumbass dog-grin.

"Daddy, its hair is so fluffy. Is it a toy?"

"Sort of. A grown-up toy, a real expensive one."

◇◇◇◇◇◇◇

I had always been relieved to touch down at Jomo Kenyatta when I was coming back from Congo, Ethiopia, Sudan, Somalia. I now added JFK to the list. Three weeks away was plenty for me. Call it spiritual jet lag. If we were gone for too long, I'd come back to Kenya feeling like I didn't belong anywhere. *Mzungu*ness is a learned behavior. It takes a lot to overlook the obvious, like how just about everyone around us was really poor and compared to them we were Bill Gates, how the world was so unequal it seemed impossible to fix it.

But more than that, I wondered if I felt more at peace in East Africa than I did where I was from. I dug the easy smiles, the extended handshakes, the casualness, and getting Richard's big-ass bear hug in the airport parking lot and hearing him finish it off with: "Karibu nyumbani!" *Welcome home!* The ambient warmth was still a major selling point of living here. I'd take a bike ride north of my house—in about three miles the suburbs opened up into farmland, deep, rich, ochre soil all around me—and sometimes when I'd see someone walking toward me along the road, I'd steer my bike close to the shoulder, right on the edge, stick out my left hand and call out "Piga tano!" *hit me five*, the Swahili equivalent of *eedack*! Nine times out of ten—smack!—I'd get it.

I relished the natural beauty, starting on my own street, draped with bougainvillea in all kinds of colors, the fallen leaves whisked by passing cars into lines along the curb like rose petals down a wedding aisle. I appreciated the lack of honking, even in traffic.

Kenyans didn't presume the earth turned for their own benefit. If the Internet went down or the electricity disappeared, they went on with their lives.

My attachment to this part of the world was kind of like a marriage. Some of the early wild passion was gone—true. It wasn't always fun. I'd been disappointed and frustrated by a lot that I'd seen. My love was still solid, but it had grown more complex.

The story was shifting, too, and I had to shift with it. Some of the big wars were ending—back in the day I covered three at a time. Now weeks would pass where I wouldn't have to type out the words "belt-fed machine gun," "gang-raped," or "dozens killed," or ask, "Where exactly did your brother get his tongue cut out?" I had gotten pretty good at bleak and troubling. I wasn't so strong on progress, and now, finally, it was all around me.

Nairobi was sprouting new buildings, new stores, new bridges, and new malls in every part of town. It was as if someone had sprinkled water over the urban area and a whole new city had popped up. The quaint colonial-era road network was no match for the 10,000-plus cars being imported each month, and men selling iPhone chargers and selfie sticks now plied the traffic-plugged highways. My nemesis Laptop, that crazy matatu, was now being outclassed by a newer fleet of minibuses with names such as Facebook, Gmail, and Password. There were even samples in the supermarket; I could've grazed all day on those little cubes of imported Gruyère and chunks of chocolate croissants that the Kenyan shoppers plucked off the tray somewhat suspiciously.

The lines out the door of Cold Stone Creamery and Domino's were evidence of why Kenya was at the forefront of a new term we started hearing around 2013—"Africa Rising." Kenya was rising, and I was happy to cover it. The country had overcome its political demons to hold a peaceful presidential election that year, the first since the 2007 disaster, and investment was pouring in. Angola was rising as well. So were Rwanda and Senegal and Zambia and Namibia and Ghana and even quiet, ex-socialist Tanzania to some degree. The reasons? Major infrastructure projects by a mineral-hungry China; new technologies that enabled money to move fast and safely around the world; the passage of Africa's turbulent turn of the twenty-first century into the more stable current era; and not in the least the 2008 credit crunch in the United States and Europe, which had reduced interest rates in the Western world to practically zero, so that those looking for even a modest return needed to look farther than ever before. And guess what part of the world was still considered the farthest.

About half an hour from our house a new restaurant appeared, called Caramel. It was beautiful: sleek wood banquettes, heat lamps, cozy cabanas in back. It wasn't cheap, either: mac-n-cheese for fifteen bucks and $450 shots of Remy Martin Louis XIII cognac (an eye-popping extravagance not lost on Kenya's *Daily Nation*, which wrote a piece about it). What interested me was that Caramel, part of a chain from Dubai, imported white waiters, and Kenya has never had many white waiters—or white working-class people—in its history. Caramel had found the cheapest *mzungus* in the world—from Macedonia—and shipped them here, banking on the fact that tweedy Kenyans would enjoy watching a white man with a bead of sweat trickling down his temple sweeping up steak scraps from the table with the flat edge of his hand. The place was packed.

Caramel's Macedonian waitstaff wasn't half as good as an all-Kenyan one. Their English wasn't exactly the queen's. "I see job in Internet, I come Africa," one told me. Another import stood at the door bowing awkwardly at the waist as customers came and left, saying "Tank you, tank you." He was the maître d'. That was his M.

The very character of Kenya was changing. For most in Nairobi, the rapid development was a positive force. But in the wilderness areas, it was more complicated. Railways and highways were now being proposed through pristine national parks. In central Africa, more roads and better infrastructure meant it was much easier to penetrate the wildest places and cart off the loot. Diamonds, gold, and other minerals were being smuggled out at a distressing pace by armed groups who were increasingly branching into business. The most dispiriting conflict resource was ivory. You don't dig it up, you kill magnificent animals for it, and the explosion of China's own middle class was spelling one of the greatest onslaughts on African wildlife in recent history.

Armed groups were fanning out across the savannahs, hunting elephants with military-grade weaponry. Some even mowed them down from helicopters, leaving their carcasses in a tight circle, the baby elephants in the center, the adults ringed on the outside in a vain effort to protect their offspring. In the span of a few years, on my watch, more than 100,000 elephants were wiped out. The tusks were sawed off and sold to African middlemen who teamed up with organized crime to ship them to China, sometimes lumping the ivory in with a consignment of chili peppers or anchovies to throw off the sniffer dogs. In underground factories in Beijing and Hong Kong, the ivory was then carved into cups, eyeglass frames, statuettes, bookmarks, and combs. The Chinese loved ivory the way we used to. It was like the nineteenth century all over again, Marlowe and Kurtz.

I'm aware that even referring to Conrad in a book about contemporary Africa may very well be seen as distasteful, but I think it's insane not to mention Conrad. *Heart of Darkness* was the first book I read on Africa—I'm sure it was the first book many of us read on Africa, though some consider it the *ooga-booga* Bible. The Nigerian writer Chinua Achebe called Conrad a "thoroughgoing racist," and maybe he was. "I am talking about a book," Achebe said, "which parades in the most vulgar fashion prejudices and insults from which a section of mankind has suffered untold agonies and atrocities. . . . I am talking about a story in which the very humanity of black people is called in question."

Conrad left out a lot about Africa, but that relatively slender book got to the marrow of colonialism. Published in 1899, not long after the Berlin Conference, when the European powers carved up Africa like a roast on the table, its focus was not the crazy natives but the *mzungus* and their murderous abuses of power that made imperialism possible. And while most of the continent, save a few islands in the Indian and Atlantic Oceans, now enjoys its political independence, things have not changed nearly as much as they should have. That's the legacy of the ruthless colonialism that Conrad thinly fictionalized. As an outsider writing about sub-Saharan Africa, this legacy puts me in a trap. If I focus on the wars, the violence, the poverty or the governments that are as rotten and mushy as an old mango, I'm criticized for getting too *ooga-booga*. But if I go on about the spirit and easy laughter, about the countless Africans I've met who are truly happy and hopeful, no matter their economic circumstances or lack of opportunity, then I'm criticized for making Africa look simple. There is so much we can learn from this part of the world that is life-affirming. But at the same time, there is so much injustice. The gap between Africa and the rest of the world—in terms of wealth, education, life span, and power—is still disgraceful.

The corruption and violence in many African countries fueled the shooting spree on elephants. Poachers in places such as Chad, Congo, the Central African Republic, and even Kenya decimated herds with total impunity. I traveled across Africa chasing dead elephants. I wanted to write the most alarming story I could about the absurdity of turning elephants into trinkets. At this rate, soon there won't be many left. Rhinos face the same fate. Many Vietnamese believe that eating ground-up rhino horn can cure cancer—even though rhino horn is made of the same protein, keratin, that's in our fingernails. Vietnam is rapidly modernizing, but the Vietnamese still respect their traditional beliefs. Rhinos are now very close to extinction.

Worrying about wildlife that we so love to observe can sound painfully quaint—this is exactly what Binyavanga Wainaina parodied in "How to Write about Africa." Well, such is the plight of *mzungus*—and, in a way, of adults. Don't we all bemoan the loss of what we first fell for in our youth? And weren't these the world's treasures? Where else do you find parades of wild elephants? Or towers of giraffes? Or crashes of rhinos? Or such spectacularly large stretches of unpolluted wilderness?

We may search the stars for life, but perhaps life's miracle was a one-off. Maybe we're it. Maybe we're floating through the universe alone. Maybe the time we're in right now is the fourth quarter of everything. Maybe in the next hundred years we will do more damage to the planet than we did during our first two million. And maybe there is no better place to see this and feel the urgency of all this being destroyed right in front of our eyes than where I live.

◇◇◇◇◇◇◇

On Saturdays, we usually took the kids to the mall. Kenyans love malls, and by late 2013, we had several: Village Market, Sarit Center, Yaya Center, Prestige Plaza, Ridgeways, Thika Road, Junction, ABC, the Mall, and Westgate. There was no greater symbol of "Africa Rising" than Westgate. It rose four stories in Nairobi's Westlands neighborhood above the one-story vine-covered bungalows and low-slung shacks selling fake Maasai shields. About fifteen minutes from our front door, Westgate contained some treats that we missed from home: a gigantic supermarket, 70 percent dark chocolate, sushi, and a six-screen movie theater with stadium seating and excellent popcorn. It was where Apollo and Asa rode their first escalator—I couldn't peel them off that thing. That Saturday—"Scatterday," as Asa called it (and as it often felt)—it was just chance that my family and I weren't there.

The first message, from the American embassy, said stay away from Westgate, bank robbery under way. More messages started coming in about a shootout. Tyler Hicks, one of the most decorated *New York Times* photographers, who happens to live with two majestic Rhodesian ridgebacks a few minutes from my house, called me and said, "Dude, get over here. I don't think this is a bank robbery." To be honest, as I jumped into my car and sped up

Peponi Road, which had been cleared by the sound of automatic gunfire, I started to think that if journalism is a history of violence, which seemed as true as it did in Brooksville, maybe it's time I do something else.

When I arrived, I saw a crumpled body lying on the same steps Apollo and Asa used to fly up, their little hands in mine. Inside, dead people were crumpled everywhere, by the grocery store where I used to buy them lollipops, by the food court where Courtenay and I used to go on dates. Westgate's gleaming floors were sticky with blood smeared into circles from the last kicks of dying women. It was disgusting, depressing, demoralizing, and terrifying.

It was a terrorist strike. It was al-Shabaab, Abu Mansoor's outfit. Maybe he had personally given the orders to shoot the women, shoot the kids, shoot everybody. Maybe he had thought it was wrong but was overruled by the real sickos. I'd be curious to talk to him about it, but I don't talk to him anymore, nor would I ever trust him again to sit down for a Fanta. In a few years, his well-disciplined militia, which had helped pacify one of the most dangerous places on earth, had morphed into a terrorist group of some of the world's most accomplished killers. In a few hours, four Shabaab gunmen with assault rifles ruthlessly massacred scores of innocent Kenyans. They separated the Christians from the Muslims and shot the Christians in the head.

It would have been so much worse had dozens of off-duty cops not come rushing in, from all directions, at the sound of the first gunshots. They didn't huddle against an outside wall, calling for backup. They charged right in, cheap pistols drawn against high-powered rifles, no flaks. Several were cut down. But these guys, who may have been, on any other day, jacking civilians for *kitu kidogo*, pressed on and cornered the Shabaab fighters in the back of a supermarket. The military response took hours, and some of the soldiers ended up looting from stores, but that was only after the off-duty cops ran out of Westgate with dazed shoppers on their backs and bloody children in their arms. They showed a courage and selflessness that I would have never guessed was inside them. In the following days, so many Kenyans lined up to donate blood that thousands were turned away. The country pulled together as I had never seen.

We were stunned by the attack, but we shouldn't have been. This was the collision of the two stories I had been living since the day I arrived. While I had been witnessing the flurry of development in Nairobi, I had also become a specialist in despair. Africa is still home to most of the world's shakiest nations. The stories I wrote on Denis Mukwege, the Congolese gynecologist, the indefatigable healer, helped raise hundreds of thousands of dollars for his hospital. Still, Mukwege was nearly assassinated recently because he dared to speak out about the hundreds of thousands of women who continue to be raped. Congo is not rising.

Neither are Somalia, Sudan, the Central African Republic, Chad, Burundi, Libya, Guinea-Bissau, Niger, Eritrea, or Zimbabwe. What we are now seeing is politics catching up with economics. Most sub-Saharan countries are still very young and poorly governed, and it is difficult for an economy to keep growing at a rapid rate if a tiny elite, often ethnically based, steals most of the gains. Some of the nations that were the fastest risers, such as Ethiopia, are the most repressive and are beginning to crack. Others are exploding. Just a few years ago, South Sudan topped the *Economist*'s list of the world's fastest-growing economies. It is now a killing field, the site of one of Africa's worst civil wars.

Kenya, on the other hand, seems to succeed despite itself. Its entrepreneurial class continues to blossom, coming up with revolutionary products like mobile money, while the Kenyan government continues to disappear millions of public dollars intended for poor people. While Africa is often seen as one, it does not move as one. Some African countries will continue to rise; others will sink. But chaos doesn't usually respect the lines on a map, so even the risers have to watch out. To live the good life in Kenya, to eat $15 plates of mac-n-cheese at Caramel while a medieval mix of famine, warlords, plagues, and pirates seethed next door in Somalia, was the epitome of willful self-deceit. The Kenyan-Somali border was miles of unpatrolled sand. We all knew what was coming across it.

The attacks continued. The Shabaab slaughtered 150 students at a national university north of Nairobi in 2015. Four assailants, light weapons—same story. The killers and the students were about the same age, early twenties, a tragic rendezvous between Kenya's generation of promise and Somalia's generation of chaos. Nothing seemed able to stop the Shabaab. American forces took out its leaders with drone strikes. Ugandan peacekeepers shelled Shabaab positions. Unlike ISIS or the Taliban or the FARC in Colombia, the Shabaab was never a militant group that controlled oil fields or poppy fields or coca fields or anything else that could turn a serious profit. Still, they had become very good at murder on a shoestring.

Sometimes we altered our routines: Asa and Apollo want to go for ice cream today, but it's Friday and it's Ramadan, and the Shabaab love to seek martyrdom on Fridays and during Ramadan, so maybe we should just stay home and eat popsicles and watch *Giggle Giggle Quack* again. That Saturday when Westgate was attacked, we happened to be at another mall. That's what was so scary. The mall we were at, with our kids, could have just as easily been hit.

"It all comes back to what that fat Zimbabwean guy said," Courtenay said one night as I was sitting in the office, finishing up another story, the word *Shabaab* on my screen a dozen times.

"What do you mean?"

"You remember the rancid donkey meat?"

I nodded.

"That's what it comes down to. These guys can keep killing and killing because they can live off nothing. And I guess you were right too. They do want it more."

◇◇◇◇◇◇◇

If this were a movie, this would be the point when the strings swell, right before the credits begin to roll. Images and captions would flash across the screen, telling you how everyone ended up in real life.

Roko continues to make movies. He was nominated for an Oscar for his first film, *Genghis Blues*, and directed another award-winning movie, *Happy*, about how different people around the world pursue happiness. One of the leading happiness researchers told Roko that every happy person he ever studied loved somebody and was loved by somebody. And, speaking of love, Roko still thinks a lot about his dad, especially now that he has his own children. But he doesn't look at that ocean rowing adventure any differently. "The best gift you can give to your kids," he says, and I tend to agree, "is to be the person you want to be." My other filmmaker friend, Chris, didn't do so badly either. Maybe you've seen some of his flicks. *Batman Begins*? *The Dark Knight*? *Inception*? *Interstellar*? That confusing idea he mentioned to me years ago when I was a reporter in LA became his breakthrough, *Memento*. One of the first films he ever shot was of the Dan summer in 1990.

Bahram, the Pakistani kid, recently married and has two sons. He lives in Lahore.

Willie Crain is one of the few people in American history to be sentenced to death with no body ever found. He maintains his innocence to this day.

The Fallujah gang who kidnapped me would not have fallen for Mr. Greck's shtick today. The Sunni insurgents in that part of Iraq are not just in ISIS; they founded it. They are tech-savvy and have made several slick videos of their beheadings, including of Western journalists.

Abu Mansoor is still alive, deep in hiding. US predator drones continue to seek him out.

Peacock still lives in Nairobi, still dreaming of a liberated Ogaden, but he's also looking for a job. He's survived more hardship, more loss, more injustice, and more defeat than anyone I know. But he isn't ruined, he isn't bitter, he's still funny, and he hasn't lost his own humanity. I realize he has killed people—that part I'm still working out, but I believe he is ultimately good, wanting the best for himself and his family. His life, and that of the Victim, will never be easy. Like many refugees in Kenya, they get constantly harassed by the police, and they don't have enough money to send their two sons to a decent school. Peacock's skill set of sabotage, ambush, and asset acquisition isn't exactly geared for a position at Caramel. Neither is his skin color. He recently asked me if I had any ideas, so I manned up. I now have a very well qualified research assistant, who sits two desks away from me, with extensive knowledge of African rebel groups.

The other day after work, Peacock and I went out for pizza, along with Courtenay and one of her new work buddies.

"So, Peacock, what do you do here in Nairobi?" Courtenay's colleague asked.

Peacock didn't miss a beat.

"I'm a member of a rebel group."

"Oh, that's nice," the guy said, not really paying attention, munching on a breadstick. Then it hit him. His eyes widened.

Courtenay has a whole new set of colleagues. Returning to her criminal justice roots, she's now running a law-enforcement program at the American embassy in Nairobi. She's off early each morning in a whirl of jangly jewelry and a blue State Department badge that conveys in code a level of security clearance I'm not allowed to mention. I haven't seen the sexy pants for years. The e-mails from her work account, at least the ones to me, always end: "This email is UNCLASSIFIED."

Her mission is to reform Kenya's police service, one of the most troubled public institutions in East Africa. She works closely with a new internal affairs department and a new civilian oversight authority mandated to pursue killer police officers. There are some good cops trying to root out the bad cops, and the Kenyan police service is now essentially at war with itself. Courtenay's often in the middle, receiving dispiriting news late at night about the most recent murder or disappearance. It drains her. She flops into bed, right eye closing by itself, and asks me a question that I continue to ask myself: "Is this making any difference?"

Courtenay is a deeply moral person and has taught me to take every action I do seriously, down to the individual words I put on the page. What happened to our marriage in real life? Why did she forgive me? How did I forgive myself? Why did we stay together?

Three reasons, mostly, and perhaps none all that satisfying. One, Courtenay, though viciously principled, is still practical, and we had just married and relocated to Africa; and the idea of "unfurling all that," as she put it, was too exhausting to contemplate. Two, we still loved each other. Three, I begged, I really begged.

Apollo and Asa now go to the International School of Kenya. Among their subjects are Swahili language and Samburu bead-work. Not far from a kindergarten classroom stands a sculpture made out of stained glass, marked with a long-ago stamp that reads "Deziree Safaris."

"What's that, Daddy?" Apollo asked.

The International School of Kenya was Dan's school, and the colored glass is a memorial to Dan. I would have never thought, back when I spent time with Dan, that he would have dropped out so early, and I would have continued along the path he had been laying. It saddens me and comforts me to think he is still close by, in his own way, the only way he can be now. Dan Eldon is watching my sons embark on the life that I so badly wanted for myself, thanks to him.

What's next for me? What do you do when the journey has taken you to your destination, exactly where you wanted to go? What happens then if your goals change?

These days, that's what I'm beginning to feel. When Ebola hit

West Africa, and my bosses asked for my help, I paused. A few years ago I would have been on the first plane out. But when I saw the early images of people bleeding out of their mouths and came home that night and stepped lightly over the Thomas trains in Asa's room and got down on the carpet and began building him a new track, I started thinking of what that guy told me years ago in Afghanistan. Being thirty is one thing, being forty another. That's how this business works. You have to be reckless to do this job. I'm now forty-five. It's a young man's game. And the worst thing I could do to my kids, the most lasting harm I could ever inflict on them, would be relatively easy in this line of work: to get Daddy killed.

But I'm hopeless. I ended up covering Ebola, and the best story I wrote was unusual for me. It wasn't about death; maybe it was an expression of what was happening inside me. I found the one place in Sierra Leone where people weren't talking about viral loads or death rates, treatment centers or moonsuits. At the Bureh Beach Surf Club, a sign at the water's edge read DI WAVES DEM GO MAK U FEEL FINE. The surfers turned to a bewitching passion to survive, and thanks to them, I stood up for the first time on a surfboard, and there's nothing like the thrill of the *shh, shh, shh* of the board's edge knifing through water, kicking up a fine line of white spray. The only thing that comes close is galloping on a horse. Surfing in the line of duty was one of the purest thrills I've felt in years, and it made me realize that if I ever tried to do anything else besides journalism, there might be too much to lose.

I ache for the days when I traveled this continent oblivious to its wars or pandemics, when I moved without advanced technology tracking my every step, when I didn't have a single battery in my backpack, and the first words out of my mouth, upon entering a new hotel, in a new city, in a new country, were not "What's the password for the Wi-Fi?"

It takes me back to the idea of life without a map. Of course maps can be handy at times, but it's also important to just go, toward sights and sounds and urges and curiosities and things people say, to put your faith in those who are guiding you, whether it is Dan or Somali warlords or Somali pirates or Yama or Peacock.

Evening used to be the most relaxing part of the day. Now it's the most taxing. Dinnertime, bath time, story time, bedtime. I glance out the window and see the sky turning violet. I yearn to hear the whoosh of the ibises, who always fly in pairs, to watch the first stars emerge. The arrival of each night on the equator is a performance—condensed, spectacular, those rich bright colors flashing by, orange to pink to purple to deep, deep blue within minutes, a haiku of a sunset.

But I am bent over in Asa's bathroom, helping him wipe away the "poopie dupe," and Courtenay's in another room reading Apollo *If You Give a Dog a Donut*. We have a few thousand more evenings together. Then our little guys will be big, leave home, and break our hearts. Instead of crawling into bed knowing exactly where they are, we will find ourselves lying on our backs, staring up at the ceiling, wondering what continent they are on, like my parents did, so many years ago.

My mom, ever the social worker, recently asked me how I thought all the near-death experiences had affected me. I said "Mom, I've only had a few," and she said, "Well, most of us have had none." I guess they've made me feel more erratic, more prone to bursts of wild inexplicable happiness over seemingly inconsequential things, like the rare weeknight escape when Courtenay and I zoom out of the driveway on a clear night to a party. I'm also more prone to flashes of depression, like when I recently watched Asa playing soccer with one of the *askaris*—Asa had insisted on putting on his uniform, shin guards, and little cleats just to kick around the ball in the driveway—and it hit me how temporary everything is.

I feel change coming. It's been ten years now in East Africa, a long time for a newspaper correspondent, and I'm not sure how many other potential moves I can duck. I'm torn by opposing impulses. Part of me wants to look up and see a new skyline, to experience more of our fast-changing world. Part of me never wants to leave. All the power and magic that I first felt I still feel, we still feel. The other day we wended along the escarpment road that hugs the eastern edge of the Great Rift Valley, the same road, actually, that Dom had spoken from years ago, when he said he'd never seen so much of the world in one gulp. As Courtenay gazed off at the miles of green veldt melting into the haze, she said: "It gets me every time."

Roads. I feel like so much of my life has happened on roads. Multiple kidnappings. Many close calls. Countless discoveries. Our first kiss.

Sometimes I see a very small one—it wasn't even much of a road, it was more like a path. It was in Congo, during one of our first trips, to speak to militia fighters who had set up a base in the middle of the jungle. We were riding along on small motorcycles, a string of minuscule figures enveloped by a huge, lush, wildly healthy forest, passing towers of bamboo that blotted out the sun and spiders the size of baseballs hanging in nets of silk, when all of a sudden the bikes in front of us stopped. Stopping in the middle of the Congolese jungle is like getting a phone call in the middle of the night. It usually means something very bad has happened or is about to happen.

"Don't move," my fixer said over his shoulder. "You wait here."

The motorcycle engines cut out. A last puff of exhaust melted into the air. The villagers got off their bikes and started heading up the path, backs stiffening.

"What's going on? What's wrong?" Courtenay said.

The Rastas? Drunk soldiers? A caravan of ivory poachers?

"I don't know," I whispered back. "Those guys up ahead heard something."

All I could hear were birds chirping, insects clicking, and my quickening breath. Shafts of sunlight sliced down through the canopy of trees that dwarfed us.

"Come on," I finally said. "Let's check it out."

She gave me her hand, and I helped her off her bike. The two of us began to walk through the cool shadows. I was comforted by the familiar sound of her nylon pants swishing behind me.

The path bent left, then right, then split into a fork. I had no idea which way to go. The forest was a tangle of vines and tree trunks and enormous leaves, so thick that if we had walked five minutes in the wrong direction, we would have been lost forever.

We went left.

In a sun-flooded grove, our crew was standing there, watching four men chop through a tree that had fallen across the path. The four men, shirtless and sweating, barely paused to look at us as they struck again and again at an old, knotted trunk.

I will never know from where these good Samaritans came, with the tiny ax they were sharing to clear what passes for an interstate highway in the twenty-first century in the Democratic Republic of Congo. No one was paying them, I guarantee.

But that wasn't even the interesting part. It was what was all around us. Thousands of fluttering butterflies, whiter than pure chalk, stuck to the men's shoulders, their muscular backs, their calves, their arms, their hands, the top of their heads. The men didn't pay them any mind. It was like they were wearing coats of butterflies. The grove was swirling with white butterflies— carpeting the grass, wrapping the tree trunks in white, opening and closing their wings, flickering in the air like falling snow.

I leaned up against a tree and watched about ten land on my arm. Courtenay held out her hand, and a pair fluttered down onto her palm. She looked over at me, her mouth wide open. I couldn't help but think that my being here and that downed tree being here and Courtenay and my being here together in the middle of Africa in the middle of a kaleidoscope of white butterflies who would probably be dead by nightfall was the outcome of a thousand accidents, some pretty dumb mistakes, and not a few deaths. The moment lasted only a few minutes, if that, but in that quiet sequence of a thousand paper-thin wings flapping, I found everything I loved about this part of the world: the unbelievable beauty, the excitement braced with a splash of anxiety, the confirmation that people, even if they have so little and so much stacked against them, usually help one another.

The men paused from their labors and wiped the sweat off their faces. They laid down their ax and lifted our bikes over, the smallest weighing several hundred pounds.

I heard the sexy pants swishing behind me. I stopped, turned around, and hugged her. I closed my eyes and squeezed.

This vision is like so many others now from years ago, intensely vivid, strange, sensual, like a fever dream, a fleeting glimpse of another world.

But I promise you it was true.

We were both there, together.

ACKNOWLEDGMENTS

◇◇◇◇◇◇◇

The best part of writing this book was getting closer to people. So many strangers have written to me to share *their* stories, and it's been wonderful to connect with people who now know a bit about me and aren't scared to expose a little bit about themselves. I definitely needed the support. I don't think I was ever so lonely as I was writing this book. I reported to a little house on a tea plantation in Tigoni (outside of Nairobi), and sat day after day in a stiff wooden chair, offline, just me and Microsoft Word. I was more vulnerable (and "wild-eyed" as Courtenay says) than I have ever been.

As I fought it out with various drafts, my friends and family supplied a tremendous amount of love, kindness, and what I really needed—feedback. I owe these people a huge thank you for giving me their time:

Damien Cave
John Corrigan
Dan DeWitt
Seth Dubin
Zachary Enterlin
Gael Firth
Howard French

James Frey
Maya Frey
Koome Gikunda
Tobias Hagmann
Parwiz Hakim
Blaine Harden
Jesse Katz

Robert Kluijver

Mike Konrad

Josh Kron

Rahel Leupin

Sarah Levitt

Ana Menéndez

Hayden Bixby

Christopher Nolan

Deo-Gratias Onyango

Daire O'Reilly

Frank Pope

Howell Raines

Kevin Riley

Henry Shue

Anjan Sundaram

Emma Thomas

Vanessa Vick

Willet Weeks

Lane Zachary

Special thanks to:

My bosses at the *New York Times*, who tolerated my chasing one long story at the expense of many others.

The dozens of editors I've committed journalism with over the years at the *St. Petersburg Times* (now the *Tampa Bay Times*), the *Los Angeles Times*, the *New York Times*, *Lapham's Quarterly*, *GQ*, *National Geographic*, *Foreign Policy*, and the *New York Review of Books*. Fragments of earlier work are scattered throughout this book, and I deeply appreciate all the help I've received in shaping thoughts, often on deadline.

The Ladies of E-Town Book Club (Cam Axelrood, Missy Hedges, Amy Kappeler Gingold, Aimee Dumas Long, Christine Long, Mary Leopold, Ann Settimi), who test-drove an early draft.

Glenn Altschuler, definitely not a more-is-more guy but thank God for him and his scalpel.

Brian Dotson, who has a genius for spelling out sounds.

Libby Carrier Doran, Tony and Gay Barclay, Emil Rolf Stalis and Raymond Weathers Stephens III, Hannah and Joseph Schwartzman, Hiwot Nega, and Jeremy Piven for their wonderful generosity in helping with book events.

Jesse Katz, an incredibly talented journalist and former marathon buddy, who put a sharp-tipped pencil to many passages.

Aaron Sampson, who emerged from the past to provide key advice and walked me through certain *mzungu* issues that only now seem obvious.

Sana Krasikov, a gifted writer and gifted critic who put down her own book to scribble all over mine.

Jonathan Jao, Jonathan Burnham, Sofia Groopman, Beth Silfin, Rachel Elinsky, Renata Marchione, and the rest of Team Harper: I was lucky to publish this book with them; to benefit from their patience, humor, counsel, wit, and publicity and marketing finesse. The first Jonathan, my editor, is one of the smartest and best-read people I've ever worked with. Even when I disagreed with him, I knew he was right.

Todd Shuster, my literary agent, who was in my corner before I even stepped into the ring and who is still there.

Elias Altman, editor, agent, literary *ndugu*, literary Yoda, actually, whose friendship, skill, and Force are evident on every page.

Roko Belic—my "other wife," as Courtenay refers to him—who saved my ass from falling off Kili and who is constantly, without even knowing it, teaching me.

Ken Morris, Virginia Morris, and Mavis Morris, my other family, who never signed up for this but treat me as one of their own.

My parents, Robert and Joyce Gettleman; my sister, Lynn; my bro-in-law Eric Chehab; all of them fighters who have stared down far more adversity than I've ever faced. They believe in me, they give me confidence, they rally to my defense, but they are also excellent at cutting me down to size.

My sons, Apollo and Asa, whom I wish I could freeze and carry around with me the rest of my life.

Courtenay, my first and only love. "Better half" could not be more fitting. I owe her everything.

◇◇◇◇◇◇◇

ABOUT THE AUTHOR

◇◇◇◇◇◇◇

JEFFREY GETTLEMAN won a Pulitzer Prize for his reporting from East Africa. He was the longest serving East Africa bureau chief in the history of the *New York Times*, based in Kenya for more than a decade. His stories have appeared in *National Geographic*, *Foreign Policy*, *GQ*, and the *New York Review of Books*. A native of Evanston, Illinois, Gettleman studied philosophy at Cornell University and anthropology at the University of Oxford, where he was a Marshall Scholar.

Insights,
Interviews
& More . . .

About the author

2 Meet Jeffrey Gettleman

About the book

5 "Not Just to Bear Witness": An Interview
with Jeffrey Gettleman
by Eric Leake

14 Letters from Readers of *Love, Africa*

Read on

18 Reading Group Guide: Discussion
Questions for *Love, Africa*

19 Suggested Further Reading

*All images are courtesy of Jeffrey Gettleman and
reprinted with permission.*

Meet Jeffrey Gettleman

No, I'm not interviewing camels. But they suffered too during a drought in Somalia.

MY INTEREST IN AFRICA was a bit of a fluke. I wasn't one of those precocious kids toying with atlases or globes at a tender age. When Joseph Conrad was a little boy, the story goes, he pointed to a map of Africa and declared: "When I grow up, I'm going there." When I was a little boy, I put my finger into my nose and declared I was going to be a fireman.

I grew up in a Chicago suburb, progressing at an average speed from Star Wars figures to Estes rockets to Roman candles to struggling with how to unclasp a bra in the dark. My mom was a social worker, my dad a lawyer, my sister a good student who drove a red Pontiac Grand Am—we were hardly the most worldly bunch. From birth to college, I lived in the same house, in the same room, and I could lie in bed and see all the stages of my life—the Walter Payton posters, the set of pocket knives, the drawers crammed with wrinkled notes, old letters, and doomed valentines. I was vaguely aware of the tumultuous throb of the world without considering I had any real place in it.

But as *Love, Africa* explains, my life took a major left urn after my freshman year at Cornell University. I went to Africa for the first time and came back a changed man. I worked summers "throwing paint" on houses (the Da Vinci Brothers' era, which I get into in Chapter Three) and raised a little dough to go back to Africa.

First, I thought I wanted to be a portrait photographer. Then I thought I wanted to be an aid worker. I had the where (East Africa), but no idea about the what. It was only after a crushingly lonely summer in Ethiopia that I seized on journalism.

An original flyer from 1991.

I've had the privilege of working at some excellent publications, from the *St. Petersburg Times* (now the *Tampa Bay Times*) to the *Los Angeles Times* and the *New York Times*. I've covered everything from small town carnage to a New Year's Eve possum drop to wars, elephant slaughters and famines. My stories have appeared in *GQ*, the *New York Review of Books*, *Foreign Policy*, *Lapham's Quarterly*, and *National Geographic*. I've been ▶

Meet Jeffrey Gettleman *(continued)*

lucky in many ways, including winning several awards: the George Polk award, two Overseas Press Club awards, and the Pulitzer Prize.

For more than a decade, I lived in Nairobi, Kenya, in a house with mango trees that were often raided by the same fat monkey. I now live in New Delhi, India, with my wife Courtenay, and our two boys. My job is covering South Asia for the *New York Times*, and though I miss East Africa everyday, India is endlessly fascinating and full of some of the warmest, most welcoming people I've ever met. ∾

www.jeffreygettleman.com

"Not Just to Bear Witness"
An Interview with Jeffrey Gettleman

by Eric Leake

This interview originally appeared in Writing on the Edge, *Vol. 23, Issue 1 and is reprinted with permission.*

Writing on the Edge (WOE): *How is reporting in Africa different from reporting in the US?*

Gettleman: The basics are the same. You want to be accurate and you want to be fair. You want to write visually and find emotional threads. But in Africa there is the sensitivity that we have to be aware of: we're writing about a part of the world that a lot of people don't know much about. It has been stereotyped and oversimplified for centuries. You don't want to reinforce stereotypes unnecessarily, but at the same time you don't want to overcorrect and sanitize what you're covering because you're afraid of these stereotypes. For instance, if I'm covering a conflict in Darfur, Congo, or Somalia, how do I write about it so that I don't give the impression that all of Africa is in conflict, that there is this inherent tendency in Africa for people to kill each other? My solution is to try to be as responsible and thoughtful as possible and to add layers of depth and to locate these conflicts on a wider spectrum of history.

I try my best to understand the roots of these conflicts, what's driving them, why they're sucking in so many people. Then, if I write about it, people can criticize me and say, "Oh, you're stereotyping Africa as conflict-ridden and chaotic." But I can say, "No, I'm really trying to study it and explain it in the most comprehensive terms that a journalist can." ▶

WOE: *As a corollary, how do you want people to read your articles? For instance, should they read them differently than how they might read an article in their local newspaper?*

Gettleman: I want people to care. I want them to care about a part of the world that they don't know much about, that maybe they've never been to, that doesn't have any direct impact on them. I want them to feel connected to the people here and what's happening in this region. To do that, you have to find reasons to make people care. It can't be dry, bloodless, or boring. We have to be objective, but that doesn't mean we have to be neutral. We don't have to be stone cold and stand back and not let our own empathy be invoked by what we're covering.

A lot of journalists struggle with that because we think that our job is to be objective, to be fair, to be accurate, and that we shouldn't let our emotions get involved. I disagree with that. I think some of the best work I've done is because I cared deeply about it. I have a sense of right and wrong. This elephant story, for example, which is one of the bigger stories I've done for the paper, is tragic. It's a slaughter. Humankind is so shortsighted that they could wipe out these elephants for trinkets. I don't want to just be like, "Oh well, there are two sides to this, there are two sides to every conflict." Well, yes and no. Sometimes one side is not sensible.

WOE: *How do you get readers to care?*

Gettleman: It's a question of connecting. Africa represents a very different way of life than what we're used to at home in the role of tradition, the levels of poverty, the levels of conflict. This is much, much different than the way most Americans or people in the Western world live. It's going to be alien, it's going to be foreign, and it's going to seem strange.

I did a story in Tanzania about albino children and adults getting killed for their body parts because witch doctors had told people that albino body parts bring you good luck. This story is a clear example of the thing I like to do—to try to find an issue where there's a real injustice, shine a light on it, and make people care. I got an enormous response. So many people emailed me to they wanted to help.

A story like that raises a lot of issues. Are you going to reinforce the stereotype of Africa as dominated by witchcraft nd being "primitive?" Since people are getting killed because of this phenomenon, you can't be afraid of these things. I think the way to make people care is to write vividly, passionately, with lots of detail, to put flesh on what you're writing about. You write in an original way and you write with care so that people do care. You have to breathe the life into your stories. I try to find stories that move me, and I write them in such a way that I hope people will be moved by them.

WOE: *Jack Shafer in* Slate *has celebrated your writing for what he calls the "Gettleman method," which he describes as direct, easy on the cynicism, and without a hint of any world weariness. Do you think that's a decent description of your approach?*

Gettleman: Yes and no. I don't embellish the material, but I also don't totally believe in understatement. I think there are times when more is more. I don't think I'm especially understated. I'm handling material that I don't need to dress up or embroider. It's really dramatic. Right in front of you children are dying of starvation and you're watching them die. You're seeing masses of people show up at refugee camps with absolutely nothing, on the doorstep of death. This is the extreme edge of what people experience and suffer. I think it is important to play it straight.

But I don't think that means you have to shy away from upsetting details. I don't do that. One way to have impact is not to be afraid to talk about people suffering, people dying, about really nasty things happening, because *they are happening*. It's part of our job not just to bear witness—that term is overused—it's part of our job to jump into these situations and make people care about them, to really get your arms around the material and present it in a way that makes people feel connected.

WOE: *I see you doing that in a lot of your pieces, sometimes in the choice of detail to humanize your subjects. I'm reading this elephant story and there is a comment about how much beer one of the men drinks as he talks about the stress of his work.*

Gettleman: When I was hired by the *New York Times* I did a story about a freak car accident in Alabama. It's a good example that you can write really dramatically and vividly about something that would be considered commonplace. These are the types of things that I like writing about, stories that deal with emotions. The challenge in Africa is this: I am the only correspondent for the *New York Times* in East Africa. If elephants are getting slaughtered at a record rate, I should be writing about that. If a huge famine is brewing in Somalia, I should be writing about that. If the politics in Sudan are breaking down and South Sudan and Sudan are about to go to war again, I should be writing about that. The hardest ▶

June 1991 London

Dear Jeff,

Thank you for the pictures and for the letter. I have never really had such a letter. You have

such nutty and interesting ideas. Yes it has taken a long time and many dodgy African continents to reach a level of understanding you, from the ghettos of Chicago and me from my small farm in Kakamega, who would have thought we would have anything in common. Your way of mixing funny nonsense together with real emotions and sincerity in your letter made me happy when I read it. I am really glad that you had a good time on the Safari and I hope that we will have more in the glorious utopian future. I would also like to check you guys in Chicago and to see the Mecca of the Midwest "The Babes Square". I have finished my semester now and I learned quite alot (Japanese politics, economics, photography) but I did not find many good people here. It is really hard to build up a network in a few months and find the good people. I really don't have much here yet compared to Kenya and it makes me feel very insecure. And when I don't have that side sorted out it makes me worry about what I am doing and what I want. But I think that Safari way of life is one of the best I know and if I can adapt some of those ideas of adventurers full living into normal life I would be more happy. O.K. please send me new news from "Stato's" Your friend Dan

News from English papers

● YOU look superb with your silicone-boosted breasts. And we hate those idiots (wankers) who call you names.
They wouldn't know real beauty if it sat on their face and blew wind.
● How about a photo of your new boobs to pin up at work? It would be something new to jerk off with.
NF, Birmingham
FIONA: Sorry son, but my super new piccies are too valuable to give away to wankers.

Bun

I am a married bint and have sex now and again with my old man.
But I'm never satisfied until I have had five knobfuls a day.
After work I catch the train to Bradford and two months ago caught three lads ogling my nice ass and jutting nipples.
When I said: "What do you fancy lads?" they pushed me in the bog and stripped me nude.
Then they knobbed me from every conceivable angle.
And I did conceive. I've now got a bun in the oven and don't know who the dad is.
Will this problem turn me off willies?
P.M. Leeds
FIONA: I doubt it. A slag like you will always want it — ALL WAYS.

Chibuku Breweries Union MALAWI 1991

SHAKE SHAKE

Jamaican Delight
262 6588

"The safari way of life is one of the best I know." Wise words from my friend Dan Eldon, killed two years after making this letter.

"Not Just to Bear Witness" *(continued)*

part of this job is selecting what to cover. There is so much that needs to be covered. Right now, as I'm sitting in my house in Nairobi, all around the region there are tons of things I should be writing about, but I can't get to them all.

WOE: *How do you handle that emotional response? Do you get caring fatigue?*

Gettleman: It's hard. I think I do have some post-traumatic stress. It's difficult to see people whose lives have been destroyed, to see people die. It takes a toll. I know the vulnerabilities of flesh and blood. I have no illusions of immortality. But I think that having an outlet for all this material helps. I'm not keeping it bottled up.

And I have a great family. I have a great marriage and two kids and I'm close to my parents. I'm not alone.

WOE: *What do you see as the public role of journalism?*

Gettleman: Americans are more empathic and intellectually curious than I think most people give us credit for. Most people would be really interested to come visit Africa for a couple of weeks—they'll never do it, but if they had the opportunity they would get a lot out of it.

That's what I see as our mission—to open up our readers. Stories have to combine a human-interest dimension that will make people care with an emotional current, and they also have to have some news, some information that has an impact. The key is blend all of that, and I think good journalism does that.

WOE: *How optimistic are you about the future of journalism?*

Gettleman: This is a moment of opportunity that could slip away or be seized. Right now more people read the *New York Times* than ever have before. But the business of the paper is not as secure as it used to be because of all the different mediums. Because of some of these changes, I'm very accountable for what I write. Back in the day, a foreign correspondent could go to a village in the middle of Kenya or Somalia or Congo, write whatever he wanted to write, come back, and nobody in that village would ever see the *New York Times*—they literally wouldn't be able to have access to the paper. But today I go to Somalia, I write a story, and local guys get on the Internet and read it because there are Internet cafes everywhere. I'm accountable to them.

It's big challenge business-wise to figure out how to make money off of the Internet and fund this journalism we're talking about because it's not cheap. On this elephant story it cost a lot of money to get to these places where they're slaughtering the elephants. It takes resources and there has to be a business that's going to support that.

But the Internet itself has also democratized journalism and information in an epic way. I'm part of that, and I like that. I like the fact that I feel connected to these areas and these people. I put a lot of work into what I do and I want people in Congo, Somalia, Sudan, or wherever to be able to read the story I wrote about them. Hopefully they'll think, "OK, this guy may not have understood everything, but he did his best to be honest and accurate and fair to what we're going through."

WOE: *For those teaching future journalists, is there anything you'd like to emphasize concerning education?*

Gettleman: I did not have an interest in journalism as a younger person. I liked to write and I took a lot of creative writing in college, but I didn't ever think that working for a newspaper would be a good outlet for that. I thought of journalism as boring. Yes, there are dry aspects to it. But there are a lot of opportunities to write well. If you're good at writing, journalism is a great opportunity because you can reach a lot of people with your words.

Another piece of advice: Seek out really good writing wherever it is— if it's literature, if it's really good nonfiction writing, if it's really good journalism—because the only way we're going to become better writers is by reading good work and thinking about it and trying to understand how these writers were able to do what they're doing. I'm not perfect at this. I'm busy and I don't always sit down with beautifully written books and try to learn from them. But I try. It's really important to be a good reader to be a good writer.

WOE: *You studied philosophy at Cornell and then at Oxford as a Marshall Scholar. I'm curious about the connection between that and your work in journalism. Was there a particular area in philosophy that interested you, and how has that study affected your reporting and writing?*

Gettleman: I think my background kicks in with my writing because a lot of what I cover is about rights and wrongs. The field of philosophy that I was interested in was moral philosophy—what is right and what is wrong. I wrote a lot about what kind of sacrifices we should make to help other people. There's a whole field of philosophy that deals with this. ▶

"Not Just to Bear Witness" *(continued)*

For example, as you walk by, there's somebody drowning in a pond. If it just takes you getting your clothes wet to save them, you should save them. But what if you have to lose your arm to save them? That's a tougher question. What if you have to risk your life? I studied a lot of that. John Rawls's book *A Theory of Justice* was very influential for me. It's all about how we arrive at the right principles to govern society.

Right now I'm living that out. I am in places where I come across injustices all the time. I see my role as trying to spotlight these issues with the hope that there will be some remedy. I'm not an aid worker. I'm not a government official. But I can use my platform as a journalist for a big paper to spotlight these issues with the hope that people will be motivated to do something. I do a lot of that. I really sit down and think which stories can I do that will help the most people or will have the greatest impact.

WOE: *Are there other ethical considerations that go into how you write about people's stories? For instance, whenever you're writing about people you're also choosing which details to include and how to construct a person for other people to read.*

Gettleman: I don't see that as a real ethical dilemma. I think you have to be honest and accurate and to try your best to represent the essence of whatever you're writing about. The tougher ethical question for me is how much to expose somebody if somebody has really important information. Let's says there's an African country where the government military is abusing, raping, killing its own people, and I have information about that. And let's say the United States government is helping this military but I'm going to put people at risk to get that information. That's a really tricky situation. I'll serve the greater good by getting that story out. But am I going to try to really push people to give me information that can put their lives at risk?

The ethics are clear-cut at many levels. We don't pay people for information. If somebody tells us not to use their name, we don't use their name. If somebody doesn't want to talk to us, we don't talk to them. It gets grayer out in the field because we can persuade people to talk to us. We can get them to give us information that maybe they shouldn't give us, just by keeping a conversation going. That's what journalists do. You get people to really open up and spill their guts, and sometimes that's not in their best interest. It's in your interest as a journalist to get your story, but it's not in their interest. Maybe later they're going to be really embarrassed when everybody knows all these things that they just told you. Or maybe they're going to be in danger.

No matter how fired up I am about the story, I'm not going to do something that will put people in danger when I get on the plane and come home. These people are then sitting in places where everybody knows they just talked to the Western reporter. They have a bull's-eye on their head. I'm very sensitive to that. Sometimes I'll leave people's names out of the story even though they didn't ask me to because they don't quite realize that even though I was talking to them in the middle of Congo, people can read this on the Internet anywhere and they could get in trouble for it.

WOE: *Is there a best piece of writing advice or lesson that really helped you become a better writer?*

Gettleman: No, I wish there were. I think it's an evolution. You become a better writer. You don't get a piece of wisdom and all of a sudden you've cracked the code. It comes from a lot of steady work and trying different things and putting a lot of care into your work. But there are certain things that we do, certain devices and tactics that we use, that you can teach: to be visual, to write in a natural, conversational way. If you read a sentence that doesn't sound like anything you'd ever utter, then don't write it like that.

You can create suspense in your work and not give away everything that happens in the top of a story. Even if you're covering a suburb or something that would seem commonplace in the States, you can still do it in a way that is visual and descriptive. Take the time to see what's hanging on the walls or the way that a lawn is mowed or how somebody cleans up their room or doesn't, what they're eating—details like that. A lot of people have this impression that either you're a really good writer or you're not. I don't buy that. I think there are ways to bring out good writing in just about anybody.

WOE: *As for future plans, is there anything that you'd like to do that you haven't done?*

Gettleman: I'm trying to work on a book. I'd like to write a good memoir about my experiences. That's what I'd like to do next. I don't want to do that totally at the expense of my journalism career, so I have to figure out a way to balance the two. But that's my goal. I think it would be really wonderful to share a lot of the experiences I've had in a deeper, more personal way than I can in a newspaper. ∾

Letters from Readers of *Love, Africa*

Upon publication of Love, Africa, *I received hundreds of messages from around the world. Here are a couple of my favorites*

Jeffrey,

I enjoyed reading about a life I once thought I would live, too. It didn't work out for me—I had kids and married young, in that order, and wound up in the dreaded throes of community journalism in a mid-size town; you dodged a huge bullet on that one.

I'm glad you wrote about the need for stories to mean something, and I laughed hearing about the "we'll bear witness on this one" advice from your editor in Los Angeles. I had an editor who used the exact same words nearly every time I really thought I was onto something.

Zachary Reid
Richmond, VA

⬦⬦⬦⬦⬦

Dear Jeffrey,

I normally don't buy newly released books because they're expensive and I'm in no position to spend unnecessarily. But somehow after reading a Kindle sample of *Love, Africa*, I was hooked.

I don't know much about Africa apart from the fact that I once walked the streets of Mombasa and swam in the waters of Nosy Be of Madagascar. The ship I was working on also had a slight pirate scare when we sailed from Salallah to Aden. Apart from all that, I'd no real idea what was going on in the countries around the continent. Shame on me!

I'm glad that you finally get to honor the two loves of your life, though I did want to punch you in the face for cheating on Courtenay.

Best wishes,
Ying
(from Germany)

◇◇◇◇◇◇◇◇

Dear Mr. Gettleman:

Your book, *Love Africa*, was displayed at the library and immediately caught my eye because I, too, love everything about Africa. As I was reading it I was struck by how the intensity of your feelings mirrors mine. My husband and I went to Kenya in 1968 (we were Missionaries, but it could be argued we were Misfits too.) We didn't choose where we would be sent but once there we were completely entranced. Although my husband and I divorced 3 years after we came home, we are still totally in sync with regards to anything African.

Of course, your experiences were different and much more exciting and dangerous than ours, but the essence of your feelings is the same. I felt like I was reading about how my life might have evolved if we had stayed. You have lived my dream.

This 72 year old woman really appreciates that you wrote a book that explains how I (still) feel.

Linda E. Gough
Toronto, Canada

◇◇◇◇◇◇◇◇

Jeffrey,

I want to tell you my story.

My name is Grace and I'm going to be a senior at Boston University this fall. In 2015, I was feeling particularly lost. I needed a semester "on." I decided to study abroad at the University of Cape Town. Like you, I fell in love with Africa; South Africa, to be precise.

One year ago today, I was on my return flight home to Washington, DC from Joburg's O.R. Tambo airport. As soon as I got on the plane, I was already charting my course back to The Continent.

Long story short, all the schemes I concocted to get back didn't work out. Life, money, school, and family got in the way, so it goes. ▶

About the book

In November 2016, I fell in love again. I became a political columnist at my school newspaper and discovered a deep passion for journalism.

I had two love affairs running parallel: my love for Cape Town and my love for journalism. Before I picked up your book, I felt like these two paths were drifting further and further apart.

I never even imagined an intersection until I DEVOURED *Love, Africa*. Every fucking word either resonated with me or inspired me.

Grace Lawless Hagerty,
Boston, Mass

◇◇◇◇◇◇◇◇

Hello,

I just closed your book and am writing to you with tears in my eyes. I feel like the question, "what did you love about the book?" is the same as when I was in Kenya in 1981 and when I returned people asked, "what did you like about Kenya?" I always changed it to love.

I want to thank you for opening my eyes yet again to how Africa has been sliced and diced and dumped and exploited. I was surprised at times to see on paper what so few people reveal in MSM.

I tried to tell my grown daughter about your book yesterday and couldn't get through a single chapter without choking up. She was 14 when I came home a changed woman and I'm not sure what she thought then. I just know that I was never the same after that summer.

All best to you and your family,

Barbara Clarke
Bellingham, Washington

◇◇◇◇◇◇◇◇

Dear Mr. Gettlman;

Your descriptions of a vigorous continent struggling to live up to its potential brought back many memories.

I spent two years in West Africa as a Peace Corps volunteer in Liberia, leaving in 1976 just before the country fell into civil war. I taught at a small upcountry college and lived in the men's dorm. During our evening palavers on the veranda, unrest was palpable between the privileged America-Liberians and the rural students. Private planes and Mercedes would drop off the Monrovia students, and those from the rural villages trudged dusty and hungry onto campus after days on the "road." The experience shaped my life (I went to medical school and married the nurse who cared for me during a bout of malaria).

Your book vividly brought back memories, both sounds and visuals, that were strong but rarely pulled up from the memory banks.

Best regards,
Mike

(I hope some day to take that escarpment road out of Nairobi to the Great Rift Valley)

◇◇◇◇◇◇◇◇

Thank you for your tribute to Africa and the hope we all share for our beloved continent!

Idy Diawara
St. Louis (via Mali) ∿

Reading Group Guide
Discussion Questions
for *Love, Africa*

1. Did reading the book make you want to visit Africa? What did you already know about this part of the world?

2. What did you learn about Africa that surprised you?

3. Who is the ideal audience for *Love, Africa*? To whom would you recommend this book and why?

4. In this book, we see things from Jeffrey's point of view. How might Courtenay have told this story?

5. Writing a memoir requires a level of painful honesty. What was your reaction to Jeffrey's confession of his indiscretions? Would you (or your partner) be capable of this degree of exposure?

6. What did you think about the portrayal of the American government in the book? How has the United States helped or hurt Africa?

7. There are so many great characters in these pages. Who were your favorites? What did you think about Commander Peacock?

8. How does Jeffrey address the complexity of his position as an outsider writing about Africa? Does he successfully steer clear of what he calls the "*ooga-booga*?"

9. What other books did *Love, Africa* remind you of?

10. Were there sections of the book where you would have wanted more description or to spend more time on the page?

11. Many scenes in the book have a cinematic quality. Who would you cast in a movie based on this story? ～

Suggestions for Further Reading

Here are some of the best books I've ever read that helped me write this one:

Memoirs

The Invention of Solitude, Paul Auster
Dispatches, Michael Herr **
On the Road, Jack Kerouac **
A Time of Gifts, Patrick Leigh Fermor
This Boy's Life: A Memoir, Tobias Wolff
Stop-Time, Frank Conroy
The Liars' Club: A Memoir, Mary Karr
Between the World and Me, Ta-Nehisi Coates

Novels

Annie John, Jamaica Kincaid
The Sorrow of War, Bảo Ninh **
Sophie's Choice, William Styron
All the King's Men, Robert Penn Warren **
The Brief Wondrous Life of Oscar Wao, Junot Diaz **

Books on Africa

Somalia

Links, Nuruddin Farah
Warriors: Life and Death Among the Somalis, Gerald Hanley
A Tear for Somalia, Douglas Collins **

Sudan

Season of Migration to the North, Tayeb Salih **

Congo

Stringer: A Reporter's Journey in the Congo, Anjan Sundaram
Dancing in the Glory Monsters, Jason Stearns
A Bend in the River, V. S. Naipaul ** ▶

** *My top ten (at this moment)*

Suggestions for Further Reading *(continued)*

Kenya

The Flame Trees of Thika, Elspeth Huxley
A Grain of Wheat, Ngũgĩ wa Thiong'o
Battle for the Elephants, Iain and Oria Douglas-Hamilton

North Africa

The Sheltering Sky, Paul Bowles **
Woman at Point Zero, Nawal El Saadawi

South Africa

My Traitor's Heart, Rian Malan
The Lying Days, Nadine Gordimer **
Disgrace, J. M. Coetzee ∾